TRANCE ZERO

TRANCE | ZERO

THE PSYCHOLOGY OF MAXIMUM EXPERIENCE

ADAM CRABTREE

ST. MARTIN'S PRESS ≋ NEW YORK

Design by Gordon Robertson / Heidi Eriksen

ISBN 0-312-24425-8

First published in Canada under the title *Trance Zero: Breaking the Spell of Conformity* as a Patrick Crean Book by Somerville House Publishing, a division of Somerville House Books Limited

First U.S. Edition: September 1999

10 9 8 7 6 5 4 3 2 1

This book has gone through a notable evolution during the period of its writing. It has taken me down paths I did not anticipate to conclusions I could not have foreseen. My wife and professional colleague, Joanne, has been crucial to this process. Although the book started out as my own project, it has ended as a joint endeavour. This is to acknowledge her special role in the crafting of this book.

ADAM CRABTREE

CONTENTS

ix *Acknowledgments*

xi *Introduction by Colin Wilson*

xvii *Preamble*

PART ONE: MICROTRANCE: THE INDIVIDUAL

  3 *Chapter One*
     The Trance

 31 *Chapter Two*
     Relating

 47 *Chapter Three*
     Doing

 61 *Chapter Four*
     Going Within

 87 *Chapter Five*
     The World of the Inner Mind

III *Chapter Six*
     The Group Mind

PART TWO: MACROTRANCE: THE CULTURE

145 *Chapter Seven*
     Cultural Trance

159 *Chapter Eight*
     Cultural Orthodoxy and Beyond

PART THREE: WAKING UP

189 *Chapter Nine*
     Little-People/Big-People Delusion

207 *Chapter Ten*
     Trance Zero: Faith

231 *Chapter Eleven*
     Immanence

261 *Notes*

ACKNOWLEDGMENTS

I would like to thank my sons, Edward and Andrew, for their thoughtful questions and helpful input into this book. I would also like to acknowledge the University of Toronto Faculty Club Group as a source of valuable intellectual stimulation as the book progressed. My thanks also go to Frances Hanna for her perseverence with the project over difficult times. Finally, I would like to express my very special appreciation to Patrick Crean who, at a crucial moment in this book's development, provided most helpful direction and encouragement.

INTRODUCTION

A DAM CRABTREE seems to me to be one of the most interesting minds in the field of modern psychology.

This conviction came to me in 1984, when he sent me the typescript of his book *Multiple Man*, a study of multiple personality syndrome. The subject had fascinated me ever since I had made a television program about the strange case of "Christine Beauchamp," described by Morton Prince in *The Dissociation of a Personality* in 1905. Later, I came upon the even more fascinating "Doris Fischer" case of Walter Franklin Prince, and made the two cases a central strand of my argument in a book called *Mysteries*, in which I suggest that we all contain a "hierarchy of personalities."

Multiple Man raises so many profound questions that even now, after reading it several times, I can still experience the same excitement when I re-read it, as I did before beginning this introduction.

He begins, for example, by talking about a young woman called Sarah, who was upset because she heard "voices" inside her head. When placed in a state of deep relaxation, Sarah spoke with another voice, which claimed to be her dead grandmother. There was no need to "cure" her; eventually, Sarah came to accept and feel glad of her grandmother's presence "inside" her. In another case, a young woman called Jean seemed to be "possessed" by the spirit of her mentally retarded sister Amy, now dead; the strange thing about the case was that Amy claimed to have "entered" Jean while she (Amy) was still alive.

Crabtree insisted that he was not looking for supernatural explanation, but merely recording what he had seen. This is not as paradoxical as it sounds; a British psychiatrist named David Cohen has recorded a number of his own cases of multiple personality in his book *Alter Egos*, and Cohen firmly insists that multiple personality is merely a complex kind of "game playing" (often it seems to me in the face of all evidence). At all events, Adam Crabtree's book confirmed in my mind the notion that had already been put there by Morton Prince and Walter Franklin Prince—that perhaps the human personality is *not* simply a product of various control units of the brain.

In 1993, Adam sent me his new book *From Mesmer to Freud*, and I found this just as exciting as *Multiple Man*. Again, I had always been fascinated by mesmerism and its offshoot, hypnotism. What interested me so much was the notion that a person under hypnosis should be capable of feats which he or she would find impossible when awake. For example, Thomson Jay Hudson describes the case of a rather ordinary young man who was told, under hypnosis, that he was holding conversations with various great philosophers, and who produced brilliant philosophical systems (which he attributed to them). It seems that, under hypnosis, his intelligence and imagination took fire, and he freely embroidered what he inaccurately believed to be the ideas of Socrates, Kant or Hegel. This seemed to argue that we *all* possess a wider range of powers than we normally recognize, and that, as William James said, our real problem is "a habit of inferiority to our true selves."

I was particularly interested by a section on Sir William Barrett, the founder of the Society for Psychical Research, who hypnotized a pupil and found that he was able to experience Barrett's own sensations, even when in another room. Alfred Russel Wallace, co-discoverer of the theory of evolution, had the same experience; when he pricked himself with a pin, the hypnotized subject cried out; when he tasted salt; the hypnotized subject pulled a wry face; when he tasted sugar, the subject smiled with pleasure. This "community of sensation" seemed to argue that this is yet another of our "hidden powers"—telepathic contact with other people—and that perhaps hypnosis itself depends upon such contact as much as on "suggestion." Again, Crabtree writes simply as an observer and a historian; but the assembly of facts he brings together in *From Mesmer to Freud* are bound to raise many questions that challenge our modern "reductionist" psychology.

So when Adam asked me if I would care to look at his new book *Trance Zero*, I was delighted, knowing that whatever he had to say would set off new trains of thought.

In some ways, this is his most challenging book so far. What makes it so stimulating is that he takes a basic and simple idea—that we all spend more time in a "trance" than we realize—and then develops it in wholly unexpected ways.

Trance, he points out, is any kind of "absorption" that makes us unaware of the outside world. Having recently been browsing in *From Mesmer to Freud*, I could grasp the full import of this notion. For the strangest thing about hypnosis is how easy it is to slip from "ordinary consciousness" into trance. I have never ceased to be fascinated by the fact that when French women go to the market to buy a live chicken, they tuck the head of the chicken under its wing, whereupon it promptly goes to sleep, and can be carried upside down by its feet. But human beings can also do this—I have always loved that story of the wife of a professor who, before a dinner party, sent him upstairs to change his tie, and half an hour later found him in bed fast asleep—the act of removing his tie had led him to undress, put on his pajamas, and climb into bed.

[margin annotation: mind-less-ness /]

Crabtree suggests that our culture induces a trance state—in fact, many kinds of "microtrances"—and that we have to awaken from this trance before we can enter the condition he calls Trance Zero, a state of being in touch with our "inner guidance." And this, it seems to me, is the essential contribution of this book. The notion that we live in a trance state can also be found in Gurdjieff, who called it "sleep." He also recognized that this sleep is due to the fact that so many of our actions and feelings are "mechanical." But Gurdjieff's point of view was in many ways pessimistic; he regards human beings as hypnotized sheep, kept in a state of trance by the butcher who wants to save himself the cost of a sheep-pen. Gurdjieff taught that we *can* wake up, but that it demands a tremendous and continuous effort, a strict discipline, akin to that of yogis and ascetics.

Crabtree is obviously far more optimistic. Like Gurdjieff, he feels that the first step is to recognize that we move from microtrance to microtrance. But we also have an important ally, the unconscious mind, and this can be used to help us defeat the trance state. In fact, his views bear some resemblance to those of Frederic Myers, another founder of the Society of Psychical Research, who believed that human beings also have a kind of "superconscious mind," as far above "everyday consciousness" as the Freudian "unconscious" is below it.

I arrived at some very similar conclusions by a circuitous route of my own. In the early 1960s, I made my first lecture tour of America, often lecturing at five or six colleges or universities per week for twelve weeks, and becoming completely exhausted in the process. (I can understand why it killed Dylan Thomas.) I would often find myself between planes in some strange airport at half past five in the evening, feeling totally discouraged by the idea of having to lecture in a few hours time. I would make for the bar and order a vodka martini, then sit at some corner table and drink it slowly. At first, the sounds of the bar would disturb me, and I would jump when someone slammed the door. But during my second drink, I would cease to be aware of the room and the sound of voices, as I went into a state of deep relaxation. With a third drink, I would be aware only of the lamp on the table, as if I was alone in the place. It was as if a circle of attention contracted slowly, creating an increasing glow of warmth. And by the time I climbed aboard my plane for the last lap of the journey (to some remote college in New Mexico or Vermont), I would find myself brimming with energy and optimism, bubbling with ideas, and looking forward to the lecture.

T. E. Lawrence made the important comment: "Happiness is absorption." And this is, in fact, what I was learning to induce in myself—a state of absorption.

It was, I should point out, not simply the alcohol that did it. It is possible to get drunk and yet remain completely *un*absorbed. Conversely, it is possible to achieve a state of deep absorption on one glass of wine. It depends on a kind of relaxation, a "plunging into inwardness."

In my first book *The Outsider*, I talked about a play called *The Secret Life* by Granville Barker. It is about people who have been made nihilistic by the First World War—and about a few people

who have *not* become nihilistic because they possesss what Granville
Barker calls "the secret life," that curious glow deep inside them
that gives them a sense of meaning and purpose. The secret life is
also the secret of psychological health. Yet because modern psychology has its roots in Freud and his profound pessimism, or Watson
and his maze-running rats, few psychotherapists have explored this
vital concept. It seems to me that when Adam Crabtree talks about
Trance Zero, he means very much what Granville Barker meant by
the secret life.

How did Crabtree succeed in escaping the pessimism that seems
to lie at the root of modern culture? I suspect that the answer lies,
to a great extent, in his own biography. To begin with, he was born
in a small rural community in Minnesota, and although he did not
think of his family as "poor," they would certainly have been classi-
fied as such by most modern city dwellers on the American conti-
nent. Yet they were hard working, self-sufficient and happy. So
Adam grew up with a kind of natural cheerfulness and optimism.

He mentions in this book his grandfather Frank Delsing, a
powerful, stable individual, who made Adam feel that as along as
he was alive, the world was a safe place to be in. This was important
for a child who was a basically an introvert, someone whose mental
energies are directed inward rather than outward.

With the idea of becoming a teacher, he went to St. John's University, run by monks, and after majoring in physics and mathe-
matics, decided that he had a vocation for the priesthood. In due
course he became a priest and a monk. And living in the small
Benedictine community was good for him, for they also staffed a
university, and he had every encouragement to think and develop
ideas. When I remember my own years of struggle, working at
manual jobs and often sleeping outdoors, I envy him.

He took a degree in philosophy, and went to Toronto for post-
graduate studies. By this time he had come upon a pamphlet describing a case of "possession" that had occurred in Iowa in 1928, a
girl named Anna Ecklund, who behaved exactly like the girl in *The
Exorcist*. This turned his mind in the direction of the mystery of
multiple personality. At the University of Toronto, he met a group

of priests and nuns who were involved in psychotherapy with a re-markable woman named Lea Hindley-Smith, who had a kind of telepathic insight into her patients, so that she could empathize with them instantly. (In due course, Adam married her daughter Joanne.) In 1965, he began to study with her, and in 1967, began working as a psychotherapist. This would lead, fifteen years later, to the writing of *Multiple Man*, which I regard as much a classic of psychotherapy as *The Dissociation of Personality* and *The Doris Case*.

Any reader of this book can see that it would be untrue to say that he has turned his back on the priesthood. The foundation of his work is a sense of man as a spiritual being, not a kind of compli-cated watch mechanism. He is also a thinker, motivated by a relent-less philosophical drive. (He comments in a letter to me: "This is something I have made no bones about, and my clients don't seem to hold it against me.") In many ways he reminds me of my own favourite among psychologists, William James, whose work always has a kind of freshness, as if he was sitting in the same room with the reader and pouring out ideas.

I suspect that, with *Trance Zero*, Adam Crabtree has hit a highly productive vein. Every page filled me with ideas, comments, new trains of thought. It seems to me that Adam is a new kind of psy-chologist—one who intuitively understands that the mind is far vaster and stranger than anyone suspected—and at the same time, stronger and more full of creative possibilities. When he speaks of imagination, he is closer to William Blake than to Freud. What is slowly emerging from his work is a new paradigm of the psyche, based upon the recognition of the "secret life."

Colin Wilson

PREAMBLE

One of the most striking features of human life is the extraordinary diversity of ways of living it. In anthropology, it is customary to register this diversity by means of the concept of culture.

– Tim Ingold, "Introduction to Culture,"
Companion Encyclopedia of Anthropology

O UR CULTURE has us in a trance. We are enthralled by the ideas and images that it generates. We are incapable of putting them aside and seeing things from some neutral point of view. The thoughts we cherish, the values we espouse are created for us. Our fashions, fads, and manners are orchestrated. Even our rebellions are expressions of conformity. Although we are capable of free choice, the alternatives placed before us are so limited that we act very much like automatons. And all the time we think we are living as free, independent creators of our lives.

Our culture is a two-edged sword. It gives us a way of perceiving, organizing, and interacting with the world. It creates a framework for understanding the complex experiences called life and assigns us a secure place in our environment. It provides institutions that assist us in the treacherous journey from birth to death. It tranquilizes us with familiarity. This edge vanquishes our enemy—fear—and makes us feel safe.

But the other edge wounds us. Its security evolves into smugness and then into a stultifying rigidity. It discourages our curiosity. It shields us from the unknown. It alienates us from those who are different. It dissociates us from our uncouth impulses. It provides no techniques for questioning its forms, but, on the contrary, isolates those who attempt to do so.

Culture induces a kind of sleep. When I sleep and dream, I am aware only of my private world. I do not know about the external environment, and so cannot interact with it. Culture too is its own private world. Those who live within it know only what is presented in its fixed forms. They are asleep to what lies beyond culture's carefully constructed universe. For them, reality lies within culture's borders. Beyond that is chaos. Anything that impinges from the outside must be an illusion or a lie. If there is evil, it comes from the outside.

This is why outside cultures are generally seen as a threat. They challenge the notion of the "other" as chaos and claim to know of another reality. Culture has no way to deal with this kind of encroachment. It must fend off the intruder to preserve its integrity.

Those who live within the culture must also defend themselves from intruders from within. Human impulses, longings, and strivings that have not been integrated into the culture are as dangerous as any outside threat. They too must be turned back.

Culture is a trance. Trance is a state of narrowed awareness, and culture is the crystallization of a specific, limited mode of seeing the world. Although there are an infinite number of ways that I could perceive, organize, and act on my environment, my culture narrows me down to one set. It is a tried and tested set that has proven serviceable. Its value is that it provides me with a relatively secure context within which I can gain an understanding of the world and find my way through life. Unfortunately, it also serves as a kind of blinder.

Our culture relentlessly communicates its constricted view to each of us. It renews the trance at every turn, for we continually reimpose our culture's view of reality on one another. This begins in the family and is continued by culture's other institutions— schools, religions, the media.

Trance admits of degrees. The more focused the awareness, the deeper the trance. Our absorption in our culture's ways is total, so our cultural trance is very profound.

Despite its scientific knowledge, our Western culture is as asleep as any other. Despite its technology, it does not know how to deal with the central issues of human existence. What our culture lacks is wisdom—an intuitive grasp of who we are and what we need. We sense this deficiency and today are groping for ways to fill the gap.

We cannot extract ourselves from our culture's trance, but we can diminish its detrimental effects. We can develop a healthy skepticism about culture's dogmas and cast a critical eye on its institutions. Most of all, we can acknowledge its limitations and explore ways of transcending them.

If our culture holds us in a trance, why do we not realize it? Because trance is a natural part of everyday existence. Our daily lives are a tapestry of trance states, and this is necessarily so. Like the macrotrance of culture, our microtrances are both beneficial and limiting. Seeing this clearly is the first step.

The next step is to learn how to transcend the limitations imposed by trance states. We do this through an inward journey that leads to the development of what I call Trance Zero. This means being in touch with an intuitive awareness that can move us safely through the complexities of life. Trance Zero implies a faith in the presence of an immanent wisdom in each person. It is a view of human existence that sees each life as the work of an inner core which is a manifestation of the divine in the world.

If we operate from the intuitive awareness of Trance Zero, we have a way to deal with the ills of culture, for then we are guided by profound wisdom—a wisdom that could only come from beyond our limited experience. That is the hope for our future.

To give the reader a sense of how I came to write this book, it may be useful to describe something of my own cultural background. Although I write this today from a large urban centre in Canada, I grew up in rural central Minnesota. From a farm outside Long Prairie I moved to the dormitories of St. John's University in Collegeville and then to the attached Abbey, where I was initiated into the monastic life of the Benedictine order. In 1964 I was ordained a

Roman Catholic priest, and a year later I travelled from the Abbey to Toronto to obtain a graduate degree in philosophy in preparation for teaching at St. John's University.

During my studies I began psychotherapy with Lea Hindley-Smith, an extraordinarily talented therapeutic innovator. Eventually I started training as a psychotherapist and, with several dozen colleagues, became involved in establishing a therapeutic community called Therafields. This experiment flourished from mid-1960s to the late 1970s, and came to an end around 1980. I had left the religious life in 1969 and in 1976 I married Joanne, who was also a psychotherapist and part of the Therafields group. Our sons Edward and Andrew were born to us in the last years of Therafields.

Around 1980 I returned to my scholarly interests, concentrating especially on the history of hypnosis and psychical research. In 1985 I published a book entitled *Multiple Man* that combined what I had learned in my clinical work on dissociative states with my academic interests in the historical background of dissociative phenomena. From my research on sources for contemporary psychotherapy and hypnosis, I published an academic tome, *Animal Magnetism, Early Hypnotism and Psychical Research from 1766 to 1925: An Annotated Bibliography* (Kraus International, 1988). This led naturally into my next book, *From Mesmer to Freud: Magnetic Sleep and the Roots of Psychological Healing* (Yale University Press, 1993), which discusses the historical foundations for present-day dynamic psychotherapy and traces the rise, from the mesmeric tradition, of what I call the "alternate-consciousness paradigm" in Western therapeutic practice.

My growing interest in hypnosis and alternate consciousnesses moved me more and more in the direction of an investigation of "trance" in general. Nothing in the literature that I had read provided an accurate understanding of those altered states, which seemed to be at once so extraordinary and so common. This book is the result of my search to grasp our experience of trances overall and to see what this tells us about our innermost being.

An order of God tells me how to act. I am not a fakir and a magician. I am God in a body. Everyone has that feeling, but no one uses it. I do make use of it, and know its results. People think that this feeling is a spiritual trance, but I am not in a trance. I am love. I am in a trance, the trance of love. I want to say so much and cannot find the words. I want to write and cannot. I can write in a trance, and this trance is called wisdom.

– *The Diary of Vaslav Nijinsky*, ed. Romola Nijinsky, London: Victor Gollancz, 1937, p. 49

microtrance

The Individual

the trance

ARE YOU IN A TRANCE?
Most people would answer that question with: Of course not! I am in full possession of my faculties. I know who I am, where I am, what I am doing, and why I am doing it. I could not possibly be in a trance.

Nevertheless, I believe we all live our lives going in and out of trances; that trances are behind what is the very best and the very worst in human beings; and that it is possible to become aware of our trances and gain greater control of our lives.

To illustrate, let me ask you a question. At this moment are you "in full possession of your faculties"? If you are really concentrating on this question, you are probably already slipping into a trance. As you continue to read this page you become less aware of the sounds and sights around you. You generally lose touch with your environment. If you are really focused here, you lose track for the moment of the other roles or identities of your life, the fact that you are a "teacher," "salesman," "lover," "friend," "mother." If you began reading with a slight headache or some other minor discomfort, the pain may disappear as you concentrate. All in all, through the experience of reading and becoming immersed in what you are reading, you lose touch with who you are and where you are. You find it hard to gauge the passage of time. You don't notice your body. You lose track of your relationships and your surroundings. These are typical features of the state called "trance."

This reading trance is so commonplace that it escapes notice. Yet it can be a truly engulfing experience. As you become progressively more absorbed in reading, your trance could become so profound that you would fail to notice important things—such as the fact that you have reached your subway stop or that the pot is boiling over on the stove.

But if something suddenly shocks you back to "reality"—if the subway lurches unexpectedly or you spill coffee on your lap—you snap out of your trance. Your attention again broadens to include a wider spectrum of impressions. You are once more aware of the place, the time, your body, the environment. You awake from your reading trance.

This reading trance is just one example of a multitude of trances. Taken together, the trances of everyday life form the fabric of our human existence. Their effects are important. They can enhance our experiences, but they can also rob us of freedom and fulfilment.

Let's wake up now and turn the page.

The Entranced Couple

I noticed the couple as I entered the restaurant. They were engaged in a quiet but intense conversation as I passed their table. The suppressed passion of their dialogue continued to draw my attention as I looked over the menu. There was obviously some trouble between them, some disagreement, and their attempts to subdue the outward expression of what they were feeling paradoxically made them more obvious.

As I looked more closely, I realized there was something familiar about this situation. Each was totally focused on the other. They noticed nothing around them. A stack of dishes could have fallen off the counter a few feet away and they would have barely heard. For them time had no meaning. An hour was like a minute. Their usual involvement with the world was suspended. They were in a world of their own, one very different from that of their fellow diners, a place filled with powerful feelings and images, memories of the situations they were arguing about. Their reality was not the furniture, food, and people of this restaurant; it was the world of their emotional involvement and the images that accompanied it. Yet their reality was every bit as vivid to them as his meal was to the man beginning to eat at the next table. The couple's reality was their highly charged relationship, and they were immersed temporarily in one of the most common and most overpowering kinds of trance that human beings experience, the *relational trance*.

What Is a Trance?

Trance is as old as the human race. Even its most recently devised version, the hypnotic trance, has been with us for more than two hundred years.[1] Although there has always been controversy about what trance is, you probably will not find a better definition than that given by Webster's dictionary: "a state of profound abstraction or absorption." With a slight modification, this definition is perfect. Let us call trance "a state of profound abstraction *and* absorption."

When we define trance this way, we can see that all of the things that have been called trance over the ages are included. In the old days the ecstatic condition of the seer or sibyl was recognized as a trance. So was the profound absorption of the monk in meditation. Trance was identified in the comatose state of the mesmerized surgical patient, about to undergo a painless operation.

In everyday life, trance characterizes the fixed attention of fascination and the glazed-eye absence of the daydreamer. Stage magicians induce a suggestible state to entertain, and medical experimenters speak of their hypnotized subjects in trances. These and many more instances of trance can be grouped under the definition I am proposing. In fact, this simple description gives us a unified theory of trance for the first time. In what follows, I will spell out how trance, understood this way, can be found everywhere in life.

What about the couple in the restaurant? It is easy to see that they qualify. They were profoundly abstracted or cut off from what was going on around them, and just as profoundly absorbed in each other. Using this couple as a starting point, we can call trance a state in which a person is absorbed in one thing and oblivious to everything else.

Some striking features characterize trance. One is seeing things that are not there—positive hallucination. Another is not seeing things that *are* there—negative hallucination. Also a person in trance can have a distorted experience of time. Minutes can seem like hours. Or time can speed up so that hours seem like minutes. All of these things appeared to be happening to the couple in their trance. They were unable to see (or hear) things that were right in front of them. Their reality was the vivid impressions of situations and people at the basis of their disagreement, and no one around them could see those images. And I am quite certain that if someone were to ask them to judge the passage of time at the end of their argument, they would have failed miserably.

Other features go along with trance, and I will get to them later. For now I would like to say something about the expression "relational trance." I believe there are a number of different kinds of trance. One of them involves being absorbed in one's feelings and thoughts about another person. That kind of absorption, with its accompanying abstraction from everything else, is what I call relational trance. Other kinds of trance are equally common in our lives. Let me give an example.

The Painter

flow?

Dan is a painter. He always paints in the same place: a studio he has designed for the purpose. When he enters his studio and begins to prepare his painting materials, he becomes very meditative. He forgets about whatever he has been involved in before and his mind fills up with thoughts about the painting he is currently working on. Even before he puts brush to canvas, he is imagining himself mixing a colour, choosing a brush, applying the paint. With each step, he becomes more and more lost in the process of planning and doing the painting.

Like the couple in the restaurant, Dan does not hear extraneous sounds. Nothing seems to penetrate his senses except what has to do with the painting. As images fill his mind and he becomes more and more engrossed in the painting process, he loses all track of time. A whole afternoon can go by without his noticing. The only indication of time passing that registers with him is the change in the light as the day grows late—and he is aware of that only because of its effect on what he is doing.

Dan tells me that if he begins painting with a headache or if his bursitis is acting up, he loses awareness of the pain as he focuses on his work. He also speaks of another peculiarity—pertaining to memory. After he has finished for the day and is relaxing with a friend over a cup of coffee, he can remember very little of what he did while painting. If his friend inquires about the thought processes that led to this or that decision about his painting, or asks about the different alternatives he considered when choosing a paint, Dan cannot reconstruct them. In treatises on trance this is usually called amnesia. Yet when Dan resumes his work the next day, all his thoughts and decisions about painting return to him in vivid detail and he cannot imagine how he could have forgotten them.

Without realizing it, Dan is using a trance state when he paints. Each day, in the familiar, well-designed setting, he eases himself into a state of consciousness that allows him to work with an effective and creative concentration. Dan's painting trance immerses him in a well-defined project or situation, so I call it a *situational trance.*

Dan's situational trance shares a number of features identical to those associated with the restaurant couple's relational trance, and a few others besides. In addition to positive and negative hallucinations and time distortion, Dan also experiences another characteristic of trance—analgesia, the inability to feel pain. This is a quality that some dentists use when they hypnotize people to carry out painless dental work. Analgesia is a much more common feature of daily life than most of us realize.

Inner-Mind Trance

Trances do not always result from involvements outside ourselves. Sometimes a trance occurs when we turn inward and become completely absorbed in our own thoughts. This is what I call an *inner-mind trance.* Let me give you an example. One beautiful June day I had been working in my office and at lunchtime decided to walk the six blocks to a restaurant. I was delighted to get out into the sunny weather, and I fully intended to enjoy the beautiful landscape as I strolled.

But then I started thinking, "How am I going to begin this book on trances in daily life that I have been planning?" My mind began to delve into my ideas, turning them over like shovelfuls of earth in a spring garden. I walked, but I did not think about it and hardly knew where I was going. I saw nothing of the beauty around me. I barely heard the traffic rushing by me and other pedestrians made no impression on me at all.

Suddenly I realized that I had walked two blocks and had taken in nothing of my surroundings, so immersed was I in my inner environment. I mentally shook myself back to the present and reproached myself for losing the opportunity to enjoy the day. With new resolution, I moved on, feeling the breeze, seeing the sights. But in less than a minute it was all gone again. I was once more walking the inner landscape of my thoughts about the book, while my body, little more than a robot, trudged through the outer.

After another two blocks I stopped. I could hardly believe it—I had done it again. By now it was becoming amusing. Despite my best efforts I could not stop myself from sliding into my inner landscape. I recognized the irony in the situation. I was thinking about issues concerning trance in everyday life, and in the process was repeatedly and contrary to my wishes falling into just one of those trances. I was the helpless captive of my own *inner-mind trance.*

By now it had become clear to me that I would have to include this experience in the book, so when I arrived at the restaurant I began to write it all down. Also, the whole thing was becoming something of an experiment that I could both experience and at the same time observe. Sitting in the restaurant and writing, I noticed that the world around me dissolved and reconstituted itself as I turned my attention to writing and withdrew it again. This building, these people, faded in and out as my reality shifted from the outer to the inner world and back.

The experience I describe here is certainly not an unusual one. Most people will be able to think of similar occurrences in their own lives. But we do not usually identify the experience as a trance.

Group-Mind Trance

American psychologist Boris Sidis wrote of a striking instance of a trance that was not limited to one person, but affected a whole group. He cited the memoirs of a Russian writer and journalist,

Ivan Ivanovich Panaev, describing the riots of military colonists in Russia in 1831. Panaev recounted that, in the course of some of the hardest fighting, he came across a corporal lying in the street, crying bitterly. When Panaev asked why he was crying, the young soldier said it was because a mob down the street was trying to kill his beloved commander, Sokolov. Panaev suggested that the corporal stop crying and go to his leader's aid. A little later, when Panaev himself brought soldiers to help Sokolov, he was astonished to see that the corporal had joined the mob and was beating Sokolov with a club himself. Panaev asked what on earth he was doing. The young man replied, "Everyone else is doing it. Why shouldn't I?"

Immersed in the energy of the mob, the corporal had totally given up his own individuality and control of his own mind. His normal perception of reality had disappeared, and he was locked into the thinking and reality of the mob. The mob possessed a corporate mind that overwhelmed the personal views of all who came under its sway. The "Group-Mind" of the rioters was so strong that even the soldier sincerely devoted to his commander could not resist it. He was plunged into a *group-mind trance* in which he was absorbed into the thought and emotion of the group and out of touch with reality as he normally knew it.

Group-mind trance does not occur only in highly charged temporary gatherings, such as riots or lynch mobs. Group-mind trance is a part of the everyday life of each one of us. We belong to various kinds of groups—families, work groups, churches, and other organizations. Each has its own group mind that entrances us, perhaps more subtly than a lynch mob, but every bit as effectively. And in the group-mind trance, we experience all the features of other trance states.

Group-mind trances give us a basis for understanding the macrotrance of culture. We can think of group-mind trances on a spectrum ranging from the family at one end to culture at the other. Culture is the group-mind trance of a whole people, and because it is so pervasive it remains largely invisible to those held in its sway.

The influence of group-mind trances cannot be overestimated. I will be talking about this in greater detail in a later chapter. In the meantime, let me summarize what I have been saying about trance.

The Four Trances

There are four main ways that we can become absorbed in something and oblivious to everything else—four main kinds of trance. We experience these four trances every day of our lives. For the sake of convenience, I have given the four trances a name and a number.

TRANCE 1

In the *relational trance* one person is absorbed in another and oblivious to other matters. Trance 1 operates in everything from concern for a friend to sickening worry about a loved one, from annoyance with a co-worker to loathing for a sadistic abuser, from flirtation to lovemaking, from interest to obsession.

TRANCE 2

Situational trance involves immersion in an activity, project, work, or enterprise to the exclusion of other interests. As a rule, the more engrossed you are in the situation, the better you do. People who are successful with their projects tend to be those capable of deep situational trance. Examples of situational trance are typing a letter, threading a needle, watching a play, addressing a staff meeting, performing a dance, and writing a book.

TRANCE 3

Inner-mind trance occurs when your attention is withdrawn from the concerns of the external world and focused on images of your inner mind (the internal world). Hypnosis and meditation are examples of inner-mind trance, but they are not the ones most commonly experienced. Dreaming is an inner-mind trance that occurs every day, although we may not always remember that we have dreamed. In dreaming, the external world is totally blotted out and

images of the inner mind dominate us completely. For that reason
it is the most profound inner-mind trance that we can have. Other
examples of common inner-mind trances include driving while
preoccupied, being "lost in thought," and daydreaming.

TRANCE 4

The trance that is least recognized but very significant in our lives is
group-mind trance. Here the individual becomes a carrier of the values and drives that characterize the group as a whole. While immersed in the group mind, people may think and act in ways that
are totally out of character with the ways they behave when separate. Group-mind trance can occur in connection with such groups
as one's family, church, or club; at sports events, rock concerts, tenants' meetings, and political conventions; or when involved with
the staff at work or friends at a gathering. Group-mind trance forms
a bridge to cultural trance, which may be thought of as a group-
mind trance on the level of a whole people.

The Nuts and Bolts of Trance

Trance involves focus on one thing and a corresponding withdrawal
of attention from another. For that reason, trance admits of degrees.
A person may focus so intently on something that he or she has virtually no awareness of anything else. That is a deep trance. On the
other hand, someone may be occupied with one thing but maintain
a moderate degree of awareness of other things. That is a light
trance. Between these two extremes lie every possible degree of
absorption/abstraction—every degree of trance.

ABSORPTION

Absorption, immersion, focusing, being preoccupied with—these
are ways of describing how our attention can fix itself on something. Being able to concentrate intently is a gift, a natural ability
that has many benefits. It allows us to take in a lecture or engage in
deep conversation. We need it to be aware of an infant's subtle

communication. Absorption is crucial when climbing a rock face. It allows an athlete to win a game of tennis.

ABSTRACTION

Abstraction, obliviousness, unawareness—these terms show the other side of the coin of trance. They describe a withdrawal of attention, a loosening of mental connection with something. The ability to be unaware is also a gift. If we were aware of everything in our experience or our environment all at once, life would become intolerable. If, as I walked down the street, I were aware of the meanings of the expressions on every face, paid attention to every sound, and examined every aspect of my body's movements, I would quickly reach overload. If I were to conjure up all my worries, ponder all my obligations, think about all my relationships, recall all of my memories, survey all my knowledge, and engage myself in all these awarenesses simultaneously, I would be overwhelmed and paralysed. It is important to be able to block out, to censor, to limit my awareness, to *not* think about things, and we do it all the time.

Both of these aspects of trance, absorption and abstraction, go together very nicely. The greater my absorption in one thing, the greater my abstraction from the rest. As my absorption/abstraction increases and my trance becomes more profound, some peculiar things happen, and these things deeply affect my experience.

The Facets and Features of Trance

Certain features often accompany trance states. These have been discussed at some length in books about hypnosis, and they apply to all types of trance. While they may not all be present in every trance we experience, they occur more frequently than we might expect.

POSITIVE AND NEGATIVE HALLUCINATIONS

One of the most striking aspects of trance is the creation of hallucinations. A hallucination is anything that is perceived by the entranced person and not by other people. If, for example, I see a dog lying in the middle of the living-room floor but nobody else in the room sees it, it is an hallucination.

Many hallucinations are not so obvious. That is because we have come to take the experience of hallucinations for granted in our everyday lives. For instance, if I am preoccupied with a particular person, I may mistakenly believe I see that person in a crowd as I walk down the street. Then when I "look closer," I see that I was "only imagining" that I saw her. This is a hallucination, but because it is such a common experience it does not upset me to have it.

There are two kinds of hallucinations, positive and negative. These labels have nothing to do with good and bad. A positive hallucination is the perception of something that is not there. A negative hallucination means *not* seeing something that *is* there.

Hallucinations can involve any of the senses. I can hallucinate that I am seeing something, hearing something, smelling something, feeling something, tasting something. These things happen to us all the time. If I smell smoke when there is none, that's a positive hallucination. The same is true if I hear an imaginary prowler in the house or feel a non-existent insect crawling down my arm. I am subject to a negative hallucination when I cannot see the jar of mustard right in front of me in the refrigerator, or when I do not hear my name called when I am engrossed in a book.

The last example clearly involves a trance, as I described it in the preamble to this book. The trances of everyday life include all kinds of hallucinations, positive and negative. The couple in the restaurant experienced both. They could not hear the conversations and noises around them (negative hallucinations) and they were engrossed in private mental images that were highly charged emotionally (positive hallucinations). Dan the painter could clearly envision his completed work (positive hallucination), but was oblivious to neighbourhood noises (negative hallucination).

Hallucinations can involve more than a simple sensation. They can include complexities of feeling and value judgments that influence the way a person experiences the hallucination. The psychotically obsessed fan perceives the movie star as madly in love with him. The guilty child sees reproach in his mother's face, although she does not yet realize he has broken the vase. The mother of the child subjected to incest does not see the telltale bruises and hopeless eyes of her daughter. The loyal parishioner does not see the staggering steps of his inebriated priest. Evidently, relational trances are particularly riddled with complex hallucinations.

MEMORY

When we leave a trance, afterwards we can experience amnesia for what occurred during the altered state. This loss of memory is quite common. The painter, Dan, remarked that when he was relaxing after a day of painting he often could not recall thoughts he'd had while painting. He also noted that when he returned to painting the next day, he could remember the previous day's thoughts very well. Why does trance amnesia occur? And why does it disappear when the person is entranced once again?

About thirty years ago, a fascinating discovery was made about how we remember: if you learn a piece of information while you're in a particular state of consciousness, you can best recall that information when you return to the same state of consciousness. This means, for example, that if someone gave you a telephone number while you were drinking at a party but you could not remember it the next day, you could likely recall the number if you again had a few drinks. Your memory of the number is keyed to the intoxicated state. This is called "state-related learning," producing "state-related memory."

But this applies to more than chemically altered states of consciousness. It applies equally well to the various states of consciousness we go through in our ordinary daily lives. Let me give another example.

I am a psychotherapist and I see clients in a quiet, comfortable office. In the course of my work with a person, he or she will give me a great deal of information. When sitting in a session with a client, I find I can easily recall details that the person mentioned six months, a year, or even several years before. The reason is that each time I begin a session I go into a particular state of consciousness—

let's call it my psychotherapy state. That state is defined by the familiar, comfortable surroundings, my readiness to listen to the person I am with, my expectation that my responses will be therapeutically useful, and so forth. Each time I go into that state, I can recall quite easily things that a person told me when I was in that state before, even long before. That is because my remembering is "state-related."

Now suppose I saw a client, Jim, for a session in the morning and then, in the afternoon, met him by chance in a nearby coffee shop. And suppose he were to sit down at my table and ask me about something that occurred in the morning session—why I made a certain comment about a situation he described. The truth is that I am likely to be at a loss for an answer. I might find it impossible to recall the situation he had described or my comment about it, even though all this happened a scant few hours before. Now, this memory lapse is not owing to dying brain cells or simple stupidity. It occurs because in the coffee shop I am in a state of consciousness so different from my psychotherapy state that I cannot retrieve the information. My state-related learning will only return if I can get myself back into my psychotherapy state.

Maybe I can actually do that. Maybe I can somehow bring back my psychotherapy state on the spot and regain the information I need. I believe we often do exactly that. Without realizing what we are doing, we use subtle tricks to bring back the "mood" of the situation in which we first absorbed the information. In this case, I try to reconnect with my psychotherapy state of the morning by picturing where Jim was sitting in my office, recalling how I felt as he spoke, reconstructing his emotional state at the time. Then it comes back to me. The memory of the session reconstitutes itself, and I can respond to his question.

Difficulties with memory are often simply difficulties with returning to the state in which we receive the information. Students are sometimes stymied by this problem, concluding wrongly that their memories are no good. They usually do not need to learn new and improved methods of memorization but rather methods for regaining the appropriate state of consciousness.

It is now quite clear why trance amnesia occurs. Each trance constitutes a separate state of consciousness. When I leave a particular trance, I will have problems retrieving what happened during that trance. When I return to that trance, my retrieval problem disappears. Trance amnesia is simply a demonstration of state-related memory.

TIME DISTORTION

When Dan was painting, he would lose all track of time. Several hours could pass without his noticing. People engaged in intense conversations (e.g., the couple in the restaurant) experience a similar kind of "compressing" of time. This time compression is a common characteristic of trance. The opposite experience, time expansion, can also take place. A dream that takes less than a minute of real time can lead the dreamer through a complex series of experiences that seem to last several years. Those who use meditation for problem solving may explore the facets of a problem, consider various solutions, and arrive at a decision in a subjective time that seems like hours, whereas in fact it lasts only a few minutes.

Time compression and time expansion in trance states are simply special instances of the relativity of time in human life. An enjoyable party is over before you know it. On the other hand, parents on a car trip with small children know very well how long a few minutes can seem when they are trying to find a rest room for a desperate youngster.

PHYSIOLOGICAL EFFECTS

Trance can affect the body in many ways. Some have to do with sensation, particularly pain. Dan said if he began painting with some kind of pain (headache, bursitis) it would fade as he got more and more deeply absorbed in what he was doing. The reduction or removal of pain during a trance can be quite startling. A person can begin a session of lovemaking (one of the most powerful relational trances) with a rather severe pain, such as a headache or stomachache, and lose all awareness of that pain as the lovemaking proceeds, only to find it returns immediately and in full force after orgasm.

With trance it is also possible to lose all feeling in the body temporarily or, on the other hand, to develop a heightened sensitivity to sensation. Strength too can be affected; entranced people have been known to lift weights far beyond their normal capacity. Trance can also affect basic functions, such as heart rate and blood pressure. There is even evidence that the immune system can be enhanced by trance.

Meaningful Reality

To make sense of the world we live in, we are constantly projecting a unity and meaning onto it. We pick and choose among the impressions reaching us, and we make our choices largely according to our past experience. This is particularly true of cultural trance. Our culture teaches us what to see and how to see it. Our culture at once focuses our attention and censors our perception. Other factors also affect how we perceive the world. These derive from group-mind influences in our lives and our unique experiences as individuals.

When we perceive the world in our limited ways, we create a reality for ourselves. This subjectively formed reality, for good or ill, gives cohesion to our experience. To avoid a useless debate about what is reality or what is "real," let me say that the trance always creates a "meaningful reality" for the person who is entranced. In the consciousness of this person, only certain things are charged with meaning. Everything else becomes insignificant and for all practical purposes fades from existence.

Meaningful reality is determined by the individual and the situation. It is easy to make the mistake of thinking we are all living in much the same meaningful reality. Two friends sitting side by side at a party can be living in two entirely different meaningful realities. Matt is happy, relaxed, optimistic. He has just come from work where he closed a deal that is going to net him a lot of prestige and a considerable amount of money. He views his friends at the party through an aura of good feeling. They are interesting, stimulating, a delight. He engages in chat with them enthusiastically and talks and jokes energetically with each one, as his excess of good humour carries him through the evening.

Next to him sits Peggy whose marriage is breaking up. She and her husband have just had another one of their "talks," full of bitterness about their past and pessimism about their future. To Peggy the world looks dull and grey. She talks with her friends lethargically. She doesn't see the humour in their jokes; she has no real interest in what they are saying. Each smiling face makes her feel oddly sad. Every happy couple reminds her of her own misery and increases her depression. Matt and Peggy do not inhabit the same meaningful reality at all. And for one of them to bridge this gap to the other's reality would be very difficult indeed.

Extreme Measures

Sometimes the psyche can play bizarre tricks on the outer mind and create a belief in a meaningful reality that contradicts all the known facts. This can occur when a person has an extreme emotional need to know something to be true.

I have worked with clients who have insisted that certain people they knew were still alive, in the flesh, when they had already attended their funerals. One man who had been very attached to his now deceased mother went through periods in which he was certain she was alive and would be coming to visit him. I have also worked with a woman who was absolutely convinced for a long time that her father had no genital organs. She was so sexually frightened of him that she could not bear to think he had the usual male equipment. In all these instances, these clients were otherwise completely sane.

It is natural that our meaningful realities shift as our trances shift. Since trances are an integral part of ordinary living, we can expect a lot of reality shifting in the course of a day. Most of us have come to accept this and are not alarmed when it occurs, even though we may not be too happy about the states we have shifted to. It seems to me that having a flexible attitude about meaningful reality is a sign of mental health.

Suggestibility

It has long been known that human beings are suggestible creatures. A child is going to sleep in his bed. In the dark he sees a bogeyman across the room, looking at him, waiting to pounce. The rest of that child's world shrinks to nothing. He calls out in terror. When his mother arrives and turns on the light, he sees only a shirt draped over a chair. The meaningful reality that dominated his existence a few minutes earlier is suddenly gone.

We tend to think of suggestibility affecting children or attached to hypnosis; the truth is that it is an intrinsic part of daily human life. From birth we are told how the world is and how we should feel about it. Those suggestions become a part of our being. We cannot easily isolate them and see how we are being influenced, so we mistakenly believe that we have some objective view of the world, garnered from some unsullied perspective.

We live our lives in the context of a meaningful reality that is reality-as-we-see-it, not reality-as-it-is, or absolute reality. We have no way of knowing a world of absolute reality. We give our world its meanings, its value, its shapes, its colour, its life. If it is alive for us, as the shirt was alive for the boy in his bedroom, then for all practical purposes it *is* alive.

How do we determine what is real? It all depends on our point of view. When the mother turned on the light, the boy made a correction to his reality. But did he then end up with the absolutely "true" view of reality? Is there such a thing as an absolutely "true" view of reality? I don't think so. Matt's and Peggy's experiences at the party were strikingly different in their meaningful realities. Was one "true" and the other "false"? No, just different.

Every meaningful reality is conditioned by our individual experiences and the group and cultural influences that impinge on us.

If, as in the case of Matt and Peggy, the differences can vary so greatly between people within the same culture, think how different the meaningful realities must be between people living in different ethnic contexts, who come from different cultural traditions, or who inhabit deeply contrasting socio-economic strata within the same society. Here the meaningful realities can be so divergent that individuals may not understand each other at all. I'll say more about this in the chapter on cultural trance.

Consensus Reality

Each group forms its own meaningful reality. Each family, for instance, has its own way of looking at things—with its perceptual clarity and its distortions—and its own sense of what is important. All of this contributes to a unique meaningful reality. The same is true of other groups. What is real will vary greatly from group to group according to the combination of experiential factors that have gone into the creation of that group.

The meaningful reality of the group comes out of the group-mind trance that focuses its members on a particular set of experiences, to the exclusion of others. One group's meaningful reality may seem very strange to the members of another group. This does not necessarily mean that one reality is right and the other wrong, although a person may be strongly tempted to see it that way.

The meaningful reality of a group maintains itself through the members continually reinforcing the group perception for one another. They encourage each other to think the same way and cement their solidarity in a variety of ways, conscious and unconscious. The result is consensus reality, an implicit agreement about what is real. A group's meaningful reality is consensus reality.

Consensus reality makes communication possible. We can only communicate to the extent that we share common images. We badly need consensus reality to create a serviceable common background against which the tension of diverse meaningful realities on individual realities can exist without creating chaos. We develop a comfortable feeling of inhabiting the same world with our fellow group members. We can take it for granted that we share with each other the same basic practical principles for daily living.

Consensus reality gives us a sense of security. We accomplish this at a certain cost. Claiming to have an exclusive proprietorship over what is real and true, the culture offers us little opportunity to explore what is unfamiliar. Those who introduce novel ideas into the culture tend to be pushed to the periphery. Therefore, the culture's consensus reality changes very slowly.

The Pros and Cons of Trance

Trances are central in our experience of everyday life. They help make our lives more effective in many ways. The problem is that trances can also impede our functioning or block our enjoyment of life. This is because trances involve both abstraction and absorption.

The absorption part of this duality of trance has many advantages. In situational trances, absorption allows the kind of focus that is needed to make things happen. The more baseball players concentrate on their game, the more effective they will be. Many pitchers, for instance, are at their very best when they are so focused on the catcher and the next pitch that nothing else intrudes on their attention. These pitchers go through a series of ritualized movements before each pitch (e.g., pulling down the brim of the cap, rubbing the glove on the right shoulder, or kicking the dirt with the left foot) to induce this profound situational trance. And it is evident in the fixed and semi-glazed look in their eyes and cataleptic (pliantly rigid) state of their muscles when they are about to pitch. If something interrupts that state (say the umpire calls time out just before the pitch), the trance is broken. The muscles loosen, the eyes once more look about at random, and the pitcher must again go through the ritual actions that will re-induce the trance when he resumes play.

Relational trances also profit from absorption. The mother's deep immersion in the care of her infant produces all kinds of benefits. An involved mother reads the meanings of different kinds of crying and responds appropriately. She can tell what each facial expression means and read the message in the different postures the child assumes. Her concentration helps her understand how to convey things to the child and allows her to grasp the child's own early attempts to communicate.

Absorption in thoughts or images of the inner world, the very essence of inner-mind trances, can be very valuable. A skilled therapist can help a hypnotized person recover powerful repressed memories. Totally uninvolved with the external world, the hypnotized person explores the emotions, images, and sensations of another time. In a deep hypnotic trance, his immersion in that inner reality can be so complete that everything else fades. The remembered event becomes so real that the person experiences the memory as though it were happening right now. All the original sensations and emotions return with full force. Memories recovery of this kind can have immense therapeutic benefit.

Other inner-mind trances occur spontaneously, without planning. A person may go into an abstracted or absent-minded state when there is some vexing problem that she has to solve. While in that state, her awareness of what is going on around her dims considerably. When she has solved the problem, she returns to normal awareness.

Group-mind trances can also have beneficial effects. Wrapped up in the group-mind trance of the spectators at a basketball game, the fan enjoys the elation of good play and the satisfaction of victory. A volunteer fund raiser for the Red Cross partakes of the prestige of that organization when speaking with prospective donors. With group-mind trances in general, the person participates in the character and energy of the group with which he or she is connected. When that character is positive and constructive, it confers that quality on the individual.

From this it is clear that, in all four trances, the entranced person can benefit from absorption. However, there is also a negative aspect of the absorption/abstraction duality of trance: a person may be so deeply absorbed in something that he or she loses touch with an important aspect of reality.

Someone who becomes obsessed with another person suffers from this kind of imbalance. The obsessed person's awareness narrows to the point that she cannot see the object of her obsession in the context of broader reality. She forfeits common sense completely and may behave bizarrely. She invests the object of her obsession with extreme qualities (extremely good or extremely bad), and no amount of persuasion can change her view. In a failed relationship, for example, a man who does not want to separate from his wife or partner may become obsessed with her, calling her and confronting her at every opportunity. All other considerations disappear and he spends every moment thinking about his former partner and planning ways to get her back. A dangerous relational trance of this kind may last for weeks, months, or even years. Families sometimes experience the dark side of situational trances. A father may become so involved in his work that he does not notice his children and their needs. Even when at home, he may remain in his work trance to such an extent that the children eventually give up expecting anything from him.

A manager may become so involved in financial worries that he cannot see the dissatisfaction developing among his staff. His excessive focus on the mechanics of the business blinds him to his crucial personnel problems.

An inner-mind trance, too, can pull a person away from involvement with other important aspects of life. A student who spends time daydreaming rather than studying sabotages her own educational goals. Her inner-mind trances entice her because she populates them with pleasant images of her own making, but in the trance she loses touch with her broader goals.

My book-plotting trance illustrates both advantages and disadvantages of inner-mind trances. It helped me in the process of putting the book together, while it took me away from what I really wanted to do at that moment: enjoy my walk.

The isolated and inward life of the cult is a good example of an unbalanced group-mind trance. The individual cult member is totally engaged in the thinking and concerns of the group and sees outside views as threatening. The more powerful the cult's group-mind trance, the more possible it becomes for the cult to abuse its members. Members surrender themselves to the thinking of the group without question and so retain little ability to resist abusive treatment.

The Phenomena of Trance

Traditionally, the phenomena of trance have been associated with a special state called "hypnosis." These include amnesia, analgesia, negative and positive hallucinations, control of autonomous bodily functions, time distortion, heightened recall, heightened sensitivity, catalepsy, effortless imagination, ideomotor responsiveness, and suggestibility. There is no basis for believing that these phenomena are limited to this special trance state. We all have the capacity to produce these phenomena, and we can experience any of them at any moment in our everyday existence. So, as it turns out, the phenomena of trance are simply the phenomena of life.

Trance Is Everywhere

Life is a web of trances, ranging from the light to the deep. Often they are layered or nested one within the other. The devotee in love with the cult leader loses himself in a powerful relational trance while enmeshed in the group-mind trance of the cult. The abused child is likewise caught in the family group mind while living in a relational trance of fear of her father and periodically escaping into the inner-mind trance of fantasy. The therapist is absorbed in the situational trance of the psychotherapy session, while at the same time he is in a relational trance with his client.

It is my contention that we are constantly going in and out of trances of various kinds, that human life itself is a tapestry of trances. In the course of one day, our concentration switches from this person to that project to this group situation to that inner preoccupation. These trances guarantee a certain narrowness of life for each of us. Our mental focus continually narrows and widens again as we move through these trances. In shifting from one focus to another, we dismiss what we have just seen in order to take in what is next. As a result, most of the time we are very limited in our mental perspectives.

We constantly experience the phenomena of trance—the amnesias, the hallucinations, the time distortions. We create our peculiar meaningful realities and then naively assume that we all live in the same world. All of this is built into ordinary experience. Precisely because these phenomena are so much a part of each of our lives, we cannot recognize them for what they are.

Trance Zero

When you get to know how trances work in our lives, one painful fact becomes clear: we live our lives piecemeal. At any moment we have only part of the story, the limited view of our own entranced minds. There doesn't seem to be any way around this, so it would be easy to come to a pessimistic conclusion about our ability to ever solve the important problems of life. Surely solutions to the great questions of our existence depend on being able to gain the widest possible perspective on things. But if we are so mired in our multitude of microtrances, and trapped in the blindness of our cultural macrotrance, how can that ever be achieved?

There is a way. It depends on our realizing that, in spite of our material involvements (a trance in itself), we are spiritual beings and there is a deeper mystery to life than we can grasp. This means that we can develop a way to be present and awake at each moment. This can happen through our attaining what I call Trance Zero. Trance Zero is a state of being in touch with our intuitive inner guidance. As do the other four trances, Trance Zero involves absorption and abstraction—with a difference. In Trance Zero we are absorbed—absorbed in what is most appropriate at the moment. In Trance Zero we are also abstracted—abstracted from everything else—but in such a way as to be able instantly to get in touch with any new concern, should that need arise. Trance Zero is an effortless movement from trance to trance through the guidance of a deep intuitive awareness that comes from our own depths.

It's clear that our ordinary trance states cannot yield the wisdom we need. Our fluctuating, limited awareness contains neither the information nor the perspective we need to achieve clarity of perception and thereby unify our lives. Because of abstraction, these states cut off our normal consciousness from the information essential to such unification. They result in feelings of fear and anxiety. No trance state can serve as an environment for dealing with the great issues.

To make this clearer, I would like to talk about our two minds, the outer mind and the inner mind. The outer mind was formed to deal with life in the world. Because its orientation is practical, the outer mind focuses on the present moment with its immediacy and urgency. It is aware almost exclusively of its own concerns and tends to consider itself the totality of the individual.

The inner mind concentrates on our inner world. It is aware of a whole range of inner experiences and feels at home with them. It can take us out of the moment and immerse us in the past or project us into the future. It can put us in contact with the inner processes of the body, the labyrinths of the psyche, and the world of dreams. It is our window on the transcendent. It can give us glimpses of other dimensions and other lives. It can put us in touch with esoteric knowledge, and it can provide a pathway to what I call the Ultimate Self.

In this life the outer mind holds a very important place. It is in charge when we look after the concerns of everyday living, for if we are to deal effectively with the affairs of this world we must be able to concentrate on the relevant matters at hand. If we were in touch with the global awareness available to the inner mind, we would be both distracted and overwhelmed. We could not carry on with the tasks, pursuits, and relationships that make up the fabric of life. The concerns of daily life must take a certain priority if we are to navigate successfully through the world.

But although the outer mind concerns itself with these matters, the awarenesses of the inner mind are crucial for achieving the full richness of human experience. We should consider that the task of our existence is to integrate the life of the outer mind with that of the inner. This integration must be gradual, for the outer mind must maintain its healthy functioning during the process.

The concept of Trance Zero assumes that we can be in touch with the world in ways other than through the conscious, thinking mind, the outer mind. Trance Zero derives from contact with the inner mind. It assumes a dynamic source of wisdom that goes beyond anything that the outer mind could accumulate. It presupposes the existence of an Ultimate Self whose perception and thought transcend our ordinary awareness. Because this Ultimate Self is always active, it can monitor our lives and guide us through our everyday trances in a most creative way and can successfully integrate our inner and outer lives.

I believe that by exploring trances and their place in human life, we will open a door leading to a more dynamic understanding and integration of those mysterious aspects of human existence that derive from living in two worlds. We can move toward a unifying Trance Zero by introducing certain awarenesses and practising certain techniques. Most important, we can progress toward Trance Zero by any step that we take to explore the mystery of what and who we are.

I suppose the ideal state of being would be to transcend trance completely—to be able to be absorbed in everything and abstracted from nothing, somehow to be immersed in reality in its totality. That is beyond what we can attain in this existence, for we live in a world that involves a division between the outer and the inner mind. Because we live and grow within this limitation, we need Trance Zero.

The Ultimate Self

Trance Zero presupposes a tremendous faith in a reliable inner source of wisdom. It involves taking what may appear to be a huge gamble. The gamble is whether I can discover that inner wisdom in myself. Can I really trust in this hidden faculty so completely that I can deliver my life and my future up to it? Can I allow it to guide me even when I cannot see where it is taking me?

Faith in this guidance from within is faith in something that I call the Ultimate Self. Here I am not talking about religious faith, but the acceptance of something within me that I cannot prove. This is the self that lies beyond all my changing states and all my limitations. It is an ultimate presence beyond direct access. We stumble across this presence every time we say "I." Our roles, our mental states, even our personalities change, yet in each of them we say "I." And each time we say "I," we acknowledge a continuity, an agent that persists through every change. This is the final doer of all our actions, the final subject of all our verbs, and the essence of who we are. This is the Ultimate Self.

The Ultimate Self is the point at which the divine manifests itself in the world. As a manifestation of the divine, each human being is in touch with an infinite wisdom which is the basis for believing in our inner guidance. If there is such a thing as a meaning for our lives, a sense of purpose that derives from within us, then the Ultimate Self is the author of that meaning and the origin of the planning necessary for realizing that purpose.

I will be saying more about the Ultimate Self later. For now, let us take a look at how the four trances work in our lives.

relating

RELATIONAL TRANCES mean involvement with another person. The type of involvement can vary greatly, as can its depth or intensity. The relationship may be pleasant, passionate, and self-affirming. All of our relationships are trances, whether they are pleasant or painful, long- or short-term. Relational trance refers to every kind of absorption a person can have with another person and things relating to that person, along with various degrees of abstraction from everything else.

Romantic Love and Friendship

For many of us, the most powerful form of relational trance that we experience in life is romantic love. When romantic love is ignited, the lover shines a powerful beam of attention and regard on the loved one and that person suddenly becomes a centre around which the lover's life begins to turn. When the feeling is mutual, this focused concentration becomes a kind of glue that bonds the two people together and may begin a lifelong alliance. The sexual expression of romantic attraction further solidifies the bond, deepening the knowledge each has of the other and strengthening their passionate desire to be close to each other.

This profound absorption is accompanied by a notable abstraction from or obliviousness to other things. In the early stages of romantic love, obliviousness occurs in two ways. The lover is less aware of certain aspects of his or her life, particularly negative ones, and experiences life in an extremely positive way. The lover is able to deal with life's difficulties much more easily than he or she could before entering the state of romantic love. Those who have just fallen in love are usually a treat to be with because their good feeling seems to permeate everything they do. Also, at this early stage, lovers are largely oblivious to the faults or defects of one another. If they do notice any, the lovers easily dismiss the flaws as unimportant. Often they believe that these are temporary aberrations that will soon pass away.

In later stages of the relationship, each lover becomes more aware of the faults or traits in the other person that he or she considers undesirable. At this point the lover may accommodate them, realizing that the loved one is human and that the faults are not important enough to seriously impede the relationship. Or the lover and beloved may realize that the things they do not like in each other must be dealt with directly. Then there may be confrontations that force each to look at themselves and come to terms with aspects of their personalities that need to be changed. When successful, these confrontations result in a working through of conflicts, and the relationship will alter in a way that benefits both. Whether this process occurs in a formal setting of some kind, such as couples counselling, or in some other way, more serious difficulties must be resolved if the relationship is to last. Those romantic relationships that have been based primarily on a fantasy of the other person, in which the lover has imagined that the loved one possessed qualities that were simply not there, the relationship is not likely to survive the working-through phase. Those that are based on a deep appreciation of the loved one and a strong desire to remain close have a good chance of success.

Even in this more difficult phase of the relationship, the relational trance is still in effect. The loved one remains an important focus of concentration in the lover's life. Even though the earlier extraordinary censorship of awareness has passed, a natural obliviousness to other things still occurs in those periods when a lover concentrates on the loved one consciously. Those romantic relationships that survive the working-through phase attain a strength and dependableness that ensures an ongoing healthy relational trance, one that can be the basis for building a family or other long-term creative projects.

Friendships are remarkably similar to romantic love relationships in the way that they arise and work themselves out. While friendships do not include sexual bonding, they can, in the earlier stages, involve a passionate feeling for the other that is very like the passion of romantic love. As in romantic love, this early passion often entails an obliviousness to the faults of the other. Eventually, a friend too must come to terms with the humanness of the other. And as in romantic love, only those friendships that are based on a realistic appreciation of the other can survive the working-through process.

Parental Love

The love of parent for child is the relational trance that ensures the survival of each new generation. In some cases, it remains a powerful determinant of life direction well into adulthood. Parental love is instinctual, and its strong emotional dimension deepens with familiarity.

Parental love may be present from conception, but it becomes fully active with birth and the parent's opportunity to know the child as a person. Absorption with the child is normally more powerful with the mother than the father in the child's first years. She finds herself attuned to even the smallest communication from the child and keeps herself ready to respond to all of the child's needs. Her absorption with the child is most profound when the child is most helpless and lessens as the child gains strength and develops social skills. As the child grows, the mother adapts herself to his or her new capacities. She encourages the child's growing drive towards independence and adjusts her responses to the child's need for more room to explore.

Ordinarily, the father's role is secondary to that of the mother in the early months of his child's life. It then becomes more prominent as the child's ability to relate expands beyond its mother. This means a gradual deepening of the relational trance between father and child.

All along the way, parents must struggle against the feeling of proprietorship that tends to come with parenthood. Even in the earliest phase of the child's life, parents must combat the temptation to feel that they somehow own their children. As the child moves through the early school years and adolescence, and into early adulthood, parents face a particular challenge. The relationship must change to accommodate the young person's growing independence. As young people become ready to make more and more of their own decisions, parents have to draw back and give them room to do so. Because of this particular challenge, the parental is probably the relational trance requiring the greatest flexibility and capacity to evolve with the changes that occur. It is not always easy for parents to let the burgeoning adult go, for it actually means allowing a gradual diminution of the familiar parental trance. Failure to do so can create a crisis in the relationship and may lead to a disastrous outcome; if appropriate adjustments are made, the relationship can thrive throughout its course. After the child has moved on to an independent life, a form of parental trance remains, and if the separation process has been successful it will probably resemble a friendship more than any other relationship.

The Spell

If you were to meet Carl casually, you would see an energetic, handsome, intelligent university professor, a cultured man who knows what he thinks and who acts decisively. These perceptions would be accurate, yet for years Carl lived the life of a virtual sleepwalker in a relationship that was a mystery from beginning to end.

Carl married Tina when he was 25. They met on the job at a Dallas high school in 1960. Carl was teaching English. Tina was the vice principal. Tina was ten years older than Carl. She was a competent administrator, an intelligent conversationalist, and an altogether likable person. When Tina asked Carl over for dinner, he accepted in the spirit of a colleague, looking forward to a good meal and good conversation.

After the meal, when Tina nestled into Carl's side on the couch, he sensed from her a more personal interest. He felt no particular attraction to her, but he felt it would be awkward to discourage her attention. As time went on, he found himself sliding more and more into the relationship, spending an increasing amount of time with Tina, moving inexorably toward a liaison.

Carl experienced his relationship with Tina in a very strange way. In retrospect, he described it as being drawn into a web and held there. His mind was not functioning as it usually did. He increased his involvement with Tina in a way that seemed robotic, as though the relationship were inevitable. He seemed to be under some kind of spell.

Carl and Tina married, although marriage came about in the same seemingly inevitable way as the rest of their relationship. Time passed, and after seven years of marriage, Carl's soul began to stir. It was the sixties, and he was aware of exciting changes in the world around him while feeling that his life insulated him from those changes. He began to feel stultified and trapped in the marriage. It did not occur to him to talk over his dissatisfaction with Tina. They simply never discussed such things. His disquiet continued to grow to the point that momentarily he even thought of killing Tina to free himself of the marriage that he now hated.

Carl remained emotionally and mentally paralysed until a business trip during which he met a young woman to whom he felt an immediate attraction. It was as though he had suddenly awakened. Feelings dead for years came alive again, and he began for the first time to wonder how his marriage had ever come about in the first place. Thinking back on it, he saw that it did not seem right from the start, but it had never occurred to him to question the events that led to the wedding. Now he actively probed the nature of his relationship with Tina and questioned its value. With this awakening came the realization that his marriage was over.

For the first time, Carl talked about his feelings with Tina. Soon they agreed on a divorce. As he described it, "The bubble of the marriage had burst and the marriage simply collapsed without the need of any rational process. It was just gone."

As Carl walked away in his awakened state, he looked back at his married life. He felt astonished at the stupor he had lived in for the previous eight years. He did not feel like the same person who had pronounced the marriage vows. This difference was reflected in physical changes that accompanied Carl's awakening. He had gained a great deal of weight during the years of his marriage. Now, within a few weeks, he lost 30 pounds without even trying.

Why had this happened to Carl? Because his life had been dominated for more than eight years by a profound relational trance, he had focused on Tina and her view of the relationship to the exclusion of every other consideration. He had completely lost touch with his own sense of what kind of relationship he wanted. Even when he felt trapped and contemplated doing away with his wife, he still focused completely on her, unaware that he could have left her if he had wanted to. When he met the other woman on the business trip, he awakened and became aware of the broader world of relationships and a freedom to choose that he had forgotten existed. Although he did not establish a relationship with the woman he met on the trip, he felt grateful to her for being there at the right moment.

Mutuality

Many relational trances involve both people equally in their trance connection. Mutual affection and love are relational trances that build positive bonds between their participants. Mutual dislike or hatred builds bonds of the opposite kind.

Bonds are bonds, and whether the relational trance is positive or negative the connection and dependency are there. To think that we are tied only to those we care for is a mistake. Some of the strongest and most lasting connections are negative.

Sometimes the relational trance is one-sided. One person may be very aware of and involved with another person without that other person knowing or caring, or caring equally.

One-sided relational trances are often unhealthy and loaded with fantasy. We see sad examples of this with people who become obsessed with particular celebrities. The pop singer Anne Murray has suffered greatly from the attentions of a male fan who for years has carried the delusion that she is in love with him. He has followed and accosted her and acted as though she has a secret passion for him but cannot let the public know. His frequent appearances in court and psychiatric sessions seem to have done little to dissuade him from his delusional pursuit.

David Letterman's obsessive fan has spun a similar delusion around the famous talk-show host. She has broken into his home and caused him great distress. She too remains fixed in her fantastic belief that she is his soul mate.

One-sided relational trances are one-sided only in terms of the present. Below the surface the celebrity is likely to be simply a stand-in for some important figure in the entranced person's early life. As long as that original relational trance is not explored, the entranced person will not be able to give up the delusion.

Transference

When a relational trance occurs as a throwback to an earlier situation, the entranced person's feelings and expectations are transferred from that earlier situation to the present. This relationship is characterized by what is called a "transference." That was the case with Julie who saw me for psychotherapy a few years ago.

One day she came into my office looking frightened and wary. Over the two years of my work with her, we had developed a good rapport. But now, for a reason she could not explain, she viewed me with uneasiness. She was embarrassed about this. As we discussed the matter, she assured me that there was nothing that I had said or done that accounted for her uneasiness. Yet there it was.

She explained that she felt as though I was going to yell at her and hit her. Although I was calm and friendly enough at the moment, she believed I was just waiting for an excuse to become enraged with her.

These feelings stayed with her for some time. During this period, she went into her fearful state as soon as she walked into my office. Between sessions, she could barely believe she was having such thoughts about me. Yet each time she was in my presence, she would be filled with dread.

Eventually it became clear what was happening. Julie was seeing me as her father. He was a violent, abusive man who constantly berated her and frequently hit her. As she opened up to me in therapy, these feelings were loosened and had become attached to me. Without her knowing it, she was viewing me as her brutal father. When she was in my presence, she was completely focused on me as her father's stand-in. Our previous good rapport was forgotten, as though it had never existed. Eventually Julie was able to resolve these feelings toward me, and once again see me as myself and relate to me on the basis of what was happening in the present. Her transference relational trance had passed.

Transference feelings are common in ordinary life. We can easily impose the image of some significant person from our past onto a person in our present lives and then respond to him or her as though the person today were that person from the past. This can occur in things small or great. Where it is powerful and encompassing, the relational trance runs very deep.

Obsession

All trances create their own universes. The meaningful reality of the entranced person is what he or she believes it to be, and may be unrecognizable to others. Perhaps this is most powerfully illustrated in obsession—a relational trance that has spun out of control.

Sometimes a relational trance can carry over from childhood. Abuse suffered then may be unconsciously sought and continued in the present. This was true of Gail. She found herself entangled in a relationship that for a period completely dominated her life.

In her final years of university, Gail had begun seeing a counsellor, Frank, to help her with fears and self-esteem. She continued her counselling with him after university and through the beginning of her marriage and raising a family. In the process of examining the possible causes of her problems, she told him about her growing-up years. She had been the scapegoat of her family in general and the object of ongoing sexual and physical abuse from her father in particular.

Over time, Frank's sympathy and warmth elicited a strong trust from Gail. Gradually, expressions of affection—hugs—occurred at the end of sessions. Then physical contact began to occur in the middle of the counselling sessions. As the months went by, the touches became more and more sensual. Eventually Frank was directly stimulating her sexually.

As things progressed, the counselling sessions became more isolated from the rest of Gail's life. Although her own family was very important to her, she did not, or could not, think of them when she was with Frank. While in his presence, she had no sense of doing something improper or disloyal to her husband. She was aware of nothing but Frank and their relationship, and she worried only about how that was going at those moments. In fact, if Frank raised some issue about her life with her husband or her child, Gail did not like it. She felt that she was losing the intensity of what was happening between her and Frank in the present. She wanted their concentration on each other to be total.

Over several years, Frank became more and more abusive toward Gail. He would routinely make fun of her ideas or interests during their "counselling sessions." He would also hint at opportunities for greater intimacy, and then laugh at her when she became excited about them. A session in which Frank was intimate and sexual with Gail might be followed by one in which he announced that all the sexual contact had to end because it was improper. While Gail struggled to accept this new arrangement, he would suddenly reverse his stand and become sexually aggressive toward her. At times he abused her physically, grabbing and constraining her, stripping off her clothing without her permission, and frightening her with threatening gestures. The "counselling" relationship had become exactly the same as Gail's abusive relationship with her father.

I began working with Gail while she was still seeing Frank. Although she eventually saw clearly that the relationship was repeating her childhood misery, she just could not give it up. This relational trance was of an extremely powerful kind, built on the foundation of the all-consuming trance Gail had originally established with her father. As her understanding of this deepened, Gail wanted to assert her rights with Frank, get him to acknowledge what was really going on between them, and end the abuse of their relationship. But each time she walked into his office, the trance state was immediately evoked, by the mere fact of her being with him, and she was paralysed, again a child responding fearfully and longingly to her abusive father.

As we discussed Frank's sadistic ways, Gail came to recognize the depth of his abuse of her. She also realized that she was addicted to that abuse and unable to give it up. This clarity would stay with Gail for a while. But as soon as she was in Frank's presence it all disappeared, and she would again be enmeshed in the false image of Frank as friend and counsellor.

Gail's two-world existence was a torture to her. In my office, she felt clarity and relief. Her meaningful reality was formed by our straightforward examination of the actions and exchanges between her and Frank. Yet when she left, that reality would begin to fade, to be totally replaced by the other whenever she saw Frank.

Gail's relational trance with Frank could rightly be called an obsession. When she was in its grip, everything else disappeared. Her concerns for her family, friends, and other activities were pushed completely into the background. She waited for hours at the phone on the off chance that Frank would call. She became fearful of going out, believing that if she took her mind off him for even short periods, Frank might not be there for her when she needed him. Her world narrowed so far that Frank and thoughts about him filled her mind most of the time. Her only respite was our sessions and the periods of insight and sanity they created.

Eventually Gail was able to build up the strength of the other realities in her life to the point that she could confront Frank directly about their abusive relationship. Complete victory over the addiction to the relationship has not come easily, however, and she faces a long struggle to free herself completely from her need for abuse. For Gail, that struggle still continues.

Triggers

Sometimes a sensory cue can precipitate a trance state. Here, a previously existing trance is reestablished. Relational trances are especially responsive to such "triggers." Hearing the voice of an abusive father on the telephone can plunge an abuse survivor into a paralysing trance. Many couples find their love renewed each time they hear a song that they heard when they first met. A child may enter a deep, secure relational trance with his mother whenever she strokes his forehead in a certain way. A particular mocking stare can renew the hatred between rivals. Sometimes the mere presence of the other person can be a trigger. That was the case with Gail, who could not be with Frank without going into her enslaving relational trance.

Rapport

Rapport is the special connection that exists between two people in a mutual relational trance. The rapport between two people in a mutual relational trance can be very powerful. When together, each may be highly sensitive to what the other is thinking and feeling. Some of this communication happens in conscious awareness, but much of it is unconscious. The two respond to the moods and expectations in each other without being aware that they are doing so.

Rapport also exists when the two are apart. Awareness of the other persists in both conscious and unconscious thought. That connection goes beyond mere remembering. A person in a powerful relational trance often reports feeling a direct connection with the other person, even though that person is physically absent. This rapport at a distance may show itself in telepathic communication or in accurately sensing what is happening in the other person's life, even though there is no way to obtain that information directly.

Anger

Anger can establish a powerful relational trance. One day Archie entered my office in a state I had never seen him in before. He was beside himself with anger, and it took him a few minutes to cool down enough to tell me what was going on. He had just received a notice of dismissal from his job delivered by his supervisor, with whom he had had an ongoing dispute for more than a year. Archie felt misunderstood, even persecuted, by this man, and for the past six months Archie's preoccupation with him had been growing. Now the axe had fallen and he was incensed.

Archie could not sit down as he talked. He paced around my office in his fury and spilled out the story. His supervisor had used some recent instances of Archie's lateness in arriving at work to seal a case he had been building with his superiors against him and had succeeded in convincing them that he had to go. Archie had explained to his supervisor that his lateness was due to a back sprain that had slowed him down in the mornings, but the supervisor would not accept the excuse. So there he was, suddenly without a job and feeling helpless about how he had been treated.

As he raged, Archie showed all the signs of a person in trance. He had little awareness of his surroundings or of me, but was totally immersed in recounting his encounter with his supervisor. At one point he was so absorbed in his anger that he began to shout at the man as though he were there. As he moved around the office, Archie showed no signs of the back pain that had been so obvious in his movements over the past week. When I eventually had to tell him we had reached the end of our hour, he could not believe how short the session seemed.

It took Archie some time to resolve his problematic relational trance with his supervisor. He was able to do this only when he realized that he had been unconsciously seeing the man as a grade-school teacher who had relentlessly persecuted him for two years.

Mothering

As mentioned at the beginning of this chapter, a powerful relational trance normally exists between mother and infant, and it is crucial for the nurturing and safety of the baby. The mother must be finely attuned to all the nuances of the infant's experiences. This sensitivity involves all of her senses. She is aware of her child's facial expressions, body posture, and any tensions that show there, skin colour and texture, and other subtleties of the baby as an organism. Much of her awareness involves processing visual cues of which she has no conscious knowledge. She also tunes in and responds to her baby on the level of touch. She immediately senses what is happening to the infant and communicates understanding and comfort to it through holding and stroking. Smells, too, convey messages to the mother about the baby's state, and probably much of this communication is processed completely outside her awareness. Ordinarily she is highly sensitive to any sounds the infant makes. She recognizes that different types of crying have different meanings and she responds accordingly. She will hear sounds made by the baby at great distances, particularly if it is distressed. There also seems to be a kind of sixth sense mothers possess through which they are aware of their babies' states even when the infants are out of earshot. A mother may wake up in the middle of the night knowing that the child needs attention even though it has made no sound.

All of this shows that there is a constant stream of communication between mother and infant, each continually learning more about the way the other conveys messages. It is instinctual for mother and infant to concentrate such close attention on each other. This establishes a powerful relational trance that will last in some form or other throughout their lives. This relational trance benefits both. The child's welfare depends on it directly, and the mother needs the connection to perform her function well.

Conflict—The Eternal Surprise

The marriage between Phil and Angie had been in trouble for some time. After a torrid start, their relationship began to cool. Nine years and two children later, they were spending most of their time at each other's throats.

My sessions with Phil were starting to become repetitive, but it took me a while to see just what it was that was being repeated. It finally dawned on me that it was his eternal surprise. The incidents between himself and Angie that he spoke about with me were all very different. Sometimes it was conflict about his long working hours. Sometimes it was about finances. The subject was constantly shifting, and what was constant was the fact that each time Phil would be angry at what he saw as Angie's lack of sensitivity to his needs, and each time he was totally surprised by her "callousness."

What was odd was that since he proved to his own satisfaction that Angie was incapable of feeling for him, how could he, week after week, be so surprised, so astounded when she once more demonstrated her indifference to him?

Why could Phil not learn from his experience? Why was he constantly expecting a response that Angie refused to give? He was immersed in a deep relational trance with Angie, a trance that he could not recognize and therefore could not shake off.

Phil was fixed on an image of Angie as she had been in the earlier phases of their relationship when she had idealized him and given him everything he hoped for. At that time, she centred her whole life around his needs and was able to perform perfectly the role of a doting mother. As their lives became more complicated, she necessarily became more independent. And with the birth of their children she no longer centred her attention on Phil, yet he refused to abandon his expectation that Angie fulfil the "caring mother" role for him. In his trance absorption with Angie, he constantly superimposed this unreal image on her and maintained his unreal expectations. Daily he recreated his mother/infant reality, and daily he was disappointed. Once he recognized his relational trance tie to Angie, Phil decided to end their marriage.

Relational Trance in Daily Life

Relationships are at the heart of human life. The intensity of the relationships differs. That means that relational trances also vary in depth. Our most absorbing and meaningful relationships establish deep trances. Our passing involvements form light trances. It is important to understand that deep relational trances may cut us off from personal awarenesses and resources that we use in other situations. That isolation from other aspects of one's life may be desirable in some cases (for instance, when you are on your honeymoon), but undesirable in others (as in Gail's self-destructive relationship with Frank). In both cases, recognizing relational trances in our ordinary lives is important for us to avoid unnecessary grief in relationships.

doing

FRANÇOISE GILOT gives this marvellous account of the legendary painter Pablo Picasso at work:

> He stood before the canvas for three or four hours at a stretch. He made almost no superfluous gestures. I asked him if it didn't tire him to stand so long in one spot. He shook his head. "No," he said. "That's why painters live so long. While I work I leave my body outside the door, the way Moslems take off their shoes before entering a mosque." When daylight began to fade from the canvas, he switched on two spotlights and everything but the picture surface fell away into the shadows. "There must be darkness everywhere except on the canvas, so that the painter becomes hypnotized by his own work and paints almost as though he were in a trance," he said. "He must stay close to his inner world if he wants to transcend the limitations his reason is always trying to impose upon him." (F. Gilot and C. Lake, *Life With Picasso*, New York: McGraw-Hill, 1964, pp. 116–17)

This is a most charming example of situational trance. Picasso's absorption in his task was so complete that he felt himself separated from his body. "Hypnotized" by his work, he was totally abstracted from the rest of reality.

Situational trance is absorption in some situation, project, happening, task, activity, or event, and being abstracted from other things. Picasso's involvement in his painting shut out everything else. He did not even want to be aware of other things in the room, so that when the sun went down, he lit his studio in such a way that the canvas alone stood out. He wanted to be in as deep a situational trance as possible, because he found that this was the best way for him to create.

When you examine how people engage in their various activities, it is clear that some degree of situational trance is always involved. How deep a trance is depends on the depth of concentration applied to the task and correspondingly, the loss of awareness of other things. Some assembly-line workers love their jobs because they are able to find ways to make them interesting. A worker may find a way to make a game of it, a game that requires a skill that she can hone. She may, for instance, set up personal productivity goals that she enjoys meeting and surpassing. She may enjoy continually finding new ways to accomplish the same task. Some workers become so absorbed in this process that they lose touch with everything else going on around them and discover that time moves by very rapidly.

Some people have jobs in which the very nature of the tasks they have to do entails variety. In an auto-servicing company, one mechanic was considered the ultimate problem solver. When something was wrong with an engine that stumped the regular staff, this man was asked to have a look at it. He approached the situation with no preconceived notion of what was wrong, but simply waited for the hidden source of the problem to reveal itself as he examined and probed the car. He was able to bring tremendous concentration to bear on the situation and shut out everything else from his mind. His combination of expertise and an ability to go into a situational trance almost always ensured his success.

Total Focus

Involvement in work as a situational trance can be a godsend for some. Will, a client of mine who attacked whatever challenges he faced with great gusto, considered himself something of a workaholic. At his current stage of life this was in part by choice. The recent breakup of his marriage had left a gap in his life that he was happy to fill with work. An entrepreneur and owner of his own company, he was able to bring total focus with him to work each day. No matter what was going on in his personal life, when he arrived at his office in the morning, he was all business. He moved into a situational trance that was a welcome respite from unhappy thoughts.

His concentration was prodigious. For him, only the business existed from the time he arrived to the last item on his agenda each day. Then, when he climbed into his car to return home, the trance broke. He began to recall the sadness of his present life and the personal matters that needed attention. It was as though in just a few seconds he walked out of a magical world of business affairs into the harsh reality of his ongoing separation.

Will chose this way to handle things for some time. Some might say he used work to run away from his problems, but I don't see it that way. He knew what he was doing and simply decided that there was nothing to be gained by bringing his personal life with him to work. After he closed the office door at the end of the day, he did his best to deal with his personal grief. Will's consciously chosen work trance was his attempt to handle the situation in the most creative way available to him.

Whistle While You Work

There is a lot of truth in the notion that if you whistle while you work, the job will be easier. In cultures with a tradition of communal manual work, the job is regularly accompanied by singing. Everybody joins in with a traditional song and the work moves ahead smoothly and efficiently. This singing is actually a way of inducing and maintaining a situational trance that allows easy, enjoyable concentration on the task at hand.

The Business Trip

Ralph learned how to set up situational trances in his work deliberately in order to do a better job. He did this especially with business travel—a skill he had to learn the hard way. Being a software salesman, he was often required to take business trips to set up new contacts and maintain the old. In the first years of his job, he did not do well on these trips. While business and social contacts usually merge in these situations, Ralph was handling the social aspect of the trip badly. He tended to drink too much and allow the party aspect of the situations to take over. In doing this, he lost his focus on what he was trying to accomplish on the trip.

Ralph finally decided that he had to do something about this situation. He concluded that it was all a matter of concentration. If he could learn to keep his focus clear from the beginning to the end of the trip, he would be much more successful in what he was trying to accomplish. He discovered that the best way to change his bad habits was to establish a routine. Just before he left on his trip, he would lie on his bed at home and think about what the trip was about, who he would be seeing, and what he wanted to accomplish with each person or company. At the same time, he determined in his mind that the whole trip would be devoted to doing only those things, and that any social situations would be treated simply as opportunities to make the contacts and get his ideas across to his clients and prospective clients. He would not see them as a chance to let his hair down and have a good time. And to cement that idea in his mind, he would plan some social event where he *could* do precisely that when he returned home. This arrangement would satisfy his partying urge without undermining his business concerns.

Ralph found that, as a result of this preparation, he would slip into a highly focused state when he got on the plane. This focused state would remain with him throughout the trip, so that he became much more effective at bringing in business and achieving what was expected of him. He felt a kind of unswerving determination within him that did not allow any distractions from his purpose. In this way, Ralph was not only more successful, but paradoxically he also enjoyed the social aspects of the trip more. No longer using the business trip to satisfy his unmet social needs, he found that he could better enjoy the people that he met and interacted with. Even though he maintained his basic situational business-oriented trance, he was still able to relax and be himself in a most satisfying way.

Getting Away

Part of Ralph's problem was that he had been neglecting his social needs. Sometimes the power of the situational trance of one's work is so strong that special measures have to be taken to break it. Otherwise, the person will have his or her life dominated by the job and its stresses.

One executive described to me how difficult it could be to leave the work trance. He found that by getting out of town and spending a weekend in another environment, he could switch out of the trance completely and enjoy a renewal of energy. So he began taking regular golf weekends with a fellow executive from the same company, with good results. However, as pressures mounted at work, the two men found themselves talking about work matters on those weekends. It got so that just being with his golf partner on the weekend was enough to induce the work trance and he would find himself surrounded mentally by the thoughts and worries he had gone away to forget. His fellow executive became a trigger for his situational work trance, and once in it he could not extricate himself from it for the rest of the weekend.

This man had to learn to be rather strict with himself in regard to separating work from recreation. He eventually got up the courage to talk with his golf buddy about the problem, and they agreed on "rules" that would help them maintain their work-free situational trance.

Play

One of the first situational trances we experience in life is play. We do not have to be taught how to do this. Watch an infant playing with toys in the crib and you will see a state of remarkable absorption and abstraction. The instinct to play operates in every waking hour of every day as the child grows and matures. Each new situation becomes an opportunity to become involved in some sort of play and helps the child learn more about how to concentrate. When a child is somewhere around two and one-half years of age, he or she begins "sociodramatic play" with other children, learning to pretend, each taking on a role of some kind (for instance, mother, father, policeman, dog). Here, the ability to place oneself in imagined situations starts to take shape.

Becoming absorbed in play often involves becoming absorbed in a task. An infant may become absorbed in figuring out how to push a ball toward her mother. As the child grows, her tasks become more complex. At two she may struggle to arrange blocks in the form of a house; at five she may become heavily involved in learning a simple card game. As the young person develops and the tasks become more complex, these latter start to look like what will eventually be called "work." The skills the child develops may be very useful in the household—learning to clean something up or set the table, for instance. If the attitude toward play and learning tasks in play is healthy within the family, the child will enjoy carrying out old tasks and learning new ones. Enjoyment in this kind of concentrated involvement bodes well for the child's eventually enjoying work.

The capacity of children to become absorbed in an activity or project is obvious to anyone who has spent time with them, and most of us remember from our own childhood how completely we could be taken over by play. The situational trances of our present lives are simply a continuation of those early experiences.

The Loner

We usually think of play as a joyful thing, carried out by children from a kind of excess of good feeling. But sometimes children use play as a way to escape from the miseries of their lives. This was the case with Ben, a client of mine.

Ben thought of himself as a loner from his childhood. He came from a Southern military family and was regaled with war stories by his grandfather, a colonel in the U.S. Army. Ben was given military toys to play with. Not toy machine guns and tanks, but toy soldiers, miniature cannons, and the paraphernalia to construct his own battlefields.

Ben would set up his battle scenes with great attention. Everything had to be perfect—the arrangement of the opposing lines, the layout of the cannons, the fortifications, the elevations. He spent hours engrossed in his military projects, much to the chagrin of his admiring little sister Clarissa.

Clarissa wanted Ben to include her in the play, but Ben would have none of that. He had to be alone, without distractions. He wanted to become so absorbed in his preparations that nothing else entered his mind. For Ben was very unhappy. He felt ignored by his mother, and his father was hardly ever around. The empty feeling in his heart was too painful, and he sought escape in his world of battle. Ben used this situational trance to take away his emotional pain.

In his adult life, Ben had to work very hard to discover how to include people in his activities. He had to face his hidden loneliness so he could then learn how to moderate his situational trance to include social involvements.

Personalities

When someone with multiple-personality disorder (dissociative identity disorder) explores the origins of those personalities, she may learn that she created them in response to traumatic situations in childhood that she could not handle. One personality may be formed to handle one type of traumatic occurrence, another to handle a different type of trauma, and so forth. These various traumatic situations evoke discrete trance states. Eventually, when the traumatic trance state has been repeated often enough, it may take on a kind of autonomy. In some instances, the resulting trance state becomes an independently functioning personality.

Creativity

Like Picasso, many creative artists enter profound situational trances when they work. They become so absorbed in their tasks that they are aware of nothing else going on around them. Some find that after they finish, they have little or no memory of what they did while working. This separation from their work trance can be so complete that they find it difficult to accept the fact that they have produced what they have indeed created.

A colleague once told me that when she was in her twenties she was taken over by the urge to write a play. She wrote for two days and nights without stopping and finished it. After she had gotten some rest and recovered from her exhaustion, she read it. She was shocked to discover large parts of the play about which she had no memory. She felt she was reading the play for the first time. She was amazed at the characters and reacted to the story as if she were reading the play of another writer. She found it very difficult to believe that she had written the play at all. She did not feel it was her creation.

A young musical composer I know describes a very similar experience. After he writes a song, he will often tell me, "I didn't write that. I don't know what it means." He feels frustrated by his difficulty in deciphering the meaning of the lyrics. He does feel some relief, however, when singing the newly composed song, because, as he says, "I seem to know what it means while I sing it." This same young man also reports the experience of sitting at the keyboard and playing music, but feeling that it is his hands that produce the music, not *him.* As he plays he does not know what will come next, and the quality of the music produced is beyond what he considers his ordinary ability.

This disowning of creative activity can be understood in part as a post-trance amnesia. In some cases it is more than that. The artistic process involves channelling profound creative resources in the inner mind into the artist's consciousness as he or she works. This is why the creative act may seem totally alien to the artist. It is as though this person were possessed by forces that are not in his or her control. This can be frightening or exhilarating, depending on how the artist looks at it. The Greeks talked about the inspiration of the muses, and modern artists describe similar processes. Mozart spoke of hearing a new piece of music unfold in his mind, totally finished and ready to play. Composers who describe similar experiences have no knowledge of developing the music they hear, no awareness of working on it, honing it into a finished product. Rather, they experience themselves as observers, watching something come forward from their inner regions fully formed. Writers such as Charles Dickens, Robert Louis Stevenson, and Enid Blyton have described similar experiences. Their productions possess an autonomy, a life of their own, and the author feels more like a scribe than an originator of ideas.

In my book *Multiple Man* I describe a fascinating example of this sense of being separate from the source of the artistic creation.[2] As a young man, the renowned viola maker Otto Erdesz received his training in violin making from an inner voice that told him exactly how to carry out the intricate steps involved. For a year, the voice came to him every time he entered his shop, guiding him most expertly in the craft. Then, it suddenly vanished. Some time later he had a dream in which Guarneri del Gesu, considered the master of masters in violin making, appeared to him and announced that it had been he who had guided Otto in his work. In the dream, he told Otto that his skill had now developed to the point that he no longer needed his supervision.

Despite the great variety of ways that artists describe the process of creation, most of them are conscious of entering some kind of trance state when they are their most productive. The artist can usually recreate the trance for him- or herself by setting the environment and introducing the proper triggers or stimuli to induce the situational trance. Bringing about the trance is crucial. Most creative blocks are nothing more than the inability to induce it when needed.

The Movie

One of the most striking situational trances in ordinary life is the experience of going to a movie. You may go there with a friend, and as you wait for the movie to begin you chat. In the back of your mind you are aware that the movie will begin shortly and you begin to think about it. As the lights go down, your attention moves to the screen. The popcorn ads hold your attention only briefly, and you may still have a few exchanges with your companion. Then the previews appear and you feel yourself becoming more and more engrossed in what is happening on the screen. Your exchanges with your friend are now about what you are seeing and whether it looks interesting or not. Then the feature begins, and your concentration increases further.

As you get more and more taken up by the movie, your conversation with your companion probably ceases. If it is a good movie, you are pulled into the characters, their lives, their loves, their predicaments. Your "willing suspension of disbelief" is your gateway to the trance. You are engulfed by the visual and auditory experience of the settings, the scenery, the camera angles, the conversations, the action. As the story develops you are intrigued, engrossed, moved, repelled, frightened, excited, or in other ways affected by what is unfolding. By now you have largely lost touch with your surroundings. You are barely aware of how your seat feels, of the sensation of the clothing on your body, or of the physical aspects of the theatre. You may briefly become aware of the other people in the theatre, particularly if someone is carrying on a conversation or making distracting sounds. But with a reasonably quiet group, you lose awareness of the individuals. You may become conscious of your companion periodically and exchange a word or two, but each time you immediately get drawn back into the movie.

All of this absorption and abstraction indicates a situational trance. The depth of the trance depends entirely on your degree of involvement. Some people disappear into the movie from the moment it starts. These people are deeply entranced and enjoy every minute of it. For them nothing else matters. They experience the movie as a kind of experience out of time, an eternal "now" during which the rest of their lives are suspended. They experience the movie as a deep trance.

Others are less involved. Some significant part of their consciousness remains aware that this is a movie, that they are in a theatre, and that this is a temporary experience. When the movie ends, their transition to present reality is easy. They experience the movie as a light trance.

Concentration

Involvement in sport automatically means involvement in situational trances. The great athletes are characterized not merely by exceptional physical ability, but also by the ability to bring exceptional concentration to their game. Sports people all agree on this point. Basketball and hockey players speak of forgetting everything else when they step onto the court or rink. Tennis players describe the challenge of maintaining concentration through a lengthy match and judge their performance on their degree of success in not allowing distractions to throw off their game. Golfers have to learn to pace their concentration in a different way. They have much more time between shots than do tennis players. They have to work at not losing their focus by the time they line up the next shot. All participants in sport have to learn to bring a single-minded concentration to bear in a way that is consistent with the structure of their game.

Chess players know all about situational trances. It seems that chess tends to draw people who are particularly adept at entering profound trances at a moment's notice. Those who play professionally sometimes give demonstrations in which they participate in many games with many opponents simultaneously. One need hardly comment on these players' ability to become totally absorbed in such situations.

Dancers and actors also know that concentration is key. Some describe their focused state as so distinct from their ordinary one that it is as though they have developed a special personality for performance. When performing, they are totally unaware of anything else in their lives. It is as though they do not exist apart from that moment.

In these cases of deep situational trance, these people may experience a striking loss of self-consciousness. They are hardly aware of themselves as individuals, only aware of the situation and the activity. They may feel a powerful sense of control over the action, yet it seems to them that at the same time they are lost in the action itself, that the activity uses them—not the other way around. They seem to disappear into the energy of the performance or game, losing themselves in the flow.

Tense Situations

Situational trances may develop instantly in emergency situations. Fear of imminent harm to oneself or another can mobilize the whole organism and focus the mind in an extraordinary way.

One man described his experience of a dangerous driving situation in this way. He was driving at dusk in early winter along an unfamiliar highway when he came over the rise of a small hill and was confronted with an unexpected patch of "black ice." He knew at once that he was in extreme danger, and yet he found that his consciousness was unusually clear. As the car began to skid sideways, he saw another car some two hundred feet ahead of him and moving at such a rate that he calculated that he was likely to collide with it in a few seconds. Luckily, his car tires caught some bits of gravel and this diverted him enough that he missed the other car by a few feet. As he passed by the car, his own vehicle caught a raised lip on the edge of the highway and began to flip over. It made three-quarters of a turn in mid-air, landed on its side, and rolled over onto its wheels. He sat there behind the wheel, stunned at what had just happened. Later he recalled that even though there were only a few seconds in which his car was turning in the air, for him time slowed down so that it seemed to take forever before the car hit the ground. He felt that his state of consciousness during this brief emergency period was very different from anything he had known before.

Fear of attack can also create an instant situational trance. People report that in ominous situations, they feel an uncanny feeling of concentration take them over. An example of this is a woman who described her highly focused and alert state when she was walking down a dark street near a park at night and suddenly became aware of a man close behind her. As it turned out, the man was not threatening, but afterward she was struck by the peculiar qualities of her state of hyper-alertness. She characterized it as one of greatly narrowed consciousness coupled with a mental agility which allowed her to visualize very rapidly a number of possible ways of defending herself.

Learning

Situational trances play a central role in successful learning. The importance of being able to concentrate is known to every student. If the student is vulnerable to distractions, he will not survive long in a competitive scholarly environment.

Many students develop helpful situational trances with little effort. They have their place to study, their study attire, their food and drink, their music in the background, and so on. This structured environment helps them produce a situational trance that they can recreate as needed. Information learned during their study trance is tied to that state and can be retrieved whenever they are able to reestablish contact with the trance. Good students are able to do that by using tricks (cues, triggers, visualizations) that they apply to induce the trance state, often not consciously aware that they are doing so.

Students who cannot create consistent situational trance for study and retrieval are likely to have serious problems. If student advisors were aware of the trance aspect of learning, they might be more able to help those with problems owing to lack of concentration.

Situations

All of the trances described in this chapter involve concentration on external situations—focusing on some aspect of the external environment and some kind of interaction with it. As we become occupied with each situation, we use the outer mind which is made to deal with the world and its practical concerns.

I would now like to draw your attention to the inner mind: that part of our mental apparatus that deals with our inner thoughts and images. The inner mind develops trances that are peculiar to it. We turn next to inner-mind trances.

going within

I F YOU CLOSE YOUR EYES and think about something that really interests you, you are using your "inner mind." The inner mind is concerned with the inner world, the world of thought and imagination.

In ordinary daily life we deal with the outer world. This is the world of our physical and social environment. When at home, at work, or involved with recreational activities, we are engaged with the outer world and are using the "outer mind."

At night, when we close our eyes in sleep and dream, all of that changes. The outer world goes completely. We have no awareness of the physical realities around us, nor of the people who may be close by. We are totally engaged in the inner world, the world of the dream. The images that populate that world are our whole reality; nothing else exists. The events that occur there can engage us utterly. It is possible while dreaming to experience the most consuming fits of rage, the most overwhelming feelings of fear, the most uninhibited surges of lust or the profoundest feelings of love. In dreams you can burn in the desert sun or shiver on a frozen lake. Dreams can display breathtaking landscapes for you or involve you in complicated plots and heartrending dramas. The dream is the most complete experience we have of the trance of the inner mind: abstraction from the outer world and absorption in the inner world.

Lucid Dreaming

Although we are normally involved in the inner world completely when dreaming, there is an exception to this rule: lucid dreaming. Lucid dreaming is a peculiar experience in which the sleeping person, while remaining physiologically asleep, becomes *aware* that he or she is asleep and dreaming. The dreamer continues to dream, but now against a background of outer-mind awareness. One of the interesting things that happens when people are awake in their dreams is that they can to some extent control what happens in the dream. People who have learned to induce lucid dreaming sometimes use that control to create pleasurable or creative situations for themselves.

Although the dream is the most totally encompassing and commonly experienced inner-mind trance, there are many other kinds that are familiar. Meditation, day-dreaming, worrying—these are all examples of inner-mind trance. I will say more about these experiences, but first I would like to turn to another well-known inner-mind trance, hypnosis.

Hypnosis

On a warm May evening in 1784, a French aristocrat named Armand Marie Jacques de Chastenet, marquis de Puységur went on a stroll through his estate to try out his newly learned healing technique on the peasants. Puységur had recently returned from Paris where he had attended a series of training seminars in "animal magnetism," a healing approach taught by the German-born Franz Anton Mesmer (1734–1815). Anyone who practises some form of "energy healing" today would have felt quite at home in these seminars, because Mesmer instructed his students in using the hands to unblock and augment the natural healing energy of the body.

Puységur, anxious to test his healing ability, found ready sub-jects among his tenants. He first cured the toothaches of two women and then was called upon to try to help a man named Vic-tor Race who was suffering from lung congestion. Puységur made the usual "passes," sweeping hand movements over the man's body, but as he worked something unusual happened. Victor fell into a state in which he seemed to be asleep and yet awake. Puységur dubbed this sleep-waking state "magnetic sleep." Sixty years later, it would be labelled hypnotism.

It was quickly noted that there was a special connection or "rap-port" (a kind of relational trance discussed in Chapter 2) between the hypnotizer and hypnotized. The hypnotized subject was very aware of the hypnotizer and often could hear only his voice. It was even believed that through rapport the subject could read the hyp-notizer's thoughts and feel his or her sensations. The hypnotizer could set the tone of the hypnotic session and introduce ideas that would become powerful suggestions to the hypnotized subject. For instance, Victor, while hypnotized, showed himself extremely sug-gestible, and Puységur could tell him that he was at a dance or shooting in a contest and Victor would believe he was there.

Hypnotic Rapport

Rapport should not be equated with transference. Rapport is a very special kind of relationship in which the hypnotized sees the hypno-tizer as a guide and source of security. The subject's awareness of the hypnotizer may not be particularly personal, for apart from a feeling of trust (that must be there from the beginning), the subject may not be particularly aware of the hypnotizer as a personality—with his particular personal traits. During the hypnotic trance, the hypnotized responds mainly to the hypnotizer as a benevolent, helpful guide.

By contrast, transference feelings involve very specific responses to the personal characteristics of the therapist. The therapist is seen as an important person from the subject's past (perhaps mother or father), and the client's transference feelings can range from love and idealization to loathing. Transference involves some degree of unreality, since the therapist is placed in the position of that past person, and may have little or nothing in common with that person. Transference needs to be "worked through," seen for the distorted view that it is. Rapport does not need to be analysed or worked through.

Although hypnotism as a systematized technique was discovered more than two hundred years ago, there is still a great deal of debate about what it is and what it can do. For our purposes, hypnotism can simply be defined as an inner-mind trance characterized by rapport.

Self-Hypnosis

The idea of self-hypnosis (auto-hypnosis) deserves some attention. If hypnosis is an inner-mind trance characterized by rapport, what is self-hypnosis? Self-hypnosis involves the private induction of an inner-mind trance with some element of rapport present. Some people learn self-hypnosis in their regular hypnotic sessions, and when they apply it by themselves they have the hypnotizer or his or her voice in their minds, which thereby reinstates rapport. Others learn self-hypnosis from tapes. Here the hypnotizer is whoever recorded the tape and the hypnotized person establishes a certain amount of rapport with that absent person.

If someone self-induces an inner-mind trance with no vestige of rapport, it should not be called hypnosis at all. It would be more accurate to consider it a form of meditation.

Blanking the Screen

If you read books about hypnosis, you will discover a bewildering array of induction techniques. When hypnotic practitioners apply these techniques, they find that some work for some people and others work for other people. None of them works for everyone. That is because, contrary to popular belief, the induction of hypnosis is not an occult rite for which one must find the correct formula. There is nothing mystical about hypnosis and nothing magical in the way it comes about. The air of mystery created by stage hypnotists and some hypnotherapists is produced for effect and does not reflect what is really going on.

The proper way to view a hypnotic technique is to see it as a path to a destination. The hypnotist's destination is the hypnotic state. Hypnosis is an inner-mind trance, so the induction technique is geared to help the subject become abstracted from the outer world and absorbed into the inner world. Through rapport, the hypnotized subject allows the hypnotist to help him find a path to that hypnotic state.

Becoming abstracted from the outer world and absorbed in the inner world can happen in any number of ways. They all involve a progressive narrowing of attention, to the point that the hypnotic subject is focused on some very limited and often trivial idea. One of the traditional ways of accomplishing that is by having the person concentrate on some small object. The hypnotist helps the subject become more and more taken up with the object and less and less aware of everything else. Eventually, the subject's attention is completely taken up with the object and everything else has faded into the background. The hypnotist thus succeeds in the first phase of the process—blanking the mind's screen, leaving only a trivial object there.

Relaxation

Although relaxation of the body often accompanies the hypnotic state, it is by no means necessary for producing this state. A person can enter a very profound state of hypnosis and still experience a great deal of muscular tension. Also, a person can be very relaxed without being in an inner-mind trance. Mistakenly equating hypnosis with relaxation has led to the equally mistaken notion that a would-be hypnotist should aim at getting the subject to relax in order to induce a trance.

Introduction of an Image

The second phase of hypnosis is fairly simple. Now that the subject's attention has been severely narrowed and the mind's screen contains only some insignificant object, it is fairly easy for the hypnotist to suggest that the subject replace that trivial object with some image. Because the remaining object is intrinsically uninteresting, the suggested image quickly expands to fill the entire screen. When caught up in a mental image that is interesting and absorbing, the subject is in an inner-mind trance.

That is just one example of how the absorption/abstraction state may be brought about. There is an unlimited number of other ways to do the same thing. Instead of concentrating on an object, the subject might be asked to concentrate on a sensation in the left index finger or the soles of his or her feet. Or the person may be asked to centre attention on an idea the hypnotist is talking about. Or be asked to focus on feelings of relaxation in the body. It does not matter what the person concentrates on, what is important is that the subject does concentrate on something and that this concentration is used as a bridge to inner-mind images, which then expand to take up his full attention.

Hypnotic Phenomena

Over the past 150 years, certain phenomena have been attributed to hypnosis. Amnesia, analgesia (lack of pain), suggestibility, time distortion, hallucinations—all of these and more have been listed as characteristic of the hypnotic state. There is no doubt that these phenomena do occur, but it is a mistake to identify them too closely with hypnosis. As we have seen, the very same phenomena occur as a part of our everyday experience, when we are definitely not in the kind of inner-mind state we have been talking about. Also, the phenomena are unpredictable and may be lacking in any particular inner-mind trance. There are those who argue that although the phenomena may occur elsewhere, they are more powerfully present in the hypnotic state than in ordinary states. They cite studies that show that suggestibility, for example, or analgesia occur more often and in a more pronounced form in a person who is hypnotized. The problem is that against those studies one can muster an impressive array of other studies showing no appreciable difference in the occurrence of the phenomena in hypnosis compared to the "waking" state.

The fact is, there is no way to prove that the "phenomena of hypnosis" characterize the hypnotic state as opposed to any other state. Rather than seeing them as exclusive to inner-mind trances, we should recognize that they belong to all trance states and to ordinary human experience: the phenomena of hypnosis are really the phenomena of trance in the sense that I have defined trance in this book.

The fact that these phenomena can occur just as powerfully in other states means that they cannot be used as defining characteristics of hypnosis. This takes us to the problem of the very definition of hypnosis.[3]

The Problem of Defining Hypnosis

In this chapter I have been using the term "hypnosis" rather freely. One might get the impression that everyone agrees about what the word means. This is far from the case. The fact is that even though the term has been used for 150 years, there is no commonly accepted definition of it, and a review of recent hypnosis literature reveals that this is not likely to change in the foreseeable future. So I would like to make two points to clarify my position on the matter.

First, I am adding my own definition to the list. When I used the term hypnosis above, I meant an inner-mind trance with rapport. My use of the term was very specific and also very limited.

My second point is that, because there are so many definitions of hypnosis, mine may not apply to some of the other usages found in medical, legal, and popular literature. To avoid confusion in this book from here on, I will refrain from using the term hypnosis, and will specify my meaning (following the framework I have been developing in this book) each time I use the term trance.

Trance Conversion in Therapy

In therapy sessions, it is not always necessary to induce a trance. Often clients bring a trance right into the office with them, for the client who comes to therapy feeling deeply disturbed about something presents to the therapist a most effective object for inner-mind absorption. All the therapist needs to do is convert that trance to an inner-mind trance.

This happened with Tony, a gay computer analyst who had been coming to therapy with me for several months. Tony had been in and out of relationships through much of his adult life, and these relationships all tended sooner or later to become obsessions. One day, Tony came to a session in a terrible state. He had been informed the previous day by his partner at the time, Ian, that he had been seeing another man for some weeks. Tony was hurt and very angry. Since learning of this, Tony could think of nothing but Ian and his "betrayal." Tony had hardly slept the night before and looked haggard. His face was very intense, and he showed every sign of someone in the grips of a deep relational trance.

In our sessions, we had been regularly doing trance work to explore Tony's earlier relationships with his parents. Normally, I would use a trance induction that included counting him down into his inner world. Today it was clear to me that such an induction was totally unnecessary. Immersed in his obsessive thoughts about Ian, Tony was already in as profound a trance as a therapist could wish. All I had to do was convert this relational trance into an inner-mind trance.

"Tony," I said, "you are very hurt by what has happened with Ian. You need to be able to talk about that. And you need to be able to see if there are some old feelings from the past intruding here and making it worse for you. Please close your eyes and picture Ian as he broke the news to you."

Tony closed his eyes, and despite his agitated, unrelaxed condition he was immediately submerged in a powerful inner-mind trance. Everything disappeared for him except his image of Ian and the devastating exchange between them. The office was gone, the noises floating in through my window from the street were gone, and I was reduced to a guiding voice as Tony lost himself in his inner world.

After the therapeutic work, it took Tony some time to reorient himself toward the outer world. His absorption in the inner world had been complete. In his imagination, he had been totally absorbed in the traumatic event. He had relived several memories that contributed to the devastation he was feeling. All of these-inner mind events were very real to him and he had been completely immersed in them. It is true that he knew he was in a therapy session. He knew that I was there, listening and at times speaking. He knew he was in my office. But his awareness of these things was very tenuous. These outer-world realities so paled in comparison to the vivid inner world he was exploring that for all practical purposes they did not exist. By simply closing his eyes and bringing to mind the distressing event, Tony had dropped into the inner world to a depth that on other occasions would have required a prolonged induction.

Unconsciousness

One of the biggest misconceptions about inner-mind trances is that in its deepest states you lose consciousness. This *never* happens. In all the trances, inner-mind and otherwise, you are always conscious. You are always aware. What changes is the object of your consciousness, what you are focused on or absorbed in.

With inner-mind trances, your focus changes from the outer world to the inner world. It is that simple. The process of going into an inner-mind trance is the process of switching concentration from the outer environment to the inner. The greater the switch and the more the person becomes involved in the inner world, the deeper the inner-mind trance.

Think of it like the liquid in a U-tube. When you increase the air pressure on one side of the U-tube, the liquid goes down on that side and up on the other side. Increase pressure on the other side and the opposite happens. Think of the right side of the U-tube as your awareness of the outer world and the left side the inner world. In your ordinary state, with your involvements with the people and situations of life, your awareness of the outer world is very high— let us say it involves 90 percent of your awareness. Only 10 percent remains aware of your inner world. As a person enters an inner-mind trance, this balance begins to shift. His or her awareness of the inner world increases progressively, with a correspondingly diminishing awareness of the outer world. If the subject of the trance state becomes very deeply absorbed in the inner world, the trance is profound. This might be represented as 90-percent awareness of the inner world and 10-percent awareness of the outer. A deep inner-mind trance is the reverse of our normal, everyday state of consciousness.

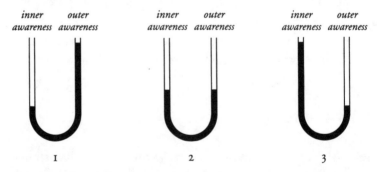

1. Normal State: the individual is mainly aware of the outer world, the physical environment, and very little aware of what is going on in the inner mind. 2. Light Inner-mind Trance: the indivual is becoming more aware of the inner world and less aware of, and concerned with, the outer world. 3. Deep Inner-mind Trace: the individual has little awareness of, or interest in, the outer world, but is very absorbed in the inner world of images, fantasies, and memories which can be very vivid and engaging. Even in the deepest inner-mind trance there is some awareness of the outer world. albeit minimal.

But note that even in the most profound inner-mind trance, *some* awareness of the outer world remains. Even when those who are highly susceptible are placed in a deep inner-mind trance, they will have a vestigial awareness of the outer world—at the very least an awareness of the therapist's voice and the fact that the therapist is with them and aiding them.

In any case, even when the awareness of the outer world is so drastically reduced, the subject maintains a very active consciousness. Just the focus of that consciousness has altered.

The mistaken notion that one loses consciousness in deep inner-mind trances follows from false conclusions drawn from what the subject experiences when returning to the "waking" state. After a person has been immersed in a profound inner-mind trance, she may have no memory of the trance session on reemerging into normal consciousness. Because she cannot remember the trance experience and the mental activity that occurred within it, she concludes, "I must have been unconscious." For the waking subject, the period of time when she was in the inner-mind trance is a blank. Her temptation, then, is to assume that no conscious thought occurred during that time. Nothing could be further from the truth.

Everyday Inner-Mind Trances

Inner-mind trances are a normal part of everyday life. If you drive, you will know what I mean. Often drivers, particularly those travelling through familiar terrain, go into fairly profound inner-mind trances. Imagine yourself leaving work to drive the forty-five minute commuter trip home. You get into the car and no sooner are you on your way than you find yourself engrossed in thoughts about some personal concern or problem that needs a solution. Those thoughts are so absorbing that when you finally arrive home, you cannot remember the drive. You recall nothing about the mechanics of driving or how you made decisions to pull in and out of lanes, stop at the traffic signals, speed up or slow down, or make this or that turn. When you climb out of your car you may wonder how you made it home at all, since you cannot remember being involved in the driving. Yet here you are, safe at home. How did you get there?

Although you don't remember the driving part of the trip, you do remember the thinking part of it. You remember very well the various scenarios you went through in your mind as you puzzled out your problem. Perhaps your deep concentration on the matter produced a creative solution. So there you are with a mind chock-full of thoughts from your inner-mind excursion and no memory of the very important matter of how you drove home safely.

In this case, you were involved in an inner-mind trance of a very common kind, the driver's trance. I am not talking here about "road hypnosis" (in which the person becomes transfixed and perilously immobile, paralysed in the driver's seat), nor about the kind of dangerous brain states brought on by flashing lights or repetitive visual impressions, nor about sleepiness arising from fatigue. Those states constitute a real hazard and imminent danger to the driver and other occupants of the road. What I am talking about is quite different, and most drivers will recognize it. In this trance, absorption in the inner mind is paramount and takes up the greater part of the driver's mental energy. Absorption in the inner world is very deep, yet his awareness of the outer world remains. The person retains enough awareness of the outer world to drive competently and safely. But he concentrates so intently on the inner world that he remembers only his inner experience.

The Sudden Realization

Sometimes we are so overwhelmed by sudden realizations that that they throw us into a powerful inner-mind trance.

In the movie *Cactus Flower* there is a hilarious scene in which actor Walter Matthau, who plays a dentist, is beset by just such a trance. In one scene he is in his office standing by the chair in which a hapless patient waits nervously as Matthau peers at his freshly developed X-rays. While looking at the X-rays, Matthau suddenly realizes that his secretary in the outer office, played by Ingrid Bergman, has just received a box containing a mink coat, a gift he intended for his girlfriend. His secretary thinks he intends it for her. This realization dawns on him as he stares at the X-rays and as it does, Matthau's expression transforms from indifference to deeply etched distress. The patient, waiting for the verdict about his dental problems, is watching Matthau's expression closely. When he sees the look of growing horror, he panics. He believes there must be something terribly wrong with his mouth. He asks Matthau to tell him what he sees. Matthau, now in a deep inner-mind trance, is so absorbed in his troubling thoughts that he cannot hear what the patient is saying. When Matthau doesn't answer, the patient becomes even more frightened, grabs his sleeve, begs to be told the awful truth, assures him that he is strong enough to know the worst. Matthau is still transfixed. He doesn't hear the begging; he doesn't feel the tugging. He is totally caught up in the shock of his realization.

Worry

One of the most commonly experienced inner-mind trances is *worry*. When you worry, you are drawn to some centre of inner concern or anxiety. For that reason, worry is truly an inner-mind trance. The source of your anxiety becomes your focal point. The further you are drawn into your worry, the less you are aware of your surroundings and present situation. As you continue to worry, you may become so absorbed that all other aspects of your life disappear from your awareness.

Sometimes worry is just a minor annoyance. It tugs on your awareness for a while and then is gone when you become involved with something else. But worry can be a truly horrible kind of inner-mind trance. It can remain as a nagging background trance in which you live, doing other things only half-heartedly. You are half-hearted in those other things because you are always half distracted, half into the worry trance.

Perhaps in some ideal world we would not need worry. We would simply meet problems with calm, creative thinking, and no anxiety. We would approach every difficulty with serenity and confidence that everything will somehow work out for the best.

But in the world we live in, it seems that worry does have its place. Some measure of anxiety is not only inevitable, but perhaps necessary. Maybe we need the experience of worry to feel that we are really doing something, that we are not ignoring the problem in front of us. In other words, perhaps we need to sweat, to see those drops of anxiety-laden perspiration on our brow and take comfort in them as a sign that we are truly concerned and responsible.

But overdone worry is counter-productive. Worry that does not lead to creative thinking about solving the problem is energy spent uselessly. So perhaps what we need to do is accept a reasonable amount of worry in our lives, if only on condition that it be accompanied by a striving for solutions. Little worries that come and go can be handled easily enough. But what about those bigger worries? What about when those problems that involve love, health, money, and the other aspects of life that can go wrong take centre stage, and produce a worry trance? Well, there is no doubt that such things can be worth worrying about. But even the greatest of problems must be given its boundaries. Otherwise, a person's whole waking (and sleeping) life can be swallowed up in worry and endless fretting.

To learn how to put worry in its place: that is a precious lesson. Granted that worry does have a place, how can it be assigned its legitimate position and kept there? Be assured that if it is a significant worry, it will want to expand its sphere of influence in your consciousness. It will seek to push out other interests and involvements. It will insinuate itself into every line of thought with which it can establish even the remotest connection. So putting worry in its place may not be easy.

The secret to doing so means understanding that worry is an inner-mind trance. The best way to reduce the worry trance to workable proportions is to shift the worrying from the inner mind to the outer world. Writing about the worry in all its aspects can help. But nothing is as effective for putting worry in its place as talking with someone about all the worried thoughts and fantasies. This breaks the closed inner circle of thought that worry so often establishes and brings the thinking into the fresh air. Exposing worry to another person places it in the outer world. There it is much easier to identify the irrational and dead-end thinking usually associated with it.

Sherlock Holmes

Arthur Conan Doyle's depiction of his character Sherlock Holmes contemplating a puzzle, shown through the eyes of Dr. Watson, is a marvellous description of a person in the throes of an inner-mind trance: "With [pillows] he constructed a sort of Eastern divan, upon which he perched himself cross-legged, with an ounce of shag tobacco and a box of matches laid out in front of him. In the dim light of the lamp I saw him sitting there, an old briar pipe between his lips, his eyes fixed vacantly upon the corner of the ceiling, the blue smoke curling up from him, silent, motionless. . . . .So he sat as I dropped off to sleep, and so he sat when a sudden exclamation caused me to wake up, and I found the summer sun shining into the apartment."[4]

Escape

Children learn easily to put themselves into inner-mind trances. Children who are subject to traumatic abuse learn this art to save themselves. An acquaintance of mine with this kind of background once said to me, "When I was young I learned to stare at the fibres in any piece of cloth I could find. I would stare at the fibres and at the space between the fibres. I would do this until everything became silent." Once in the inner-mind trance, she was oblivious to all that was going on in her life; she was safe, for a little while at least.

Children learn to use inner-mind trances to relieve not only emotional pain but also physical pain. As a nine-year-old, Jacob Grimm had to be operated on for the removal of a tumour. This was in 1794, long before the development of chemical anaesthetics.

During the surgery he was told a story so engrossing that he felt no pain at all. His inner-mind trance produced complete analgesia. I suppose it is not surprising that he would eventually become such an advocate of fairy tales and publish his version of that very story, "Snow White."

The power of inner-mind trances to deal with physical pain was used to great benefit by Josephine Hilgard and Samuel Lebaron in their work with children with cancer. They devised techniques to help children develop vivid mental imagery during procedures that ordinarily cause a great deal of pain. In a significant number of children, the pain was either completely removed or greatly reduced. They found this approach successful only if the child's involvement in the inner fantasy was intense. Mere day-dreaming was not enough. The imagined events had to be so vivid that they seemed real. They called this state "believed-in-imagination."[5] Put another way, the "depth" of the trance was the degree of the child's involvement in the imagined experiences. In the case of Jacob Grimm, his immersion in the "Snow White" story must have been very deep indeed.

Ultradian Rhythms

Recent psychological research has confirmed something long suspected: that we go through natural cycles of activity and rest throughout the day. There are periods in which our bodies and minds are geared for action, and there are periods in which they shift into a state of rest, renewal, and healing. The cycles last for 90 to 120 minutes, about 20 minutes of which are devoted to the resting part.[6] It seems that the average North American is good at the activity part of the cycles, but a miserable failure at rest and renewal. We make good use of that flow of energy available for work and movement, but when the nervous system switches to renewal mode we tend to think something is wrong. Our organism is saying, "Slow down, take it easy, veg out for a while!" but we tend to register that message as an undesirable fit of fatigue, sleepiness, or—worst of all—laziness.

Children have the knack of these rhythms. They will play with great energy for a time, and then suddenly start doing something quiet and inward. They may just stare blankly out the window for a while, or fiddle listlessly with some toy. Both body and mind have gone into the rest phase of the cycle.

In the rest phase of the ultradian rhythm, people often slip into an inner-mind trance. They may appear to be awake and involved, but in fact most of their energy is involved in inner, unconscious activity, while their conscious involvement with the outer world is greatly reduced. That inner activity includes physical rest and rejuvenation, as well as mental and emotional processing of the preceding phases of activity. In addition, there is evidence that physical and emotional healing can be going on at a level beyond the person's conscious awareness during this phase.

The ultradian inner-mind trance may be profound or light. The person may remain somewhat involved with the outer world, but really show little energy for it. For that reason, he or she may complain abut being unable to concentrate on the undertaking at hand. The person may notice feeling tired and easily confused, sensing the sudden loss of energy for work or exertion.

It will help a lot to realize that this is simply a part of the natural rhythm of life. If we take that natural rhythm into account and give each phase its due, we will be able to make much better use of our time. If we fight it, we do not really win, because during the rest phase everything in us is being pulled inward and we will feel in conflict with ourselves.

Meditation

In his book *How to Meditate* Lawrence LeShan says that meditation is like "coming home."[7] It involves the attempt to find something of oneself that has been forgotten or lost, without being able to say what was lost or when it was lost. Meditation gives us access to our deeper self and a greater reality than we ordinarily recognize in daily life. We seek to expand our ability to love, to elevate our capacity for living, and to attain a more profound knowledge of life and the world.

Meditation is practised all over the world by people from the most diverse backgrounds. India, China, and Japan have their ancient traditions of meditation. The Sufis of the Near East have practised meditation for centuries. So have the mystics of the Jewish tradition. Also, Western religious communities of the Christian faith, such as the Benedictine order of the Roman Catholic Church, have always included meditation as a central part of their daily practice. Nearly every "New Age" group or philosophy views meditation as an essential part of spiritual development.

Meditation is a special kind of inner-mind trance with inner concentration. While the object of concentration, the reason for the concentration, and the means for bringing about concentration vary, the goal is always the same. The work of meditation is to perfect one's ability to concentrate and avoid distractions. This can be difficult work, and much of what is taught about meditation is aimed at helping the person meditating improve that ability.

As a person becomes better able to concentrate, he also becomes more adept at giving himself over in an undistracted way to the activities of daily life. The discipline of meditation carries over to more focused living. The practice of meditation helps the person see himself more clearly and objectively. It makes it possible for him to identify both what is "good" and "bad" in his personality in a realistic way. Meditation also brings with it a fresh view of the world, less encumbered by the prejudices that family, culture, and other group minds tend to impose on one's thinking.

Meditation always involves inner concentration of some sort. The object of concentration varies according to the method chosen. One method entails focusing entirely on a particular physical object, such as a leaf. The purpose of the exercise is to look at the object actively, alertly, but without words. It is hoped that the person meditating will become more and more completely involved in the looking, so that distractions are gradually eliminated and the looking itself becomes the only thing the meditator is doing. Another method involves concentration on breathing. Here the person might count his breaths, for instance, and strive to think of nothing else. Other methods of meditation include focusing on the stream of one's own thoughts, using a "mantra" (a word or phrase that is repeated over and over), and concentrating on the sensations in the body. Each has as its purpose the radical narrowing of attention so that a new way of perceiving reality has room to manifest itself.

Confession of a Mall-Walker

I have to confess that I am one of those people you might see in the early morning at a mall, speed-walking in endless circles to get my day's exercise. For me mall-walking has become the next best thing to that cavernous, perilous fresh-air mall we call the out-of-doors in the city, and a great way to avoid the all-too-frequently inclement weather. My mall-walking serves another purpose for me, one just as important as exercise. It provides me with my most profound meditation experiences. Those early-morning circuits, round and round the nearly deserted mezzanine level, provide just the rhythmic movement and mental monotony perfect for inner concentration. After feeling an initial vague interest in what the display windows are showing, I find that my environment no longer holds my attention. At that point I can pop any issue or concern I choose into my mind and away it goes. I am often surprised by the results, which are often really original answers to questions that have eluded resolution up to that point. I totally lose track of time in these perambulations, which reminds me of a further advantage to this mode of meditation—the exercise period is over before I know it. I return home doubly exercised, invigorated in body and satisfied in spirit.

Depression as an Inner-Mind Trance

Many who suffer from depression say that it puts them into a world unto itself. Depressed people may seem to live in the same world as their neighbours, but really they do not. They are trapped in an inner world that nobody else knows about, an inner-mind trance of the most unfortunate kind. This is most clearly seen in the condition commonly termed "major depression." This inner world is of a particularly nightmarish kind.

William Styron's essay "Darkness Visible" describes how the torturous inner world of his depression appeared to him.[8] He undertook the task of detailing his personal experience because the pain suffered by one caught in the grip of major depression is "quite unimaginable to those who have not suffered it." He believes that those who have not endured that anguish often misunderstand and misinterpret those who are driven to commit suicide. He depicts depression as a "veritable howling tempest in the brain" which eventually saps all vitality from the body. During the period in which he was descending into depression, Styron experienced an "unfocussed dread" and an "immense aching solitude" that robbed him of his ability to concentrate. He describes the despair that eventually overtook him as like "being imprisoned in a fiercely overheated room. And because no breeze stirs this cauldron . . . the victim begins to think ceaselessly of escape."

Styron pleads for an understanding of the depressed person's experience from the inside. He makes it very clear that within the unrelenting agony of this interior pain, barely glimpsed by those around, the sufferer's view of living alters radically and his or her meaningful reality differs immensely from that of those not in that state.[9]

If you talk with people who have experienced severe depression, it becomes clear that their world has its own values, rules, fears, explanations for happenings, and solutions to problems. Those who love and esteem the victim of depression find his or her unique ways of understanding things very hard to fathom. The depressed person may dread movement or action of any kind and go to great lengths to avoid it. This sets up a whole set of procedures to make life minimally bearable, procedures governed by rules known only to the depressed. The inability to interact with people and life is most painful, but the depressed person is largely helpless to do anything about it. He or she suffers, motionless and silent, in a pit of misery, trapped within an inner-mind world impossible to convey to another living soul. The meaningful reality of the depressed person is so different from that of friends and family that it does not seem possible to build a bridge between the two.

As Styron points out, sometimes the depressed person reaches the point where the only thought, the only driving motivation he or she can muster, is to find a way to end the agony once and for all. This thought, too, is trapped within the closed inner-mind world. It is often not talked about because the depressed person believes, with some justification, that the logic of his thinking will be questioned and the desperation behind the thought will not really be understood. So, while the depressed person operates one way on the surface, even perhaps appearing "OK," yet in the powerful meaningful reality of his inner-mind trance, he is carefully planning his own final demise.

Within that meaningful reality, everything seems logical and even necessary. No perspective from the outside can make any difference. No connection with the joys of life can be established. From the point of view of the depressed person, life is intolerable. So it simply must stop. All of the person's inner-mind resources are put to the task of finding the best way to do the deed. The mind works calmly and methodically, considering the possibilities. The person feels relief when finally settling on a plan, and because of this may appear to those around to be coming out of the depression. His mood has indeed shifted, but not in the way they imagine. Rather, he feels the lightness that comes from knowing that the agony will soon end.

Carl, whose relationship with Tina I discussed in Chapter 2, knew this agony well. He was subject to periodic bouts of depression that would last from three days to a week. These depressions could come seemingly out of nowhere, suddenly and drastically altering his whole view of life. Normally a cheerful and optimistic man, he would become lethargic and hopeless. Everything seemed a great effort. When he thought about doing things that he ordinarily enjoyed, or at least had no difficulty with, he felt utter lassitude, told himself that everything was just too much trouble, so "why bother?" Every once in a while, he would move into a state of agitation and anger, during which he would wander restlessly and could not tolerate the slightest frustration. Then he would slip back into the lethargic state and spend most of the time frozen and immobile.

Carl's depressed state was complete and self-contained. He often described it as a trance, within which he was unreachable. He did not consider his state and the hopeless feelings that characterized it as something to be questioned. His negative circular thinking seemed to him perfectly normal. It did not occur to him to seek help. Neither did it occur to him that the state he was in would eventually end and he would return to his former affirmative attitude toward life. If anyone spoke to him about concern for him, it had no effect, unless he was in the irritable phase, during which he would respond with anger, for then he was especially loath to allow anyone to come close to him or affect him.

In his normal state, Carl viewed his thoughts during his depressed states as so unlike his usual ones that he could not imagine himself taking them seriously. He described his depressions as trances because they were characterized by a dramatic narrowing of awareness and a pattern of thinking that nothing from the outside could interrupt. Within the tiny reality he constructed in his depression trance, his ideas seemed perfectly rational; it was only from the perspective of broader reality that he saw them clearly as disturbed. Carl regularly developed suicidal feelings during the depressions and often rehearsed plans to act on them. In his normal state, Carl believed that he was not likely to execute those plans when he was in the lethargic phase, but he was concerned that he might impulsively put them into operation when he was in the agitated phase.

Carl realized that when depressed he gave little indication of what he was thinking to those around him. This allowed him for the most part to continue within the distorted meaningful reality of his depression trance undisturbed. He also believed that if he was going to conquer these bouts of depression, he would have to find a way to begin to communicate with the outer world from within the trance. Only in that way could the trap of his inner-mind trance be broken.

While Carl chose to struggle with his depression by entering psychotherapy, many people who are subject to depression try a combination of medication and psychotherapy. Medications have proven effective in some cases for reducing the dangers of the depressed state and aiding people in their trek back to mental health. Psychotherapy is particularly useful when it concentrates on breaking into the inner-mind trance. It is so important that the depressed person be able to talk about his or her inner meaningful reality, to begin to let some fresh air into that enclosed cavity. Even though the depressed person may feel pessimistic about it, he or she must not avoid the inner world in psychotherapy. On the contrary, it must be explored in detail so that ways can be found to bridge the gap between that reality and the common social reality within which the person lives life.

Trance and Memory

THE MAGIC OF REMEMBERING

We know little about the subjective experience of remembering. Remembering is to me a magical thing. I do not really know how to remember. I just know that at some point I decide I want to remember something, and then I employ some magical rituals that I have put together over the years and hope for the best. I wait, trusting that the gods of memory will grant my wish and bring to mind the memory I am after when I need it. Although they usually do, I can never be certain that they will grant my wish.

The rituals are quite simple, perhaps even silly. I might stare ahead of me, thinking something like, "Now what was his name anyway?" Some point out that this fixation of the eyes is common in trying to remember and that the direction of the stare (up to the right, or down to the left, for example) indicates the kind of information I am trying to recall (for example, whether it is concrete or abstract). It seems that the gods of memory are pretty specific about their rituals. In any case, this type of ritual often does the job, and I remember what I want to remember.

Sometimes I am not so lucky and the gods do not smile upon me. I try and try, but cannot remember: Where did I leave my wallet? What *is* the capital of Luxembourg? What did my grandfather give me on my twelfth birthday? I formulate the proper intention. I stare in the proper way. To no avail. The gods of memory require more.

So I close my eyes. Perhaps the sacrifice of sight will be sufficient propitiation. Then I try to work my way into it: Where was I during the six hours in which my wallet was misplaced? What are the names of some cities in Luxembourg? Where was my grandfather living when I turned twelve?

Often this further effort on my part satisfies the gods of memory that I am serious and worthy of a response, and the memory comes to me. Yet sometimes even that does not work, and I am left unenlightened, frustrated and helpless. At that point it is again brought home to me how little my conscious processes are involved in remembering.

I know the rituals and tricks that can trigger memory but not the actual inner operation. It is like that with so many things: because we do them we think we know *how* we do them. Take physical healing, for example. If we have a cut, we can clean the wound and protect it from contamination, but we do not consciously know or participate in the healing process itself. So, too, with memory. Luckily for us, the healing process seems a bit more predictable than the process of remembering.

LIVED MEMORY

Sometimes a memory comes to me totally unbidden. A song that I learned in grade school pops into my mind and repeats itself again and again. The smell of a certain hand soap produces a vivid and detailed image of my aunt's bathroom. I wake up suddenly in the middle of the night reliving the time my grandmother knocked over a tree in our yard while she was trying to learn to drive. Unbidden memories may arise when triggered by some present experience or without any obvious trigger. They may be charged with emotion or entirely without feeling. They may strike me as useful or meaningless. But in any case, I recognize them as memories and respond to them as images relating to my past.

But memories can come to us in disguised form, so that we do not recognize them as memories. Because of this, we do not acknowledge their past-time quality. Instead of coming back in familiar form, the memory is woven into a present life experience. The memory is lived out, not recognized as a memory. This can get us into trouble.

Marge provides an example of lived memory. One day she called her friend Helen and proposed that they take a weekend trip to New York. Marge had put a lot of thought into the idea. She knew that Helen loved New York and had planned the stay down to the last detail. When Marge proposed the trip, Helen declined. She had other plans for the weekend and could not change them. Marge was devastated. She felt flooded with feelings of rejection and hurt. Her mind filled with thoughts that Helen did not value her and that everyone else was more important. She kept these thoughts to herself and ended the conversation. Over the hours that followed, the thoughts became more and more intense until Marge felt suicidally depressed. Then came the anger.

When Helen called the next day, Marge felt rage toward her and could hardly speak. She had to cut the phone call short so that she would not say something she would regret.

Marge was an intelligent woman. She knew that her reaction was way out of proportion to the situation. She had made her plans without consultation, feeling sure that Helen would be able to comply. That Helen had made other plans was not *so* surprising, and there was no rational reason to take it so hard. Yet that is precisely what Marge did. Although reason told her there was no justification for her desolation, she could not free herself of the feelings.

Marge, without realizing it, was living a memory. She was reliving a moment of crisis regarding her mother when Marge was three-and-a-half years old. At that time, she came to an inner decision about what she would expect from her mother. After Marge was repeatedly ignored and rejected by her mother over a long series of attempts to win her mother's love, Marge had finally decided it was no use to continue to hope. She had decided to silence her longings and expect nothing of her parent. The hurt that accompanied this decision years ago was enormous, as was the anger that followed. The memory of that decision had been sealed away from Marge's conscious awareness, and now, when Helen declined her invitation, that memory was resurrected.

The memory of that crucial moment in Marge's childhood, with its crushing emotion, was now brought back as a lived memory, an event recalled through revivification, not through conscious recognition. Marge was engaged in psychotherapy at the time, and she eventually came to recognize the source of her response.

The therapeutic potency of inner-mind trances is very great. As I mentioned earlier, when an inner-mind therapeutic trance is first induced, outer-mind concerns dissolve and the subject's attention is riveted on some inconsequential inner-mind experience, such as the subjective sensation of heaviness. This amounts to creating a psychic vacuum or an expectant space in the mind. Any image or idea can then be introduced into that space and expanded to command the person's full attention. When dealing with a lived memory, a past problematic trance can be introduced into that space and dealt with therapeutically.

This was the case with Marge. First Marge was asked to recall the feelings of the lived memory as she has been experiencing it in the recent present. She was asked to bring back the experience with Helen as vividly as possible, letting the emotions and thoughts return without censoring them. Then Marge concentrated on those emotions and the despairing thoughts that came with them, to allow them to grow to their fullest intensity. When she did this, Marge was flooded with memories of being three-and-a-half years old, when her despondency about her mother had peaked and she vowed never to need her again. Once Marge had recovered this direct memory, she was able to explore it and reduce its influence by viewing it according to present perspective. As a result, the lived memory she experienced in relation to Helen quickly dissipated.

Inner-Mind Reality

When we experience inner-mind trances, we are in touch with an area within us that seems both familiar and mysterious. The inner mind possesses qualities that appear at odds with the ordinary reality of daily life. The inner mind's reality is our next consideration.

the world of
the inner mind

I F WE ARE GOING TO UNDERSTAND the inner mind and how it works, we have to go back to the problem of meaningful reality. Specifically we have to ask: What is real for the inner mind?

Meaningful reality is personal. It is what is real for me, here and now. Right now my meaningful reality is this paper, this pen, the table and chair, insofar as they allow me to write, and my ideas. Everything else is pretty insignificant at this moment, and for all practical purposes it does not exist for me. Let me emphasize again: I am not talking about reality in some final metaphysical sense, but meaningful reality, which is the reality of our experience.

Outer and Inner Reality

The outer mind is at home in the physical, social, interactive environment of our lives. Working ceaselessly to make things happen, to accomplish what it wants to accomplish, to relate to others as it wishes to relate, to handle life's situations as it chooses, the outer mind is a true citizen of the world, and, like it or not, the outer mind cannot escape this involvement. The world is its home, its theatre of operations, the place where it lives, and the job of the outer mind is to find the best way to deal with worldly affairs.

The outer mind's reality is not just the physical world and its occupants, but also the expectations, rules, and protocols that operate

there. In the next chapter I will discuss these factors as they emanate from our group-mind involvements. For now let me just
say that the outer mind is very concerned about fitting in with
these demands. And why not? If it is going to negotiate this complex world successfully, it has to know what works and what does
not.

The hallmarks of the outer mind are rationality and determination. Reason dominates every outer-mind experience and willpower
provides the force to get things done. When reason or willpower
breaks down, it is because something else has entered the picture—
the inner mind.

The inner mind operates in a world of interior impressions. Its
meaningful reality consists of the ideas and images of that world.
Everything there seems immediate and self-evident. The inner
world is occupied by our everyday dreams, fantasies, and memories. It is also the arena of telepathic awareness and spiritual vision,
and the place where we may encounter past-life memories or near-
death experiences.

The inner mind is fully aware of the outer world. It is affected
by what goes on there and it reacts to the outer world. But the outer
world is not really its sphere. The goals and values of the inner
mind may be quite different from those of the outer mind and at
odds with outer-world culture. In our culture it is common to dismiss many things that the inner mind experiences as unreal. Being
a law-abiding citizen of my culture, my outer mind speaks up and
rejects those inner-mind experiences—often with irrational fury.
The outer mind is our most vocal protector of cultural trance.

The inner mind can sense things not noticed by the outer. It
picks up cues, feelings, "vibrations" from other people that the
outer mind misses. A whole world of communication occurs between people's inner minds that escapes their conscious awareness.
I may be overwhelmed by the feelings of silent anger in a friend sitting next to me. I may know "telepathically" what my partner is
thinking. I may sense that a certain person is about to phone me.
However one might explain these experiences, they do occur, and
the inner mind feels very much at home in this intuitive realm.

The inner mind is the font of all creativity and genius. It is the author of artistic productions, the inventor of original ideas, and the source of spontaneous solutions to problems. When it comes to creativity, the outer mind is subordinate to the inner. The outer mind does the Joe-jobs—corrects the grammar, checks the measurements, and smooths the outer surface of the creative product—but the product itself comes from the inner mind.

The inner mind is where the heart is. It is there that we discover our deepest passions and our subtlest desires. Affection and love arise from the inner mind, as do anger and hatred. When we want to understand the mysterious doings of our emotions, it is the inner mind that we must explore.

Inner-mind reality is completely subjective. It can never be adequately grasped by objective knowledge or directly observed by another person. We can try to communicate our subjective knowledge. We can describe the inner experience to others or allow our bodies to be hooked up to machines that measure physiological changes as we experience something, but we cannot pass on the subjective experience itself. In that sense, our inner-mind reality remains totally personal and incommunicable. When we die, our inner-mind reality dies with us.

Nevertheless, the inner mind's world is very real. Inner-mind realities have a quality of presence and vividness every bit as insistent as that of the physical objects and people of the outer world. In fact, the inner mind's reality often seems more real than that of the outer mind.

A person who suffers from agoraphobia—fear of open spaces—may realize, from all the evidence of her senses, that there is nothing to fear in leaving her apartment and stepping onto the sidewalk. Yet some image from the inner mind completely overrides that outer-mind perception and paralyses her with fear. It makes no difference how eloquently her outer mind reasons about the outer-world situation. It makes no difference what physical preparations she might make or what safety precautions she might put in place. Her fear is unshakeable and immovable. The strength of her inner-mind reality is such that no outer-mind realization can change it.

Sources of Inner-Mind Reality

How is inner-mind reality created? We can only guess at the answer, because most of what occurs there is hidden from awareness. If we knew exactly how inner-mind reality creation worked, we could cure all mental disorders and emotional problems arising from that reality. Unfortunately, the operation of the inner mind remains largely unknown to us. Nevertheless, we can say something about factors that help to shape inner-mind reality.

The Three Selves

Some light might be cast on the functioning of inner and outer minds through the view the practitioners of the Huna religion in Hawaii hold of the psyche. According to Huna, there are three selves that operate in each human being.

There is the Middle Self that functions in the ordinary affairs of daily life. This self has no inner existence. Its sole purpose is to deal with those things that make life in this world possible; to that end the Middle Self has the full power of reason and a strong will. This makes it virtually impervious to the power of suggestion. We tend to identify with this self. It corresponds to what I call the Outer Mind.

Then there is the Low Self. This part corresponds largely to what in Western psychology has been called the subconscious mind. Although capable of rational thought, its mental processes are not ruled by reason, as are those of the Middle Self. The Low Self is highly susceptible to suggestion—from both the Middle Self and from outside sources—and can maintain false or distorted ideas about things acquired through suggestion indefinitely. For this reason the Low Self is the arena of neurosis within a person. The Low Self is also the seat of all emotions. Any feeling experienced by the Middle Self in fact emanates from the Low Self. In addition, the Low Self is the source of memory, and the Middle Self, which has no memory of its own, is dependent on the Low Self for all remembering. Finally, the Low Self controls all the functioning of the physical body and can powerfully affect the person's state of health.

The third self is the High Self, a wise superconscious spirit that oversees the life of the person. The High Self is a kindly parental presence and is considered to have elements of both male and female. The High Self is capable of extraordinary, even miraculous, acts of healing. It possesses supernatural faculties, such as the ability to see the future and to control the forces of nature. The Middle Self may contact the High Self through "prayer," which must be channelled through the Low Self. This prayer may not always be successful because the Low Self can harbour neurotic distortions or "complexes" that block access to the High Self.

The Huna view of the human psyche is most interesting in light of our discussion of the inner/outer duality. The outer world is the domain of the Middle Self. The inner world is where both the High and Low Selves operate.

Inner-mind reality is shaped by influences from within and without. From within we are affected by our own biology, by those biochemical exchanges that are part of our existence as physical organisms. We are also affected from within by all of those dynamic factors that psychological researchers—such as Sigmund Freud, Carl Jung, Wilhelm Reich, and many others—have spent the past hundred years trying to map out. Repressed or dissociated memories, infantile and adult desires, interiorized family and cultural expectations, collective archetypal representations: these and other factors are active within us to create and reshape the reality of the inner world. Beyond these known dynamics are others as yet unrecognized by conventional depth psychology. They include paranormal experiences, healing experiences that affect both body and mind, flights of creative genius, spiritual and mystical experiences, and the mysterious movements of love.

There is also the seemingly endless production of stories, myths, and poetic images by what has been called the "mythopoetic" faculty of the inner mind.[10] This is an aspect of inner human experience that accounts for the sagas generated by dreams, the fantasy dramas presented by mediums and channellers, and the poetic images and mythological stories that sometimes spontaneously arise in our imaginations. It seems that this mythopoetic activity is going on all the time in some region of the inner mind, with only a small part of it reaching our conscious awareness.

From outside come other shaping forces. Our daily involvements with people and situations provide the basic material for our inner-mind creations, but the form they take owes in large part to that mysterious thing called "suggestion."

Suggestion

The power of "suggestion" has been recognized from time immemorial. It is described in ancient treatises on imagination and contemporary scientific articles on the placebo effect. In modern times, suggestion is universally acknowledged as an integral part of human experience and is invoked to explain a host of mysterious phenomena that science cannot account for.

Animal Magnetism

Suggestion has often been used to explain what is scientifically opaque. An example of this can be found in the history of a healing system called "animal magnetism" that flourished for a hundred years from about 1780. This technique produced tens of thousands of cures and treatments, documented in thousands of books and pamphlets. Animal magnetism explains health and disease by a universal energy (magnetic fluid), which permeates all living things. When this energy is blocked or hindered in its flow through the body, the body can contract disease. When freed through animal magnetism's healing procedures, the body can cure itself.

Animal magnetism is just one in a long line of healing approaches that today extends into New Age energy-healing systems on the one hand, and Reichian bioenergetic techniques on the other. Scientists have always had a hard time with the notion of a life energy as the foundation for healthy organic functioning, and so have felt obliged to seek out other explanations for the undeniable effects of these approaches. The power of suggestion became the explanation of choice and remains the standard way of dismissing the positive results of alternative medicines.

Suggestion is the conversion of an idea into a reality. An idea is introduced to a person in such a way that he or she develops the impression that the idea is real. For instance, I may say to you that in the next sixty seconds your nose will start to itch. If you accept this as a suggestion, you will find your nose does begin to itch; you will have converted the idea of an itching nose into a reality. Or a stage hypnotist may ask you to clasp your hands together and then tell you emphatically that you cannot separate them. If you cannot, then you have accepted his suggestion and converted the idea into a reality.

Sometimes suggestions are not intentionally imposed. For example, we are continually being bombarded by physical stimuli that become influential suggestions. Advertising companies know that boxes of popcorn and containers of Coke on the big screen make our mouths water and propel us to the candy counter. Many people cannot read descriptions of diseases in a medical dictionary without their inducing imaginary pains. For me the smell of salt air can trigger powerful images of a pleasant holiday I spent at the seashore. And we all know that a healthy yawn is irresistibly contagious. Our family and cultural involvements are also laced with suggestions. A Haitian woman grows sick and takes to her bed when she hears that she has been cursed; a child labelled stupid by his father cannot pass an examination; and for years, the mere knowledge that no one had ever run a four-minute mile prevented many great athletes from breaking that invisible barrier.

Many suggestions come from the outside, from people, situations, or even simple sensory experiences. But suggestions can also come from the inside, from images that we elaborate in our own imaginations or from ideas that we deliberately dwell on. Stores are heavily stocked with auto-suggestion tapes that help people do everything from developing self-confidence to giving up smoking.

In professional literature about suggestion, there is often an association made between suggestion and hypnosis. Some say that people are more suggestible when hypnotized than when in their ordinary state. However, studies of hypnotic suggestion indicate that suggestion received in the normal state may be just as effective as hypnotic suggestion. Many researchers claim that hypnosis itself is not a special, altered state of consciousness, but a social relationship, with suggestion at its heart.

Probably the most surprising effects are those that occur in the physical organism. How is it possible, for example, that medical hypnotist Dr. David Cheek, when dealing with traumatic vaginal bleeding in an emergency ward can say to the patient, "Look up there at that spot on the ceiling . . . and stop that bleeding," and the bleeding immediately subsides and then stops?[11] How can Victor Rausch use auto-suggestion with such effectiveness that, with no anaesthetic, his gall bladder can be removed surgically without pain?[12] How is it that hypnotherapist Milton Erickson can suggest to an eighteen-year-old woman whose breasts have not developed at all that she will grow breasts—and she meet with dramatic success in two months?[13] How does an idea implanted in the mind get translated into physiological effects that a person could not deliberately produce in a million years?

And what about the famous placebo effect? A placebo is something given to a person to gratify or please him or her. The placebo effect refers to the physiological changes that occur when an inert, harmless substance is given to a patient who believes it is a potent medication. The expectation causes the effect. Typical is the harmless sugar pill given to a patient who is told it is a powerful painkiller. In a significant number of cases, the sugar pill will be as effective in reducing pain as the real thing, simply because of the patient's belief. Beneficial results are known to occur when placebos are used to treat a wide range of illnesses. In fact, the placebo effect is so common that every time a medication is tested for effectiveness, control groups must be set up in which all participants are administered either innocuous placebos or the real thing without knowing which, and the results are compared. In this way the mysterious placebo effect can be isolated from the results the medication actually produces.

Recent research shows that placebos and other suggestive procedures can enhance the strength of the immune system. There are even reports indicating that suggestion in some cases may be instrumental in bringing about remission in cancer. Techniques involving relaxation and suggestive images depicting the body fighting and destroying cancer cells have produced promising results. All in all, the overwhelming conclusion of studies involving treatment with placebos and other suggestive approaches is that we have an extraordinary ability to bring about profound organic changes in ourselves through suggestion.

Suggestion and Memory

When we remember something, we are not dealing with an objective record of an event engraved in our brains, but rather a personal experience moulded and shaped by a host of internal factors and returned to our attention in a subjective format. In a sense we are not dealing with the event at all, but with our present take on the event. In other words, we are dealing with an inner-mind reality.

How We Remember

There are two kinds of memory: explicit and implicit. Explicit memory is recall of the details of an event: who, what, when, where, why. Implicit memory involves the effects of past experiences, including emotional associations, skills and habits, conditioned responses, and the raw perceptual input of events. As an example, if someone were assaulted, his explicit memory would be of the place, time, and sequence of events. His implicit memory would not come back as direct recall, but as changes in behaviour, so it might show up in nightmares or flashbacks, depression, or feelings of anxiety triggered by sights, smells, or sounds reminiscent of the assault.

One of the problems with memory is that implicit and explicit memory are served by different systems within the brain. This means that recalling something is not like looking at a snapshot in the mind. Rather, remembering is a process of reconstruction: retrieving components, validating them, and assembling them.

There is evidence that explicit memory is more fragile than implicit memory. A person may have undergone a traumatic assault in a woods, for instance, and retain no explicit knowledge of what happened, and yet experience powerful feelings of fear and anxiety at the smell of dead leaves. It is as though the emotions remember, but the mind does not. There is an apt saying among students of memory that "emotional memory is forever."

It has been discovered that the more intense the emotional stress of the incident, the stronger the emotional memory of that incident. This means that traumatic events will be more indelibly stored as emotional memory than will ordinary events. The problem is that there is no evidence that the *explicit* memory of the event will be stronger. In fact, some research indicates that storage of the explicit memory of an experience that involved excessively high stress may be impeded. So we could have a situation in which the explicit memory is unavailable but implicit, and the emotional memory is powerfully present. This would create a real predicament, because a traumatized person would be triggered emotionally by situations that recall the trauma, but would not know what was causing the upset. Psychotherapists who work with recovered memories of trauma frequently encounter this situation. The explicit content of the memory has been dissociated (separated) from the person's awareness, but the emotional, implicit aspect of the memory is excessively active in the person's life. Before the explicit memory is recovered, the person is subject to "emotional triggers," situations or experiences that cause unaccountable anxiety and fear. This can have a negative impact on their lives, since the triggering is unpredictable.

It is important to note that, given the right conditions, explicit memory may be once again restored where for some time only implicit memory existed. Here the dissociation is undone, the original cause of the unaccountable anxiety or fear is brought back into the person's awareness, and the memory is complete. Where this occurs with a formerly dissociated memory of trauma, the person has a chance to resolve the emotional knots that have been tied around the memory and to integrate the experience into his or her personality.

As simple as this sounds, the process can, in fact, be perilous. Because the retrieval of memory involves a reconstructive process, the wrong elements can be put together and produce a distorted or even false memory. We are particularly prone to making mistakes about memory because of something called *source amnesia*. With source amnesia the person remembers the core of the event but cannot recall its context—the time, place, and circumstances surrounding it. For example, a person may remember a man's face, but not be able to recall where he saw that face—its original context.

The problem of source amnesia makes the accurate remembering of traumatic events particularly difficult—especially since the source is probably the quickest aspect of memory to decay. Think of the person who has been assaulted in the woods. The high level of stress in the situation might lead him to create a powerful implicit memory, on the one hand, and to destroy an explicit memory on the other.

Now add to that the fact that the person may also experience source amnesia, and what do we have? Well, let us say that the emotional memory is triggered, perhaps by the smell of decaying leaves or by a therapeutic technique that brings the person into contact with the traumatic feeling. What then? The brain tries to determine the source of the memory, but if the source has deteriorated, the recall mechanism may make mistakes and generate faulty source memories. The fabricated source may be constructed of bits and pieces of things the person saw or experienced, or it may even consist of elements the person imagined or that were suggested to him. Here the real and the fabricated combine into a false memory. The implicit, emotional memory is true, whereas elements of the source and/or explicit memory are false.

Like other inner-mind realities, memory is subject to the influence of suggestion. Experiments show that if a person has witnessed an event, recall of that event can be altered by suggestions introduced about the event. So if someone sees a car accident, for example, and then discusses it with other witnesses, her recollection may be mixed with elements taken from their accounts. Also, if someone is interrogated about something he has witnessed, he can be affected by the way the questions are worded and by the emotional tone with which the questions are asked. In other words, suggestions conveyed during questioning can lead us unwittingly to recall something inaccurately.

Suggestions from questioners need not be delivered deliberately. In most situations where we are asked to remember something, the interrogator is genuinely trying to get at the truth. The problem is that the questioner may have preconceived ideas about what the answers should be and may unconsciously telegraph cues about his expectations. The suggestion is conveyed in such a way that neither the questioner nor the questioned person is conscious of what is going on. In recent years, there has been a growing awareness of the dangers of unconsciously "leading" someone who is trying to recall an event. Now police officers, social workers, and others who act as interrogators are warned about them.

Unfortunately, the way suggestions are conveyed can be very subtle, and it takes more than a manual of how to phrase questions to overcome the problem. A surprised look, a raised eyebrow, an intake of breath can convey powerful suggestive messages to the person responding, so to ask questions free of suggestive influence is particularly difficult to do. We are very responsive to suggestive cues in dealing with others. There is great survival value in being able to recognize even the smallest indication of what is expected of us, particularly from a person we see as an authority or upon whom our welfare depends. We are particularly alert to cues in situations of danger, when we believe we may be harmed physically, emotionally, financially, and so forth, and we are very observant when we want the questioner to like us.

Because this suggestion/response interplay occurs largely beyond our conscious awareness, the use of interrogation to gain accurate memory information is particularly risky. Despite our best intentions, our recall of events is likely to be shaped by the expectations, real or imagined, that we perceive in the situation.

Recovered Memory

In psychotherapy, a client sometimes unearths memories of traumatic events forgotten since the events occurred. This is commonly called working with "recovered memory." Memories uncovered in this way can be problematic because the operation of this kind of memory is anything but simple. A few words about this kind of memory work is in order.

Some memories from childhood are straightforward and clear. For example, I can recall an incident when I was four years old. My grandfather and I were leaving my parents' house by the rear entrance. He was taking me for a walk in the little town where we lived. I was excited about this because my grandfather was my hero. As we left, my grandfather made a comment that included a mild profanity. I remember that word and I recall very clearly that my mother was annoyed at his using it in my hearing. This memory has always been with me. It is something I have always known, even if I rarely think about it.

Not all memories from childhood are this straightforward. I can also remember being about two and a half years old and standing in the dining-room of our house, looking out the window at the back yard. I saw the grass strewn with ice cubes, the kind you make in a refrigerator. As I looked, the ice cubes suddenly rushed to a central point on the lawn and clashed together there, making a tremendously loud noise. This is another memory that has been with me my whole life, yet I know it cannot be literally true. I realize that I must have distorted or misinterpreted what I saw. I now believe that what really happened was that I saw hail falling on the back lawn, dancing about as it landed. At the same time I must have heard a loud clap of thunder. The whole thing combined in my childish imagination to produce the hallucination-tinged memory that has stayed with me.

Obviously, our childhood memories can be distorted. In the case of the ice-cube memory, I was not sophisticated enough to interpret the sight accurately. The distortion came from my limited perceptual capability. Childhood memories can also be distorted by those mechanisms that affect how we process and recall what we have perceived (see box "How We Remember"). So, a childhood memory can be true in its kernel but place an event in the wrong location or substitute one person for another or in other ways misplace peripheral elements.

Memories can also be false. We have the capacity to fabricate events unconsciously in our inner minds and then introduce them into consciousness as true memories. I have seen striking instances of this. I have known clients to describe, in great detail and with powerful emotion, memories of events that I know for a fact did not happen. Although an exploration of the unconscious meaning of these pseudo-memories sometimes leads to an understanding of why they were fabricated, it is still shocking to realize how deeply we can deceive ourselves.

What part might suggestion play in recovering memories of traumatic events from childhood? This is an extremely important question. In cases of abuse, what is being recalled has serious implications for not only the client, but also for any other people who may be implicated in that particular memory.

A therapist who is well trained in the art of psychotherapy will be keenly aware of the potential for influencing memories of clients and go to great lengths to avoid that. He or she will take into account the factors I mentioned above regarding the dangers of unconscious cues. Unfortunately, some therapists are not well trained and might make serious mistakes in this regard. This appears to have happened in some cases reported in the media.

But even if the therapist is careful not to influence her client, recovered memory work is still hazardous, because the client is exposed to repeated powerful suggestions from sources beyond anyone's control. Encounters with media, family, friends, and acquaintances—virtually all social contacts—are laced with suggestive ideas. Today, every psychotherapy client has seen sophisticated media dramatizations of child abuse, multiple personality, recovered-memory therapy, and a host of related topics, so that it is impossible to carry on a therapy untainted by outside suggestion. Add to this the availability of magazine articles and books that go into these matters in depth, and it becomes clear that recovered-memory work, free of suggestive influence, is a myth. These sources of suggestive information present contradictory ideas, in some cases promoting the acceptance of recovered memories of abuse, and in others arguing against their validity. In this matter, suggestions pro and con are often presented with highly charged emotions, and those who are exposed to them can hardly go away unaffected.

Because of the ubiquity of suggestive ideas and the problems inherent in the recall process itself, working with recovered memory must be carried out with great care. Although in some cases the client regains memories that are clear and leave no room for doubt, this is not always the case. Where this certainty is lacking, the client must be allowed to go through the very arduous and difficult process necessary to determine the objective reality of the memories of abuse being recovered. This process requires time. In many cases it takes years to complete. Over that period, clients sometimes experience cycles of contradictory feelings about the validity of their memories, now doubting them, then accepting them fully. The process must not be rushed, no matter how long it takes the client to arrive at a final position on the matter.

Recently, I have become concerned about the apparently increasing number of cases in which a premature stand is taken in public—parties making accusations, laying charges, or launching civil suits—about alleged childhood sexual abuse. In these cases therapy clients act against their purported abusers before they are absolutely sure about their memories. Clearly this can have very undesirable consequences. If people have not completed the recovery process, they take a terrible gamble in making the matter public. The gamble is that their present judgment may not be the final truth about the memories. And if the recovery process is short-circuited, how can they know whether that judgment is or isn't the final truth? By taking a public stand, they freeze their own positions, and it is difficult to continue the recovery process to an unbiased conclusion. Because the stand is public, it is hard for these people to admit, even to themselves, new doubts that may arise.

Like all memories, recovered memories bear the indelible stamp of the inner mind. Recovered memories are inner-mind realities that sooner or later have to interface with outer-mind realities. The client is the forum in which the confrontation between inner and outer worlds takes place. The client should be informed that the re-call process is complex and fraught with problems. That way both client and therapist can take the care needed to arrive at a satisfactory outcome.

False-Memory Syndrome

"False-Memory Syndrome," an expression in widespread use today, is a term without status as a psychiatric diagnosis and without cogency as a conceptual framework. The term purports to describe a syndrome in which psychotherapists and their clients treat recovered memories of childhood sexual abuse as if they were true, whereas they are really mutual delusions initiated by the therapist and taken up by the client. According to this way of thinking, the client is so suggestible that even slight hints on the part of the therapist will be elaborated into full-blown detailed descriptions of sexual abuse, often perpetrated by a parent. Those who promote the idea of a False-Memory Syndrome also oppose the notion that traumatic incidents of childhood can be repressed or dissociated from awareness for years, only to reemerge into consciousness in psychotherapy sessions as an adult. They base their opposition on the skimpy research done to date on this subject and ignore the massive clinical evidence of dissociation reported over the past hundred years.

The problem with a False-Memory Syndrome is that it is only believable if you ignore the complexities of memory. This approach emphasizes the suggestibility of the client in a one-sided way, rightly pointing out that a therapist could introduce suggestions that influence a client's memories, but ignoring the fact that the vast majority of therapists are aware of this and take proper precautions. It also overlooks the fact that clients are equally subject to suggestion from those who want to deny that the clients have suffered any sexual abuse. The original abuse was often sealed with the perpetrator's strong threat to the client never to mention the incident—a powerful suggestion on an impressionable mind. Also, alienated families of those who believe they recall childhood sexual abuse sometimes introduce their own powerful suggestions. They isolate the accuser emotionally, indicating that she or he will be accepted back into the fold only after giving up the notion that abuse occurred. The tremendous complexity that develops around recovered memory has to be taken into full account if justice is to be done, and any approach that reduces that complexity to a simple formula, such as False-Memory Syndrome, is naive.

Inner-Mind Anomalies

We are always dealing with inner-mind realities. We usually don't reflect much on them because they have been incorporated as an ordinary part of life. However, some of our inner-mind realities may strike us as unusual, even odd. They involve experiences that our culture does not identify as "normal," and so when we have them we are taken aback. I am talking here about paranormal experiences (such as telepathy and precognition), spiritualistic experiences (channelling, spirit possession, and communication with the dead), alien-encounter experiences (UFO sightings and alien abductions), extraordinary multiple identity experiences (multiple personality disorder or dissociative identity disorder), and unusual spiritual experiences (past-life memories and near-death experiences).

What these inner-mind experiences have in common is that they are considered bizarre by our society. We do not have any acceptable cultural category that they fit. Other cultures may readily accept some of these phenomena; ours does not. This is important: the problem we have with these experiences and the reason we feel odd about them is not that they are a priori impossible, but that they do not fit into our cultural categories. People who have these inner-mind experiences may for that reason feel alienated from other people and society at large. Because these odd experiences are not assimilated into our North American culture, I am going to call them "anomalous inner-mind experiences."

In calling your attention to anomalous inner-mind experiences, I do not mean to pass judgment one way or the other as to their "objective truth." These phenomena have a personal truth—at least as ways of explaining the world to those who have them. They are certainly experienced as genuine, and one might say that in a way the person having the experiences has no choice but to have them.

There are those who believe that anomalous inner-mind experiences can be "proven" to be objectively real. They attempt to show that they correspond to outer-mind happenings or that inner-mind phenomena may leave palpable traces in the communally accessible outer world. Perhaps they are right.

Research of this kind leaves me unmoved. I believe that much of this kind of investigation, usually done under the banner of science, is carried out to lessen that sense of alienation from the broader community that a person inevitably has who claims to have had anomalous inner-mind experiences. There is the hope that, by amassing anecdotal or circumstantial evidence in favour of the phenomena, those who are skeptical will be convinced and our culture's unbelief will be overcome.

I believe this approach sidesteps the problem of inner-mind/ outer-mind duality that is an unavoidable part of human existence.

The experiences of the inner mind occur on a subjective level, and so cannot be put under objective observation. Any objective verification of subjective events is indirect and never totally conclusive. Rather than pursue that course, effort would best be spent investigating anomalous inner-mind experiences on their own ground and placing them in the broader context of inner-mind realities of every kind.

How Unusual Are They?

Although anomalous inner-mind experiences may be considered odd in our society, we cannot conclude that they are rare. Gallup polls conducted in 1990 and 1994 show that belief in anomalous phenomena is widespread, and a significant number of people report having anomalous experiences of their own. According to the 1990 poll, one-half of the population believes in extrasensory perception (ESP). More than one-third believes in telepathy and one-quarter in clairvoyance. About half of those polled believe that people are sometimes possessed by the Devil. Slightly fewer than half accept the reality of UFOs. The 1994 Gallup poll revealed that 28 percent believe in communication with the dead, while 27 percent accept reincarnation, both of these figures showing notable increases since 1990.

Neither poll asks questions about near-death experiences, and there seems to be no comprehensive information about their frequency. Studies on the frequency of reported out-of-body experiences vary greatly, but the best is probably that conducted by Susan Blackmore, which states that 13 to 14 percent of respondents believed they had had at least one such experience.[14] Neither Gallup poll posed a question about the participants' personal experiences with possession. There is good reason to believe that possession experiences and feelings of intrusive influence are, thankfully, uncommon, but it would be a mistake to think that they are confined to "more primitive" cultures. While the 1990 poll reported a fairly high rate of belief in the reality of UFOs, it is hard to evaluate what percentage of the population actually claim alien abduction experiences.

To summarize, we would have to conclude from these surveys that a significant portion of our society accepts the existence of anomalous inner-mind experiences and that millions of North Americans actually report experiences of anomalous inner-mind realities.

When Outer and Inner Minds Do Not Agree

As I mentioned above, when a person experiences anomalous inner-mind phenomena, this frequently sets up a tension between outer and inner mind. The inner mind has the experience and simply accepts it as reality. Just as we accept our dreams as real while we are dreaming, so also when the inner mind has a past-life memory, for instance, it experiences it as real. But, with anomalous inner-mind experiences, our outer mind is not completely out of the picture. Rather, it is present as an observer, offering its opinion about what the inner mind is experiencing, and usually that opinion is skeptical, dubious.

The outer mind is, after all, a denizen of the outer world with its values and criteria for measuring truth. Because the outer mind is geared to make do in this world, it must conform to reality as determined by its culture. If the outer mind's culture were India, for instance, it would not be inclined to introduce doubt about a past-life memory. But in our North American culture the idea that we have lived before and have been reborn into various lives is not acceptable. Even though one in four among us believes in past lives, our society as a whole rejects the notion, as does the scientific community in particular. This latter community is such a dominant force in determining orthodox beliefs and makes a point of dismissing such ideas as superstition.

Since the beliefs of this culture are so frequently and so forcefully inculcated in us from every side and, since it has to live and relate in this culture, the outer mind becomes a mouthpiece for cultural orthodoxy, opposing unacceptable ideas that emanate from the inner mind.

The Imaginal World

Islamic scholar Henry Corbin writes of an "imaginal world" described by Islamic philosophers of the Middle Ages, Philippus Aureolus Paracelsus, and Emanuel Swedenborg.[15] The imaginal world is not an imaginary world: it is a world of reality beyond sensible experience, yet perceived in the form of images. Corbin says that we have lost touch with this world, which is known through "active imagination" or "spiritual imagination." Our active imagination is a form of cognition and perceives imaginal reality as directly as sense cognition perceives the physical world and intellectual cognition perceives abstract concepts. Ancient Islamic philosophers took pains to distinguish between the imaginal and the imaginary, but we have no language availabe in our culture to allow us to have the experience they describe. If we were to accept the existence of the imaginal world, we would perhaps see certain inner-mind experiences as dealing not with the imaginary (combinations of sense images left over in memory) but with a reality separate from yet as real as the physical.

The inner-mind/outer-mind conflict can make itself felt as the experience happens or it can arise later. One of the criticisms frequently levelled against the validity of anomalous inner-mind experiences is that many people begin with an ordinary experience and, over time, embellish and elaborate it into something extraordinary. It is said, for example, that a person might see an unexplained glow in the sky one night, and by the next day believe he saw a spaceship of some kind. Then, as he describes his experience to friends, he elaborates on it further and now believes he saw little creatures alight from an opening in its side. Soon the account turns into an alien-abduction incident.

Although I am sure that this kind of imaginative elaboration can occur with certain personality types, I also believe that the experience of most people is much the opposite. On a number of occasions people have told me about an anomalous experience of some kind that was so vivid and shocking at the time that they could hardly admit to themselves that it was happening. Then as time passed, they invented all kinds of reasons why it must not have occurred, since it is just too bizarre. Still later, the originally extraordinary experience is reduced to the ordinary and is thus relieved of its disturbing quality. By now the person passes judgment: "I must have been imagining things." This happens not because of any new insights into the matter, but simply because, when it comes to anomalous inner-mind realities, the outer mind must retain its domination over the inner mind if it is to function unperturbed in our culture.

I believe that because there is such great tension between our outer minds, which so steadfastly reflect the skepticism of our culture, and our inner minds, it will be a long time before we will be able to give anomalous inner-mind realities the impartial attention they require. Only then will we be able to develop a truly comprehensive understanding of them. As long as there is so much cultural censorship, we will not even be able to acknowledge data from the inner mind, much less learn what those data mean.

Our culture needs to lose its fear of the inner mind. That fear seems to be based on a conviction that if we ever listen seriously to accounts of anomalous inner-mind experiences that people are having all the time, we will be seduced back into the dark ages of primitive superstition. I think the opposite is the case: unless we pay attention to these data, we will secretly harbour the fear that they are, after all, true.

I believe that the fear of recognizing anomalous inner-mind experiences as psychological data worthy of study is itself the manifestation of a hidden superstitious attitude in our society. Our culture, having so heavily invested blind faith in science, secretly feels the fragility of that faith. It secretly fears that the demons banished by science over the past two centuries will rise again if not fought off at every turn. Our culture is not confident that science has disposed of the occult and the spiritual as thoroughly as it had hoped. It may claim to fear the demons of superstition in people's minds, but I believe that the taboo it imposes on looking at the data of the inner mind shows that, on an unconscious level, it harbours a real fear of real demons. In a neat projective defence, it has repressed its belief in their existence and attributed that belief to others. The result is that, in the culturally accepted view, anyone who pays attention to anomalous experiences is a dangerous true believer in blind superstition, whereas anyone who prejudges the case and flees from these data is a hard-nosed realist.

So as it turns out, the problem of the inner-mind/outer-mind conflict is in the last analysis a cultural problem. It revolves around the conditioning imposed on the outer mind by the various group minds of which it is a part. We are dealing, then, with the power of group-mind trances in our lives and the inner split they can produce. This is what we must examine next.

CHAPTER SIX

the group mind

THE DESIRE TO BELONG, to be a part of something: that is essential to what it means to be human. We instinctively form groups and join groups. From birth to death, we live our lives in relation to groups.

When firmly established as part of a group, the individual feels strengthened and supported. There is a sense of being more, of partaking of the resources of the whole. This sense of expansion is one of the main benefits of membership in the group and is perhaps the main reason we seek it so desperately.

We want to belong to the in-group, the clique or inner circle. Even when we feel painfully excluded, we still live in relation to them, lamenting a happiness lost or never attained. Sometimes rejection by a group is so deeply wounding that a person may spend the rest of his or her life gossiping about the offending group, nursing bitterness, and plotting revenge.

Group Mind

A group mind is an entity built up by many individuals who together focus on one idea or activity. A group mind is not just a collection of individuals. It is a kind of organism that carries on a life of its own, above and beyond that of the individuals who comprise it. The group mind exerts a powerful influence on the thoughts and actions of the group members. They may behave in ways totally out of character with themselves in other contexts or individually. And even if the individual in the group deliberately strives to maintain independence of thought within the group-mind, he or she may find that very difficult indeed.

Group-minds may be natural, spontaneous, or planned. The family is a natural group. The members have been brought together by the circumstances of life and form a group sanctioned by both nature and society. As children are born into the family, they become a part of the family group mind, but not by choice. They are immediately immersed in the practices and thinking that characterize their particular family, and they do not reflect on the rightness of those traditions. As the child grows, he or she seldom questions the tenets of the group mind. A family member may appear to reject the ways of the group, but often that rebellion is only apparent. Even in the rebellious teen years, the adolescent's rejection of parents and family ties is seldom more than superficial; the powerful emotional ties, the ones that really count, remain largely intact. For the most part, those ties are not seriously reviewed or examined in the course of the adult life of the family member.

Other natural group minds are those formed as people gather together in tribal or social units for the sake of physical survival and to improve their quality of life. Racial and ethnic groups can form group minds that exert tremendous influence on their members.

A spontaneous group mind was described in Chapter 1, in the episode of the Russian corporal who was so caught up in the mind of the street mob that he began beating his own superior officer that he revered. Another spontaneous group mind is that of the crowd at a soccer game. People can be swept along on the energy of the crowd to such an extent that they become involved in fights and other dangerous conduct that they would not otherwise engage in.

Churches, cults, clubs, unions, political parties, and work situations are examples of planned group minds. These groups are formed with conscious intent, and they are organized around a particular belief, goal, project, or person.

Many group minds are just temporary. Some last for a few short hours, or even minutes. A lynch mob might form, act, and disperse within one hour. Sports crowds usually have a life span of several hours. A political convention may last a weekend.

Some group minds endure for long periods. It is difficult to measure the span of a family group mind. Since they tend to remain consistent over many generations, family group minds can be hundreds of years old. The group mind of the Catholic Church has existed for nearly two thousand years. Although it has altered over that time, the same group mind has endured, evolving with changing circumstances. The group mind of ethnic groups and races may be even more ancient. The Jewish group mind can be traced back three thousand years. The Arab group mind seems to be at least as old. Other ethnic groups point to histories that reach back many hundreds of years into the past.

Group-Mind Trance

Group-mind trance means being absorbed into group-mind thinking and abstracted from or out of touch with other thinking patterns. The corporal of Chapter 1 who beat his superior officer was out of touch with his usual feelings toward him as he beat him. The office worker who gets caught up in vicious staff gossip may be appalled by his conduct when he returns home. The cult member, when freed from the bonds of that group mind, can barely imagine how she could have thought as she did. The group-mind trance encloses the member within a limited sphere of thought that allows the individual little access to broader awareness. This can have advantages, and can also be destructive.

It must be emphasized that group-mind thinking is not abstract, objective, rational thinking; it is thinking charged with emotion. The group mind operates on a visceral level, and much of its influence never reaches consciousness at all. It is known only through the feelings it generates, the responses it stimulates, and the actions it compels. If you want to get a sense of what a particular group mind is like, pay close attention to what kind of emotions bind the participants and what kind of actions are produced. The conscious

thinking of the group members is less important than the unconscious thinking indirectly revealed in this way.

Group minds are built on the basic human emotions and needs.
If the emotions and needs that engage the group mind are constructive and supportive, the ideas and actions the group generates
will be positive. The opposite will be true of groups based on destructive thinking.

Because the group does not reflect upon the emotions on which
the group mind is built, the thinking that arises from those emotions is largely unconscious. The group's true values and motives
are silently embedded in group life and are difficult for the members to identify. It is precisely when ideas and motives are unexamined that they are most influential. That is why the group-mind
trance is so powerful. Those who are entranced by a group mind do
not realize how much their awareness is narrowed and how radically their thinking is altered. Only after having been separated
from the group mind for some time do former members realize the
depth of the group-mind trance they have been under.

Group-Mind Communication

The influence of the group mind on the individual is conveyed
along several pathways. Those pathways can be defined in terms of
the mutual interactions of the outer and inner minds.

The most obvious pathway for the influence to travel is that
between the outer mind of the group and the outer mind of the individual member. A new staff member, for instance, is informed
about the rules of the company, what is expected and what is
frowned on. Here information is imparted deliberately and consciously, and the new group member can clearly identify the corporate influence.

This is followed by an exchange between the member's outer
and inner minds. The information conveyed to the member's outer
mind makes an impression on his inner mind which, as we saw in
the last chapter, is very suggestible. The message from the group

might be: If you follow these rules, you will be appreciated and re-warded. This is conveyed to the inner mind which, in its need for acceptance, takes the message very much to heart. An image of being needed and loved is activated, and the inner mind responds to it with enthusiasm.

Images may be activated that produce fear or even resistance to the group suggestion. But the group mind is so strong that those images are usually overpowered. The reason such individual resistances are usually overcome is that the group-mind influence is also conveyed along another, less obvious, pathway, with more effective access to the member's inner life. Here the group's inner mind operates directly on the inner mind of the member. Influence travels this pathway silently and mostly unnoticed. This action occurs outside the awareness of the outer mind of both group and member, and for that reason is doubly effective. If the member's outer mind were aware of the unconscious suggestions imparted by the group's inner mind, that awareness would reduce the strength of the suggestion. But unnoticed, the group's message affects the inner mind of the member almost without resistance. This is why, under the group's influence, the Russian soldier could join the group beating up his own beloved superior. This is why people in sports arenas yell things they would blush to repeat later on. This is also why the members of dysfunctional families find it so hard to identify the insidious influences that operate long after they leave their home bases. Suggestive influences that never reach consciousness are many times more effective than those that are presented straightforwardly.

In my experience as a group member, group leader, and group therapist, phenomena that happen in a group context are much stronger than when they happen outside. Two people will respond to each other with much greater vehemence in a group than when by themselves. Trance states are much more quickly and easily induced in groups than in individuals. Suggestions from a stage hypnotist are more effective on people responding in his audience than if he tried the same suggestions when he and a subject were alone. Emotions are stirred more deeply by an impassioned speech to a mob than by that same speech heard by separated individuals. Group "contagion" is an old concept. Speakers, whether evangelists or demagogues, count on the rapid mobilization of emotion in a crowd to achieve their success. Emotional energy of any kind moves through groups very rapidly, and in a closely packed crowd it seems to travel with the speed of light.

Group members affect one another with an astounding immediacy, as though a powerful energy were constantly circulating among them. This energy is an inner-mind phenomenon, one that cannot be identified or measured with outer-mind instruments. No wonder we have failed so miserably in our attempts to understand group phenomena through psychology and sociology, or sociobiology. Group-mind phenomena are principally generated by inner-mind interactions, and the devices of science have never been able to penetrate this sphere significantly.

But although the inner world of group-mind interaction remains obscure, we can still say quite a bit about the group mind and its trance. The best way to explore this matter is through experience. Each of us has a great deal of group-mind experience, and once we recognixe the reality of the group mind we can evaluate our personal experiences in a new light.

Influence of Group Minds

Over the course of my own life, I have been a participant in many group minds. There is no doubt that the thinking of those groups has had a powerful part to play in forming who I am.

I was born into a family whose group mind had its own peculiar cast. My father and my mother came from very different backgrounds. My father's family had been in the United States for many generations and was made up largely of low-income farmers who were not particularly concerned about advancing their fortunes in the world. My mother came from a family with third-generation Dutch immigrants on her father's side and second-generation German immigrants on her mother's side. Her values included a belief in a lot of hard work to better one's position in life. In our family there were four children: three girls and me. The values of the two ancestral-family group minds had a tremendous influence on us and affected our conduct every day of our lives, establishing expectations of life that have endured to the present.

Our family lived in the bosom of the group mind of a small Minnesota rural community. We constantly felt the influence of that group mind—its unwritten laws, its rigid protocols, its moral judgments. If you lived by them you were a respected member of the community, a "decent person," someone who posed no threat to local order, someone who could be trusted. If you succeeded in staying within proper bounds for a long period of time, and if you vocally promoted the values of the community, you might eventually find yourself appointed to some office of trust or voted to a position of power. If you violated them, you were "uppity" or "wild" or "peculiar" or "ornery." In any case, you were not to be trusted, you were dangerous, and you would have no chance of being promoted in the local hierarchy.

At the same time, our family lived within the influence of another powerful group mind—that of the Catholic Church. This organization with its clearly defined and ancient group mind made its presence felt locally in the parish and its priest. My experience of the church group mind as it reached me through family practices and liturgical exercises was not a happy one. I knew the church as a heavy thing, a morally restrictive and form-riddled entity that principally elicited fear when I thought about it. Yet, with its emphasis on what is "right" and its attempt to say something about the meaning of life, I felt drawn to it. When eventually I attended a university run by Benedictine monks, I also recognized the ancient connection between the Church and the pursuit of knowledge. Love of learning had become a central reality for me, and I found myself moving toward deeper involvement in the life of the Church, the university, and another significant group mind—that of a Benedictine monastery.

Half-way through university I joined the monastery and began studying for the Catholic priesthood. The group mind of a monastery is formed by three converging traditions: the Catholic Church, the Benedictine order with a history almost as ancient of that of the Church, and the local history of the particular monastery. The structure is both hierarchical and democratic. The head of the monastery, the abbot, is elected by the monks, and major decisions that affect the whole community are put to a vote. The community has its official hierarchy consisting of abbot, prior, subprior, and so on, in descending order. And it has its unofficial power structure, which operates within the various areas of work undertaken by the monastery. In my monastery, one of the main projects was the running of a university and, as time went by, it was decided that I would be trained to teach there. That decision resulted in my exposure to another influential group mind.

My monastery sent me to graduate school at the University of Toronto to study philosophy with a view to my teaching university students a few years down the road. Things did not work out that way, however. In Toronto, I became involved in a completely unforeseen situation. By this time I was an ordained Catholic priest, and on campus I became acquainted with a group of other priests and nuns who were also attending university. Some of them were undergoing psychotherapy with Lea Hindley-Smith, an extraordinary psychotherapist with a powerful personality. It might have seemed strange that members of religious orders of the Catholic Church were undergoing psychotherapy, but this was the mid-1960s and the second Vatican Council had indicated that it was all right to be adventurous. In the process of doing psychotherapy, some of us realized that we would like to be trained as psychotherapists ourselves. Lea Hindley-Smith had for some time contemplated starting a training program and the influx of interested religious people was impetus enough to convert the idea into reality.

This was the beginning of a therapeutic community—a rarity even in the tumultuous but creative 1960s—that eventually took the name Therafields. In the early years of its existence, it was guided largely by its charismatic leader, but as time went on, Therafields formed a hierarchical structure of its own that handled day-to-day operations. Therafields centred around psychotherapy, and in its heyday had more than eight hundred members, with several dozen psychotherapists. Members were all engaged in individual therapy, but there was also group therapy. The various psychotherapy groups formed the core of the larger community, and within an impressive array of therapeutic groups with varying purposes the most dynamic and influential was the "house group."

Therafields was the focal point of most members' lives. Many belonged to groups that lived together in large houses in an area of Toronto called the Annex. These house groups had daily contact within the group and weekly group psychotherapy. For members of house groups, Therafields was a way of life. Even for a great number of those not living in house groups, it constituted the central involvement of their lives, with opportunities to associate with other members and work together on various projects.

The Therafields group mind became very strong indeed. In my opinion, it was a striking example of a group mind with both positive and negative aspects. On the positive side, there were many who were helped greatly through their personal psychotherapy. Also, Therafields provided social contacts that were equally stimulating and supportive. It was easy to find someone among the members to talk with about your interests, your future hopes, and your problems. Since everyone was involved in psychotherapy, there was a sophisticated level of awareness that could be counted on when you spoke your mind. And a common language developed that facilitated communication.

Unfortunately, the very elements that provided positive experiences within the group mind could also produce negative ones. Therafields' common language could reduce itself to jargon, words that had lost contact with their original meanings. Community support of and interest in individual members could become community gossip, pressure to conform, and interference in each other's lives. The hierarchical structure that originally developed to handle day-to-day management could also be experienced as the unfair exercise of power of one group over another. Concentration on psychotherapy could mean neglect of other interests.

In addition to these problems, the relationship of the community with its charismatic founder became troublesome. In the years of her most active involvement, Lea Hindley-Smith was an unusually skilled psychotherapist on the individual and group level and was able to mobilize energy behind community projects with great effectiveness. But as her health deteriorated in the late 1970s, so did her effectiveness as a leader.

The negative aspects of the Therafields group mind, combined with changed socio-economic conditions, led to the demise of this therapeutic community in the early 1980s, but the memory of the experience of the Therafields group-mind trance is very much with me. The Therafields group mind created a way of seeing the world that permeated my life for many years. It involved viewing everything in terms of the unconscious mind, believing that unconscious motivations and dynamics are a part of all human interactions. It involved believing that psychotherapy could solve most of life's problems, and that almost everybody could profit from psychotherapy. It involved believing that group meetings could bring forth the truth in any situation and that groups could be completely objective in their views. It involved believing that since we, as a community, were involved in psychotherapeutic self-examination, we would always know if we were getting on the wrong track and we would be able to find our way back. It involved believing that the community had the resources to meet all its members' needs and that there would be little reason to look elsewhere for anything. It involved believing that the language we used was completely accurate and in no way a jargon. It involved believing that our leader was a font of wisdom so comprehensive that anything she believed must be true. In other words, it involved believing things that could not hold up over the long haul.

In this narrative I have not mentioned all the group minds of which I have been a part, since that would be a long, unnecessary exercise. I mention my personal experiences with group-mind trance because I think that they contain elements that are common experience, and it is crucial that we become aware of how group-mind trance permeates life.

The Elemental Group Mind

The most basic group mind is a group of two. When two people are emotionally engaged with each other over a period of time (an enduring relational trance) they form a seminal group mind—a third thing produced by the two people yet separate from them. They are not aware that their relationship is giving birth to a seminal group mind, and so that "third thing" operates on a totally unconscious level. Once formed, this elemental group mind influences the two participants and affects their responses to each other as the relationship develops. A loop is formed in which the two people feed into the group mind and the group mind feeds back to them.

As time passes, the group mind of the couple can grow so strong that it dominates the relationship in an unhealthy way. The two people may change and mature as individuals while their group mind retains the outlines of its original structure. This unfortunate situation can produce a painful tension as the individuals outgrow the confines of their now outmoded group mind of two.

Charles and Edna met each other and married in the early 1960s. In many ways, it was a different world then. In that world, marriage was an institution with clearly defined roles. The husband earned the money and was in charge. The wife looked after the home and children, and she respected her husband as the head of the household. For a wife to work was a disgrace, a sign of weakness on the part of the husband. The wife could develop hobby-like interests outside the home or she could be involved with temporary charitable undertakings, and that was it.

This cultural view of sex roles was built into the group mind resulting from Charles and Edna's relationship and marriage. And for quite a while it worked. Edna was dependent on Charles, financially and practically. She looked to him to make decisions and provide direction. He was glad to do this, to bask in the power iterated by St. Paul: "Women, be subject to your husbands."

But times and the culture changed. The altered situation put increasing pressure on the relationship—and their group mind. In the early 1970s, struggling to care for four small children, Edna began to question the whole set-up. She felt vaguely discontented with being so confined to the home and resentful that Charles could not understand her discontent. He still felt comfortable in the structure of their couple's group mind, while Edna found it difficult.

By the early 1980s, with their children grown to independence, or nearly so, the pressure on Edna and Charles's group-mind structure had increased to troubling intensity. Feminism was by now a force to be reckoned with, and Edna's discontents were stronger and more clearly focused. Their marriage was looking more and more tattered and worn, more and more anachronistic. Edna was back in school, taking courses in education, hoping to parlay a bachelor's degree in English into a teaching career. Charles had reluctantly agreed to this move, but it was clear he was not wholeheartedly behind a change that would so drastically alter their way of life. He felt his importance in the family was being eroded, and he did not know how to connect with a woman who was determined to establish a degree of independence from him. For her part, Edna was enthusiastic about her new direction, but felt guilty, as though she were betraying an unspoken contract that had been established between them when they married.

It was clear, however, that the old way simply would not work any more. Edna could not maintain the role of subjugation to her husband that she had learned from both her original family and her culture. She was feeling stirrings toward independence and self-realization that could not be denied. But because of her guilt, she often found herself responding to Charles's resistance in ways that she did not like. Either she would draw back from expressing her real thoughts about the matter because she felt she could not "arbitrarily" change the terms of their agreement just because she felt frustrated, or else she reacted with anger and sarcasm. In this way she contributed to the stalemate they were at when they began counselling as a couple.

Edna and Charles truly loved each other, but they were trapped in a group-mind trance that bedevilled them both. Though their individual thinking was changing, they both felt haunted by the old way of seeing things. While they had painfully evolved, their marriage group mind had remained rigidly fixed. Their therapy involved ceasing to blame each other. Instead, they had to recognize that they were in the grip of a group-mind trance and work together to educate their unevolved group mind to fit the realities of the present.

Establishing the Group Mind

There are certain elements that contribute to the establishment of an enduring group mind. The first is the passage of time. The group mind might have begun as a bunch of people gathered to concentrate on some project—for instance, to establish a corporation. But then the sheer fact of their being together, engaged in a focused activity over a lengthy period of time, helps to solidify their cohesiveness as a group. During that period, the group develops an individuality of its own and becomes an independent reality. Once that has happened, the members cannot easily withdraw from the group mind. The attention of each member is held whether he wants it or not, and the group engenders feelings in its members whether they want to feel them or not. Members can no longer think about issues that relate to the group's concerns without being influenced by the group mind. At this point the group attains ascendency and the individuals within it have to some degree lost their ability to think independently. Individually, the members might not agree with the thoughts of the group, but under its influence they succumb. The group mind is truly more than the sum of its parts.

A group mind gains strength by identifying what differentiates it and sets it apart from the masses. A distinctive set of beliefs, an unusual purpose, a unique ancestry, or anything else that segregates it from the rest of humanity will add to its cohesiveness and influence over its members. That is why if a group mind suffers opposition or persecution, it grows stronger. That is also why secrets held by the group add to its unity. Information known only to the group members separates them from other people and makes them feel special to each other. The need to protect secrets from outsiders creates a unifying energy that binds the members and focuses their resources to protect the group. Secrets and a sense of being persecuted are characteristic of cult groups, for instance, and account for their special cohesiveness.

Other elements that help establish group minds are leaders, writings or stories, and rituals.

Leaders

Some group minds are brought into existence through the efforts of one person. That individual may become the focal point of the group's attention in such a way that his or her personality strongly defines the character of the group mind.

Many of the world's religions were formed in precisely this way. The personalities of Buddha, Jesus, and Muhammad became inseparably linked with their spiritual messages, and the holy writings of these religious traditions convey not only religious doctrine, but also information about the founder/teacher.

Most cults are identified with a leader/founder and make use of the charismatic qualities of that leader to focus the imaginations of the members. The magnetic Jim Jones was the founder and focal point of the People's Temple. Devotees of the Unification Church had the Reverend Sun Myung Moon, and transcendental meditation (or the Science of Creative Intelligence) had Maharishi Mahesh Yogi. The tragic and controversial Branch Davidians were led by the outspoken, magnetic preacher David Koresh.

Books and Stories

Long-lasting group minds will usually have writings that maintain their groups' sense of identity and continuity. The great religions of the world have their holy books. Modern cults have their manuals and collected speeches of their leaders. Writings are particularly effective in preserving the cohesiveness of the group mind because the members can use them to stay in touch with the mentality of the group even when they are not in the presence of the leader or other members.

Stories are equally important. In an article that appeared in the *New York Times Magazine,* Andrew Greely asked: Given the repression of dissent and other significant problems within Roman Catholicism, why do Catholics stay in the Church? His answer: Because of the stories.[16] The Catholic tradition is full of stories about saints, miracles, healings, holy places, holy people, and holy paraphernalia. These stories create vivid images that stick in people's minds, and no matter what problems they may have with the doctrines of the Church they are still attached to the images that go along with being a Catholic. In the Jewish tradition, stories play a central role in teaching and passing on religious and cultural values. The stories of the Talmud, for instance, and anecdotes maintained through the oral tradition are rich sources of wisdom and inspiration.

Families, too, have their stories. There are those oft-repeated tales of the adventures of the children, stories about the grandparents and other ancestors, stories of hard times and good times, of accomplishment and failure, and family myths, fabricated stories that convey what the family *wants* to believe about itself, even if it is not true.

Many other groups use stories to enthral their members. Cults have their tales of persecution and victory. Corporations have their myths of the importance of the individual worker and of devotion to the good of mankind. Workplaces have their office gossip. Wherever group minds exist over time, they generate stories that strengthen their bonds.

Rituals

In his article, Greely also mentions religious rituals as a way that members remain bound to the Church. But rituals are not limited to religious contexts. They are employed in a wide variety of groups.

Rituals are special actions that are repeatedly performed. Within the group, they are performed in the presence of the members to strengthen the bonds of the individual to the group. Everything is geared to engage the members' emotions and imaginations. As rituals are repeated over time, they become more and more effective. As the participants grow more familiar with the symbols used, the effects are more deeply imprinted in their nervous systems.

In churches, cultures, and cults, rituals may involve readings, songs, artwork, special dress, or symbolic actions. In families, there may be special ways of greeting each other, specified actions or attitudes during meals, or defined forms of punishment or reward. Workplaces have their protocols. Clubs have their rites. And most other enduring groups have developed some sort of ritual that symbolizes and fortifies group unity.

The Suit and Tie

The corporate group mind has ways of emphasizing conformity and cutting out individuality. One of the most obvious is the use of the corporate uniform, the suit and tie (or the feminine equivalent, the business outfit). The message of the suit-and-tie uniform is conveyed each time group members meet: I'm OK and you're OK and we understand the rules and we will keep each other safe within those rules. The person who doesn't wear the uniform in the corporate environment is looked upon with fear, but treated with scorn. That person represents non-conformity to the rules of the group and threatens the security that conformity ensures. Uncontrolled clothes may mean uncontrolled thinking, a questioning of group values, even—God forbid—unpredictable actions. Group mind demands the enforcement of group thinking. Anything that symbolizes independence of thought must be removed. Corporate-sanctioned "jeans days" are fine. They are no threat because non-conformity is not involved. As a matter of fact, the illusion of individual freedom within the corporate context is created by mandating days of official exception. Paradoxically, the group mind thereby succeeds in painting a picture of freedom through an imposed practice.

The Family

The first and most influential group mind that we experience is our own family. It has its own unique history, and by dint of its long evolution has developed distinctive characteristics. It manifests a kind of personality and unique way of being in the world. Most of us are acquainted with families that are a delight to be with. We have probably also known families that we would just as soon avoid. That is the way with group minds. Of themselves, they are neither good nor bad, but in their concrete forms they manifest as wide a variety of qualities as individual people do.

In what follows, I am going to be describing family group minds that are more on the negative side. This is not because I think that families or group minds are negative, but because I believe that certain important characteristics of group minds are most clearly demonstrated in situations where something has gone wrong. Also, while I hope that this does not amount to a bias, I must admit that my involvement in therapeutic work has made me particularly aware of group-mind problems. I do believe, however, that by understanding how groups become disordered, we can learn something about how to keep them healthy.

The Engulfing Family

Marlene, a client of mine who grew up in a particularly abusive family, wrote this about her experience of her family group mind:

I have a strong image of myself physically wrestling with a large, powerful, physically strong shape. It has enough form to seem somewhat human and it has a personality. Its personality feels made up of power, anger, authority, hostility. It demands submission, respect, loyalty, subservience.

It feels very difficult even to think of standing up to such an awesome figure, to ever think I could gain any ground, let alone defeat it. To defeat it would be to break free from its grasp, to feel no link with it, to be able to clap my hands, look at it disdainfully, turn my back on it, and walk away free.

It is important to be able to see the figure for what it is. There is nothing good or pure or real or nurturing it has to offer me. It holds me in an uncompromising posture of bowing, forfeiting any sense of self. It needs me, but I can have no healthy need of my own met by it. "I" as an individual am not looked for, not regarded. I am required to be a piece of it, a piece that has no voice, no mind outside of what it speaks itself.

Of course this figure—it feels an ugly creature—represents my family's group mind. I think it's important to be able to see it as a creature, something that has a life. It is experienced by me as a thing having a life in and of itself. All six of us make up the whole, but it seems to me to also have a life of its own.

My mom is the head, the ruler of the kingdom. My dad is the one who is to be protected, never questioned, given reverence and respect and, especially since his death, to be idolized.

I know my place is that of the scapegoat, but I have a difficult time trying to know the place the other three siblings fill. I think I see Joel as the defender of the family, Eileen the one who is given respect and support and is admired. She is the one they saw a future for—their golden girl. Howard, I would say, gets to be the baby—not a lot expected of him, always protected by mom, at least verbally and emotionally.

I'm feeling angry. Who do I kill—them or me? That's kind of what it comes to. They win (and I lose) or I win (and they lose). I think of the group mind we have and I *hate it!* I want to destroy it. I want to stand in front of them and say, "Look at what we've created. Look at what it's done to us. How comfortable all of you are within it. How can any of us continue to allow ourselves to be ruled and restricted like this?"

But I meet with blank stares. This is where I falter. Here I am standing alone, facing them, screaming in anger and frustration at them. Really, even when I present myself in opposition, railing at how we work, I place myself in my designated place: the one who doesn't fit in.

Family Group Mind/Family Roles

How can I say that the family group mind makes everybody think the same way when it is obvious in most families that the members think so differently? It is well known that family members tend to have their different roles to fill, and that means their outlook on things is very different. How can these people all be shown as under the sway of the one family group mind?

Take Marlene's family. Marlene's role was to be the one who was emotionally disturbed and always doing things wrong, an embarrassment to the family. The father's role was the honest hardworking man whose failures and abusiveness were to be ignored and denied because he put the food on the table. The mother's role was that of the long-suffering saint. She endured her trials with stoic patience. Her Christian spirituality was her mainstay and helped her through the troubles caused by fortune and the problems caused her by her children, especially Marlene. Marlene's sister's role was that of the girl who could do no wrong, who followed in the pure Christian path blazed by her martyr mother, whose setbacks in life were just a sign of her being specially loved by God.

These diverse roles, far from dividing the group mind, were its chief source of unity. They all agreed on the roles assigned to each. The mother thought of herself as a saint and martyr, the older daughter as a good girl, and her husband as the stolid breadwinner. The father saw himself and the others in the same way. The sister agreed wholeheartedly. And for much of her life Marlene, too, accepted these roles as accurate portrayals of the qualities of each. This is important. Even Marlene, who came out badly in the assignation of roles, fully accepted them. Although in her therapy she

fought to expose the falseness of these roles, for a long time she remained a slave to them. She saw the others as described, and she
saw herself as the weak, disturbed, embarrassing, unloveable one.
In this she was every bit as much a mouthpiece of the group mind
as were the rest.

Group-Mind Damage/Group-Mind Healing

A family group mind can cause a great deal of damage. Family
group-mind thinking can be so distorted that abuse and neglect are
accepted as normal. Damage delivered by the family group mind
goes unchallenged because everyone is trapped within the same
thought patterns.

But if damage can be caused in a group mind, so can healing.
For people who work in the helping professions, some of the most
powerful experiences of psychological healing happen in groups—
such as therapy groups, support groups, and 12-step groups.

The truth is that effective healing from group-mind damage
can only happen in a group context, for only a group has the power
to generate healing of such depth. And only a group has the power
to break the subtle hold that damaging family group minds—or
other destructive group minds—still exercise over the individual.

A person may clearly recognize his family group mind as the
source of the damage and yet be secretly tied to that group mind.
His need to belong was satisfied in that old group mind, even if in a
very distorted way. None of us can exist in a social vacuum. We
must be part of something. If the alienated member has rejected
the family abuse but not replaced membership in that group mind
with membership in another, he will still be extremely vulnerable
and will not be able to remain in that position for long.

This was the case with Marlene. In moments of clarity, she recognized the damage done her by the family. The family had subjugated her needs to its own. There was no recognition of her as an
individual, no encouragement for her to develop her own life and
attain healthy independence. She was to consider herself first and

foremost a member of the family for the rest of her life. No loyalty to husband, children, friends, or her own sanity were to take precedence over that. She was to preserve the family myths and tell the family lies.

In the course of her therapy, it became clear to Marlene that her attempt to get at the truth of her life was considered a threat to the family. Marlene was continually torn between continuing her course of self-exploration and recognition of the family myths and lies on the one hand and returning to the bosom—and oblivion—of the family on the other. Again and again the invitation was proffered: Forget what you have seen of family abuse, return to the family and be loved once more. The invitation was tempting because her family was still Marlene's strongest experience of group-mind belonging. Her only lasting way out was to establish group-mind bonds elsewhere that were equally engaging.

The Therapeutic Relationship

Healing from group-mind damage demands a person's participation in a healthy, supportive group-mind experience that replaces the original. I have mentioned some kinds of groups that can perform this function. But there is another very important healing group mind: the group mind of *two* that is formed by the alienated individual and his or her therapist, counsellor, spiritual teacher, or other healer.

Earlier I spoke of the smallest and most basic group mind, formed through a relational trance—the couple. I said that two people who are emotionally engaged form a group mind of their own, an entity separate from them as individuals that strongly binds and influences them. The same is true of the healer/client group mind. They form a group-mind entity of great power—power to heal (or, if abused, to damage again). This group mind has the capacity to push out and replace the old group mind for the beleaguered client. Unless it can do so, no healing will take place.

That is why therapy cannot be successful if it is purely intellectual. An emotional bond between therapist and client must be developed to generate true psychological healing from old group-mind wounds. Because the healing process must overcome the present active unconscious influence of the original family group mind, a counter-group mind must be formed in the therapeutic relationship.

Group members do not need to be in everyday contact with each of their members to enable the ties to function. They can be far away and out of communication and still exert their influence. This situation holds good even if all of the members of the old group mind are deceased. Ties to a defunct group can be at least as strong as those to a living group. In fact, the task of recognizing the distorted thinking of the group is even more difficult with a defunct group. With no ongoing reality check to correct her ideas, the person tied to a defunct group can idealize the members and hold on tightly to these ghost comforters.

As mentioned above, for the first fifteen years of my practice as a psychotherapist I was involved with a very powerful group mind in the psychotherapeutic community called Therafields. The community aspect of this therapeutic undertaking was very potent. There were nearly 30 house groups where members lived together in the centre of the city, four farms in the countryside, and a few city office buildings for sessions and groups. The members of Therafields were constantly interacting with each other, living together, working together, recreating together, doing therapy together.

The group mind of Therafields grew very strong. It provided powerful support for the members as they struggled to get to know and free themselves of emotional impediments to health. As members fought to break unhealthy group-mind involvements with their original families, they drew powerful support from this counter-group mind. In the years since that experiment ended, I have continued to work as a psychotherapist, and I must confess that I have often wished that I had some equally dynamic, healthy group mind to offer some of my clients to aid them in their struggles. So many times I have watched clients leave my office after a courageous confrontation with their destructive ties and realized that they were walking out into a vacuum. They had no meaningful supportive group to go back to—at least not one of any emotional weight. On occasion, I knew there was a good chance the client would find being cut loose from those destructive ties too terrifying, and before the next session, would find some equally destructive involvement to take its place, however briefly. It is important not to sit in judgment on those who cannot stand the emotional vacuum and have to tread a long and torturous path to their freedom.

The Cult

Many cults are patterned after the family. That way they make use of the unfulfilled longings and aspirations of individuals who have been disappointed with their personal family experiences. Charles Manson made that connection explicit, calling his infamous cult "The Family" and claiming that inclusion in its circle would allow his followers to overcome all divisiveness and attain true brotherly love. Charles Manson and The Family provide a spectacular example of how a charismatic leader can induce a powerful group-mind trance and manipulate the entranced members to perform the most bizarre actions.

Jim Jones and his People's Temple also laid heavy emphasis on what he described as family values. He promoted ideals of communal love and service that enticed extremely bright, capable people. His emphasis on the importance of children in the cult and his attempts to control through multiple sexual liaisons with key group members were echoed in a more recent tragic cult phenomenon, the Branch Davidians of Waco, Texas, under David Koresh.

We are disturbed and uncomfortable with the events of Waco, and Jonestown, and other cult situations gone violent, and we need some way of explaining them to ourselves. The explanation is that we are dealing with a *group-generated alternative reality*, and we are dealing with a *trance state* that makes the development of an alternative reality possible.

Let me repeat that we are dealing with an alternative reality created within and fed by a group-mind trance. David Koresh and his followers lived and eventually died in a trance state. Within that trance, they created a reality that generated such power that it was impossible to question it. The trance state held them tightly in its grip, and no force from outside the group could loosen it.

Let me recall a few facts about David Koresh. He grew up as Vernon Howell in rural east Texas. As a boy, he spent many hours praying alone and wanted to be part of a Christian church. He joined the Seventh Day Adventists, but was often in conflict with church members. In the 1980s, he started a group called the Branch Davidians. He saw himself as fathering a new house of David, and to that end, he took sexual partners from the wives of his sect members and fathered a number of children. As time went on, he became more and more self-obsessed and autocratic. He also became more fearful of outside influences and began to stockpile weapons to fend off imagined invaders. Into this tense atmosphere came officials of the Federal Bureau of Alcohol, Tobacco, and Firearms with weapons charges. They met armed resistance and set up siege around the buildings of Koresh's centre in Waco. The eventual outcome was a fire that killed Koresh and more than 80 followers, including 25 children.

The methods Koresh used to form and strengthen his group were very effective. He was charismatic, and when speaking he could mesmerize his listeners. He preached a doctrine of imminent apocalyptic catastrophe and based his ideas on his peculiar interpretation of the Scriptures. Those who were drawn to him were quickly isolated from their usual social contacts—separated from family and friends—so that Koresh became the total focus of their lives. They were deprived of food, sleep, rest, and privacy. They were treated arbitrarily and unpredictably, and were given "inspired" but contradictory explanations about events around them. They were exposed constantly to talks about how the world was against them and about to destroy them. The world of each inductee rapidly shrank to a very small point. Then with the introduction of a stimulating set of beliefs presented by the leader, the inductee fixed on the startling new reality being proposed and made it his own.

This new reality—the doctrine of Koresh's mission, the end of the world, persecution by external enemies—became the only meaningful reality. The trance was now very deep. The Koresh-defined reality was the only reality, for no other reality could penetrate the very powerful group-mind trance. The members were drawn closer and closer together in an atmosphere of excitement and fear. This burgeoning terror of the outside world isolated them further and encouraged them to stockpile arms. The tragic results we all now know.

We have seen that over time the group mind takes on a life of its own, an existence beyond the existence of its members, and functions as a living organism. In most cases the group mind moves beyond even the control of the leader; even the most charismatic leader cannot encompass the group energy that is generated. It appears that this is precisely what happened to David Koresh, so that he himself became subject to the power of the monster he had created and was destroyed by it.

Jean Jacques Rousseau said, "One thinks himself master of others, and still remains a greater slave than they."[17] Nowhere is this truer than with the cult and its leader. There is great arrogance, and greater naiveté, in thinking that you can mobilize the powerful forces of a group mind with the kind of binding techniques used in cults and remain in control of those forces. Because the cult leader experiences his power daily in such a palpable way, he foolishly believes that this power actually belongs to him. In fact it belongs to the group mind and, as Rousseau said, he is an even greater slave to that group mind than are those he governs.

What the cult leader does not realize is that the group mind arises from the unconscious mind of the members, and from his own unconscious mind, too. This means that much of the pattern of thought, much of the motivation, much of the agenda of the group mind is hidden from everyone, including the leader. Listen to the tapes of Jim Jones as he encouraged and harangued his People's Temple members to drink the poisoned punch and go to their deaths. This was not a man operating from clearly formulated thoughts arising from clearly established goals. This was a man driven by something that he himself surely did not understand. In the last months of his life, Jones moved further and further into the dark world constructed by his cult's group mind. He was a major contributor to the negativity and destruction that was growing there, but he was not its sole author. In the end he was little more than its pawn.

When the People's Temple group-mind reality became dark and sinister, neither he nor the other cult members made any attempt to grapple with the negative elements as they evolved in the secret places of the group's inner mind. It is difficult enough for anyone to examine a group mind critically from within. Jim Jones's faults as a human being made it impossible for him to be the one to recognize the group's accelerating move toward self-destruction. On the contrary, his thirst for power and control blinded him to the sinister elements and contributed to their consolidation in the group mind's inner world. By the time the poisoned drink was handed out, everyone was in the grip of these negative forces of the cult's group mind. By then it was the group mind, not the leader, in control. One man with a handful of henchmen could not have forced hundreds to take that poison and feed it to their children. The group mind itself was the executioner.

Everyone who becomes leader of a group should avoid the naive thinking that has proven so common among cult leaders. A leader should have a healthy respect for the power of the group mind and the ubiquity of the group-mind trance. The stronger the group mind, the less individual people operate according to the framework of thought that governs the rest of their lives. The more they embrace the group-mind experience, the less will reason and common sense win out over their group thinking and group-mind induced reality. The leader must be aware of how easy it is for everyone to believe that the meaningful reality of the group is all there is. The leader must realize that in the group context, people will do things they would not dream of doing elsewhere. The leader must know that while in the grip of the group-mind trance, members are operating largely from motives and impulses that are not conscious to them. They might rationalize them and convince themselves that they are being perfectly reasonable, but that is just the front a person puts on when in the grip of a compulsion and he or she needs to justify some action. Most of all, the leader needs to know that he himself is subject to all of these influences. To believe that he is immune from them is disastrous, both for the group and for himself. For that reason, the leader must become something of an expert at understanding how unconscious thinking influences conscious life, so that he can help mobilize the unconscious energy of the group in a positive direction, and spot destructive elements at an early stage.

The Broader Group Mind

Group minds exist on the tribal, regional, and national levels of association. They are products of the cohesiveness that develops over time in larger geographical areas through common genetics, common language, common religions, or other common interests. History has shown that when a geographical group already has some loose affiliation, its cohesiveness is powerfully strengthened by the shared experience of oppression or conquest by an outside power. By suffering together at the hands of a common enemy, people who otherwise might be less sympathetic toward each other forge bonds and develop myths, rituals, and other cultural expressions that cement their solidarity.

The Marine

George joined the U.S. marines at age 19. He had been well prepared for this step. George came from a Midwestern immigrant family that had fled the communist regime of an eastern European country and maintained an active interest in what was going on in their homeland. From childhood, George had been groomed to become a fighter whose combat skills would eventually serve the anticommunist underground in the family's native land. He learned how to use guns before he entered high school and developed mechanical skills that would be useful for a future soldier. As a Catholic, George considered himself a soldier of the Church, ready to sacrifice himself without hesitation should the Church need defending. These two group minds—that of his ethnic culture and that of the Church—worked together on George's impressionable psyche. In boot camp, George's instructor told him, "A marine is a highly trained, underpaid juvenile-delinquent killer." It was clear that George had found a new group mind that could bring to fruition the military ideals so highly prized at home.

How did the marine corps create its human fighting machines? By forcefully indoctrinating them into its military group mind. Reflecting on his experience years later, George points out that the first thing that happens to the recruit is that he loses his hair. He is shaved as bald as a baby, newborn into the world of the marine corps. The clippers also shave off all individuality—one bald head looks pretty much like every other bald head. The recruit's encounter with his trainers continues the shaving job. He is constantly screamed at and criticized for every small fault, every deviation from the norm. The screaming maintains its intensity all through the training period, so that the inductee never gets a chance to catch his breath and question the validity of this constant humiliation. All the communication, says George, is one way. The trainer screams at the trainee, but the trainee may not in any way answer back or even initiate communication. Also, the trainer stares—or rather glares—at the trainee relentlessly. The trainee is never allowed to make eye contact with the trainer. Any gesture that conveys anything other than subjugation and obedience is severely punished.

The marine group mind makes you a part of the "green machine," says George. Being a member of the marine corps means that you are invincible. But you are not invincible as an individual. As an individual, you are nothing. You are invincible as a marine, part of a fighting unit that obeys orders unquestioningly and reacts automatically.

George came through boot camp with flying colours. His sergeant told him that he had achieved the highest scores in the camp in all of the required skills—marksmanship, physical fitness, endurance, knowledge. But the sergeant also informed him that he was not going to receive the coveted award of top trainee. The reason was that he had an "attitude problem." This meant that he had not become the unthinking robot they had hoped he would. He had continued to show undesirable signs of individuality throughout the training. Not that he was in any way insubordinate or disobedient. But he had done things that showed that he was thinking for himself. He had, for instance, carried the weapons of his comrades when they were exhausted in the march. This and other equally objectionable actions had removed him from consideration as top soldier. The marine group mind and George remained a difficult mix. Although he was successful in his military career and was respected by peers and superiors, he never sufficiently subjugated his individuality to become a true and full member of the corps.

Recent revelations about sexual abuses in the military have made us more aware than ever of the problems inherent in the relationship between officer and subordinate. Emotional and physical abuses have always been there, but for the most part they have been ignored, dismissed as the price you pay for military "discipline." The military has tended to justify imposed humiliation as "constructive force." But force is force, and a more enlightened view is emerging from the recent exposure of cases of sexual misconduct in the military (rape and other sexually contexed crimes). It is now being recognized that the relationship between superior and subordinate in the military is characterized by a devastating and paralysing inequality. If this insight can be applied to sexual acts, perhaps the routine physical and emotional abuse in the military that has been tolerated for so long will also come up for scrutiny.

Today, when nationalism is in the ascendency, it is helpful to remember the power of the group-mind trance over those who belong to the various "nations" that are asserting their identity and independence. For many participants in modern nationalist conflicts, the events that forged the identity of the national group took place before they were born. There is evidence that national identities originate not so much from diverse racial or religious traditions but through the experience of fighting a common enemy.[18] The unifying power of the common enemy should be familiar to us, because we have seen it portrayed so often in the movies. The common enemy used to be the "red man" in the ubiquitous westerns of the 1940s and 1950s. The Germans and the Japanese served that role for a while. So did the Vietnamese and, more recently, the Iraqis. But for a long time the enemy of choice was communism in general and Russia in particular. With the collapse of world-wide communism, we were in trouble, because we immediately felt an enemy vacuum. We tried the South Africans for a while, but that soon fizzled. So today we have alien invaders, effectively portrayed, for instance, in films such as *Independence Day.* We have had to leave behind our flirtation with the benevolent alien of *Close Encounters of the Third Kind* and *E.T.*, because our ability to find a unifying common enemy on earth has finally failed.

In any case, the memory of those formative battles is kept alive by the group in stories, writings, public ceremonies, and everyday conversations. The youth of these national groups are caught up in a powerful energy of patriotism that often leads to a readiness, even eagerness, to sacrifice their lives for their national cause. This patriotic immersion in the national cause is almost universally applauded. Unthinking loyalty to the position of one's national group ("My country, right or wrong") in regard to international conflict is rarely criticized.

Few better examples of subjugation of individual thinking to that of the group mind could be found. This subjugation is often institutionalized in laws (conscription) and cultural arts (the glorification of American military action in Viet Nam in movies in the 1970s). Although protest movements in the United States in the 1960s and 1970s made some headway, recent events on the world scene show that unthinking patriotism is still highly regarded. The nationalistic battles raging in Eastern Europe and former Soviet countries, along with continuing conflicts in the Near East, Africa, and elsewhere, indicate that the national group mind is still capable of marshalling the hearts of its members to battle while silencing their questioning minds.

The group-mind trance with the broadest reach is that of our culture. Here the group involved is a people. Cultural trance is about a way of perceiving and interacting with the world that extends over a wide geographical area and through an extended period of time. The power of this most invisible of trances is our next consideration.

2

macrotrance

The Culture

cultural trance

CULTURAL TRANCE is the group-mind trance of a people. This trance is so pervasive that it is virtually invisible to those living in the culture. It is so profound that it can rightly be called a sleep.

When I sleep and dream, I am totally involved with the dream and my dream world. To me it is completely and unquestionably real. For instance, I dream I am five years old, standing on the front lawn of my grandfather's farmhouse. It is a summer day and the sun is very bright and a bit hot. I see my grandmother at the wheel of the family car. She is trying to learn to drive the car, and she looks very tense as she motors up the driveway from the barn to the house. When she reaches the place where the driveway turns to the left she panics, and instead of putting on the brakes she steps on the accelerator. She does not turn the wheel, so the car lurches straight ahead, off the driveway and toward a grove of poplar trees. My uncle, her son, is standing in front of one of the trees and the car pins him against the tree, killing him instantly and knocking down the tree. In horror I watch the death of this beloved uncle. I wake up in a sweat. The dream seems so real that, for a few minutes, I am sure that my uncle, instead of dying from a ruptured appendix, as I had always been told, was in fact killed in this way.

In the dream, everything is vivid and real to me. I can feel the heat of the sun and the cool grass under my feet. I hear the car as the motor races. I see the agony in my grandmother's eyes when she realizes what she has done. There is nothing in the dream that does not seem as real as in my waking life. Until I wake up, that *is* reality. End of story.

But is it all of reality? No, it is not. The part of reality I cannot be aware of is my body lying in my bed and existing in time and space outside the dream. The dream is not the totality of my reality, but for now it is all I know of reality, my meaningful reality.

The meaningful reality of cultural trance can be every bit as compelling as that of my dream. As in my dream, my waking reality is what I perceive. Even though the environment around me has an irreducible physical existence beyond culture, yet my perception of it is determined by my culture. I cannot step outside my culture and perceive the world from some objective position any more than I can step outside my dream and talk about my dreaming.

Saying things about what I perceive also has its problems. I cannot find any terms exterior to my culture to talk about it. While language is a marvellous enabling tool, it is also a kind of straight-jacket. Every word I use is conditioned by its history and present cultural significance. My words censor my ideas as much as they give them scope for expression. Even the way I put words together creates a limitation and has an arbitrariness; this is evident from an examination of the great variety of syntaxes to be found in the languages of the world. Add to that the importance of intonation, body posture and gesture, and the physical context of the spoken word, and I am soon disabused of any notion that my language exploits the full potential of human communication. So when I speak here about culture, I must acknowledge my own very limited perspective.

That is the hard thing about being a part of any culture. Our perspective is limited, but we do not tend to think of it that way. We are likely to believe that we have some uniquely true view of reality, when in fact it is just one of many possible versions. We are likely to disparage the views of other cultures, simply because we cannot see things from their perspectives. We cannot put ourselves in their shoes. Yet other cultures may be able to see things to which we are blind.

Cultures develop unique perceptual sensitivities. The subarctic-dwelling Inuit distinguish between more than one hundred kinds of snow whereas we discern but a few. It is vital to the well-being of the Inuit that they be able to recognize subtle variations in weather and ground conditions, so their culture has educated them to this degree of sensitivity.

Although the human animal seems to have evolved a much diminished awareness of smell in North American culture, in some cultures this sense is actually of central importance. The people of one of the indigenous tribes of New Guinea are very much oriented to personal scent. They use their heightened sensitivity to send socially important messages to each other. One friend taking leave of another, for instance, will place his hand in the armpit of his comrade and then stroke it over his own body in order to carry his friend's scent with him. Such practices indicate that communication and bonding through smells are a natural part of that culture's everyday life.

Variations in education of the senses can have a profound effect on the forms of culture. Detailed information is communicated by means of complex drumming among the Kaluli people of Papua New Guinea. The natives of Sumba Island of the eastern islands of Indonesia have developed a versatile vocabulary of tastes and flavours that they use to communicate a variety of messages. These cultures inculcate awareness of subtle sensations that are simply unknown to us. On the other hand, in the North American Indian language of Maidu, there are only three words to cover the whole spectrum of colour.[19] Their meanings most nearly approximate our words for "red," "green-blue" and "yellow-orange-brown." This means that the modern North American discerns many colours that would have looked the same to the people of this tribe. It is all a matter of education and language. Human beings are physically capable of distinguishing millions of different colours in the visible spectrum, and if our culture were to educate us to distinguish them and supply us with a vocabulary to express them we would have that special sensitivity as a unique cultural feature. This would undoubtedly affect our everyday dealings with the world and with each other. There are indications that we may be moving in that direction. While the English language has a basic vocabulary of eight colours, we continue to add more words for subtler colours. In recent decades, we have been giving our children boxes of crayons with dozens of distinctive shades. And now the computers we use daily boast of being able to produce hundreds of thousands of shades of colour. While we have not named them yet, that may not be too far in the future.

The point is that we see and sense what our culture prepares us to see and sense. If we have not been given the opportunity and the language for the experience, we cannot have the experience itself. It may be there to be had, but it is simply not accessible to us. So my culture, the framework within which I experience life, confers on me both sight and blindness. It gives me the means of having many subtle experiences, but the very fact of its limitations also blocks me from having many others. And this does not apply to just perception of sensual aspects of the physical world. It also affects our perception of other people and of the intricate social situations that surround them.

We react to the way people dress, for instance, and deem them alien to our society if their mode of attire differs too far from acceptable standards. Standards of grooming and hygiene are also ways of identifying cultural kin. The armpit ritual of that New Guinea tribe would seem both repulsive and invasive in our culture. The use of cattle dung as a hair-styling aid among the Masai of Africa would be equally repugnant to us. Courtship rites and sexual behaviour also vary greatly from culture to culture. The sexual promiscuity encouraged at festivals of some African tribes would not be accepted here. Neither would the arranged marriages of children that are an honoured tradition in parts of India.

Religious beliefs and practices integral to many of the world's cultures our own culture finds disturbing. Ritual sacrifice, worship of a multiplicity of demon-gods, communication with the spirits of the dead, and sorcery are all seen as primitive and unworthy of human beings. Even shamanistic and spirit-based healings are thought by our culture to be empty superstitions, even though a significant percentage of people in our own society report similar beliefs and practices (Chapter 5). Our culture rejects their experiences as a whole.

When people of other cultures behave according to what appear to us to be strange customs, we interpret them in light of our own meaningful reality. We are not aware of *their* meaningful reality and so cannot experience the world as they do. This is why so many anthropological studies of other cultures fail. The observers are incapable of putting themselves in the cultural shoes of those they are studying, and so they simply end up interpreting their practices in terms of our own categories. A similar thing happens when people within our own culture speak of having unusual experiences or manifest culturally condemned behaviour. We then have dangerous alienation within the culture itself. I will say more about this in the next chapter.

Creating and Preserving Cultural Trance

Our culture not only puts us to sleep; it has to keep us asleep. This is accomplished largely through the great cultural institutions: the family, the school, religion, the ethnic group, and the political unit.

When you consider how we are indoctrinated into the cultural trance it is not surprising that it has such power. Charles Tart has called this broader group-mind trance "consensus trance."[20] Rightly pointing out that our "normal" state of mind is a trance, Tart says that this consensus trance is induced by our culture and that our induction into it begins at birth. In general, we are expected to be "good citizens," members of society who conform to cultural-trance expectations and who, in our turn, teach our children to do the same. Yes, we are expected to induce the same trance in our children, so that by the time they are released on the broader society (usually around age four or five), they conform so well that they will not stand out, nor threaten the unanimous view of the nature of reality that our culture embodies.

This alarming state of affairs has been decried by a number of social critics. Robert Lindner, in his classic *Prescription for Rebellion,* graphically describes the pressures to conform that are applied to every person in our culture from cradle to grave.[21] In a thousand ways, we are taught that we must adjust to the requirements of society, to align our thinking, feeling, and action with the situation as it presents itself, submitting to existing "realities" as inevitable. This requires an attitude of passivity and resignation. Above all, we must not protest, but must quietly and meekly go along with things. Lindner says that this pressure to adjust and conform aims to reduce human beings to an indistinguishable formlessness, a sameness, an amorphous homogeneity, so that group domination over our individuality will be complete.

The individual feels the pressure to conform from every direction. It begins, says Lindner, with the message parents deliver to their children, that they must adjust. He claims that parenthood has come to be little more than a campaign against individuality, with fathers and mothers trembling lest their children be seen as different from others in their thoughts or actions. Lindner exempts few from this conspiracy. Educators, philosophers, and especially behavioural scientists continue to teach the lesson of conformity begun by parents. Lindner is especially hard on his own profession, claiming that psychotherapists have by and large joined with the power elite in our society to stamp out the healthy spark of rebellion and individuality that is natural to human beings: "Most of the accomplishments proudly claimed by members of these professional groups—most of the magic advertised by psychiatry, some of what passes for psychoanalysis, much of clinical psychology, all of religion, and a good deal of the less pretentious arts of medicine and social service—is based upon a cult of passivity and surrender."[22]

Wilhelm Reich decried the same mindless imposition of conformity on the individual in his book *The Murder of Christ*.[23] Where Lindner concentrated on the ills of society in the present, Reich identified the forces of adjustment as age-old, and he believed that a hatred of life itself motivates these forces.

Reich says that people find themselves in a trap, a trap that prevents them from attaining full realization of their potentials as human beings. He says that the trap is the emotional structure that we develop early in life. The child is born with an abundance of life energy: God is life and all newborn infants have this life flowing freely in their organisms, "but it [is] killed right away by the people in the trap who either [do] not recognize God's Life in their infants, or [are] frightened to death at the sight of living, moving, decent, simple life."[24] What people don't realize is that every human being in this sense has God within. According to Reich, the feeling that God or the energy of life is within them produces a state of severe anxiety in people in this trap. Because of this anxiety people in the trap armour themselves against their own inner life-energy. In this state of tightness and rigidity, they find themselves beginning to hate life in all its forms. They particularly hate the manifestations of life in children and in loving adult sexuality. This current of hatred and repression, says Reich, is abroad in our society and determines our social structures. It has spread to every segment of human life, like a spiritual pathology, and for that reason he calls it the "emotional plague."

Reich, like Lindner, talks about adjustment and conformity. Like inmates in a prison, humanity in the trap has learned to adjust to life in that trap. Instead of finding its way out of the trap, a project they gave up long ago, people are content to try to make life in the trap liveable: "One can decorate a trap to make life more comfortable in it. This is done by the Michelangelos and the Shakespeares and the Goethes. One can invent makeshift contraptions to secure longer life in the trap. This is done by the great scientists and physicians, the Meyers and the Pasteurs and the Flemings. One can devise great art in healing broken bones when one falls into the trap. The crucial point still is and remains: to find the exit out of the trap."[25]

Tart, Lindner, and Reich indicate that when we try to identify the ways that group minds affect us in our daily lives, we must look into the most profound levels of our conditioning. We must question the cultural "truths" we normally take for granted. We have to employ a scalpel of self-analysis that cuts extraordinarily deep. And culture will resist. Look at the experience of feminism, which has made a radical incision and encountered a stunning backlash. It looks as though it will take some time for that surgery to be completed and healed.

How does cultural conformity/adjustment/consensus trance/the "emotional plague" work? Fully conforming to the cultural way of seeing things elevates people to "normalcy." Now they are full members of society and can count on their basic acceptance by others wherever they go. Other members of the culture recognize them because they are constantly, in a thousand ways, giving the "secret handshake" that reveals them as among the initiated. Those who do not conform or who come from another culture are looked at with suspicion and generally avoided. If the presence of these nonmembers is perceived as in any way impinging on the welfare of members, these nonmembers will be speedily put in their place.

And what is this "place" that they are put in? It is often something based on superficial, rule-of-thumb judgments that enable the society to accept and reject or rank its members. These often cruel judgments are based not on the personal qualities of the person but on such things as how much money she makes, what kind of job she holds, what clothes she wears, what religion she adheres to, what school she went to, how well she fits the current standards of beauty or physical attractiveness, whether she knows the right people or speaks with the right inflection, and other equally arbitrary criteria. Because of the unfairness of the basis for these judgments and the harshness with which they are delivered, those who are the object of negative evaluations may suffer deeply.

People want desperately to be considered "normal." They fear the label "abnormal," which has come to denote the socially deformed, a hideous creature to be avoided by all. One of the most frequent questions clients ask me in my psychotherapy work is "Am I normal?" The question usually follows on the heels of a painful revelation, the description of some emotion or some way of seeing things that is not approved of in our culture. The client's question arises from an inner anguish, a fear that "maybe I don't fit in. Maybe people will look at me and find me unacceptable." I usually have the impression that the client would do anything to make sure this doesn't happen, for being socially shunned is still one of the most devastating punishments that can be inflicted on a member of society.

Social shunning is accomplished in many ways. One of the most effective is through gossip. Gossip is a powerful agent of conformity. Gossiping about the sins and shortcomings of group members produces a suffocating atmosphere of social timidity. The subjects of gossip are those who stand out in some way or other, who do not follow the rules, or who are too free and easy. If you want to avoid being talked about, then don't do anything remarkable. We don't want to be gossiped about; we don't want people laughing at us, or pitying us, behind our backs. We will go to practically any lengths to avoid that. Gossip is the group's cattle prod, generating painful shocks in us to force us into the proper pens.

So conformity with the cultural trance is brought about and preserved by several means: by word, example, reward, and punishment. We have developed ways of carrying out this task in our contemporary society that are perhaps more powerful than any in history. These involve technology, particularly as it applies to the communications media.

The Media

Today the media play a central role in inducing and preserving cultural trance. We take for granted our ability to communicate to large segments of the population immediately and graphically through the technological means now available. It used to be the radio and the newspaper. In our time, it has been television, and now the Internet.

The Internet

At this moment I am typing at my notebook computer. With a few keystrokes I can plug into the Internet and, while I continue to write, my computer can locate web sites that will give me the latest Gallup polls on television-watching in North America, information useful in the next section of this book.

The Internet has been fittingly hailed as a means of democratizing knowledge, a liberation of society from a top-down control of information. I can be wowed by this immediate and almost unlimited access to information, but I believe there should be some caution in my enthusiasm. Even though I have achieved a certain freedom from control through it, the information I am receiving is as culturally conditioned as anything else. To a large extent my enthusiasm may turn out to lead me even deeper into my cultural trance.

There are a lot of illusions created through the Internet. When people hook up to each other and communicate about areas of common interest, an illusion of intimacy is easily created. There can be a feeling of directness that rivals being in another person's presence. But it is not the same at all. When people are physically together, they communicate in a million unconscious ways about themselves. They provide a physical/emotional context to their communication that conveys nuances that the other party or parties would otherwise miss. In this way, they also give away things about themselves, both good and bad, that could never be picked up through the computer. There is simply no replacement for the immediate interaction of two unconscious minds in the world of human relations.

Another illusion the computer world creates with its attendant network is that you have solved a problem when you know something. We can be seduced into thinking that if we can just gather together enough information, now available in such vast amounts, we will be able to solve any problem. I recently heard a version of this naive view in a radio commercial promoting a technique for speed-reading. The blurb was that by now just about every human problem has been written about and solved in books. The reason we still have our problems, so goes the blurb, is that we simply do not have the time to read the books we need to read. So if you want to master all of life's problems, all you have to do is learn to speed-read. The temptation to buy into this simplistic notion that information-gathering is the road to happiness is probably nowhere more enticing than when you surf the Net. The fund of information has gone way beyond books now. The amount of hard, soft, and truly soggy information available at the touch of a finger is staggering. Yet information is not wisdom. Knowing is not doing, and it never will be.

Television

In October 1945, the U. S. government lifted its wartime ban on the construction of TV sets and new TV stations. Television had not had much chance to develop before that time. There were just 7,000 sets in use and nine stations broadcasting at the time. At the end of the same month, Gimbel's department store in Philadelphia held a large-scale public demonstration of television and 25,000 attended over a period of three weeks. From that point, television never looked back.

Within 10 years, television had expanded into a popular and powerful communications medium that was leaving both radio and newspapers in its dust; in 1963 television was for the first time rated as the source of information North Americans preferred above all others. Since 1945 there have been many technical improvements: colour television has become the norm; the quality of reception has been progressively enhanced; VCR recording is a part of everyday life; cable has made dozens or even hundreds of channels accessible to practically anyone. Over the past four decades, significant new programming formats have been invented and turned to success. Daytime talk shows, soap operas, sitcoms, nighttime dramas, entertainment news, prime-time magazines, miniseries, all-news, all-sports, all-movies channels—a fantastic variety of information and entertainment awaits the touch of the channel-changer buttons. Television has become an incredibly rich source of stimulation, and there is every reason to believe that what we have seen since 1946 is just the beginning.

But what happens when we sit down in front of the TV? We move into a very special kind of trance state. Our eyes become "defocused" and almost motionless in order to take in the whole screen. We tend to become less "active" in our looking and listening than in other situations. TV passivity is also characterized by the absence of language and other forms of interaction that we use elsewhere. Our imaginations are stirred, but usually not in a creative way: fantasy is stimulated but there is little incentive for us to develop images creatively.

This particular trance combines stimulation and passivity in such a way that the television viewer is likely to end up more vulnerable to suggestion than usual. This heightened openness to suggestion is largely put at the service of our cultural trance. By age 18 the average North American will have watched 18,000 hours of television, as opposed to spending 11,000 hours at school and 3,000 hours getting religious instruction. Television wields tremendous power to affect our whole culture. Its effects could be of any kind, but when you look at what is viewed, it becomes clear that it renews cultural trance and preserves cultural conformity.

True, the effects of television are uneven. Some viewers are more actively involved in the viewing experience, interacting with the television content and/or with other viewers. Some viewers bring a natural maturity to the medium, a mental/emotional toughness that makes them less susceptible to its suggestive power. But by and large, if you watch television, you cannot be completely immune to its trance-reinforcing effects, for we are affected not just on the level of conscious involvement, but also the unconscious. On that level we remain vulnerable and can be drawn in and influenced despite our determination to keep our distance.

Television has so far shown itself to be the friend of cultural trance. It is not a force for countercultural thinking. It does little to invite the viewer to question our cultural assumptions or to examine the basic premises of life as we know it. This is necessarily so, given the financial structure on which television depends.

In the same year that television was given the go-ahead by the U.S. government, major advertising firms were gearing up to make full use of the new medium. CBS was setting up a Television Research Institute, which invited advertisers to make use of network personnel and studios to test new techniques for commercials.

From the beginning, it was clear that money would be the main engine driving the new medium and that advertising would be its source. In the late 1940s, investment in TV commercials mushroomed. By 1952, television-created commercial characters were becoming more widely recognized by the public than movie stars and political leaders; Borden's Elsie the Cow attained a greater recognition rating than actor Van Johnson or Senator Robert Taft. By 1954, television had become America's leading advertising medium.

The goal of the sponsor is simple: Reach as many viewers as possible with your message. The more people watching, the bigger your financial return. Programmers at the networks and local stations know that they are only going to get advertising money if their shows are popular. They also know that they do not draw viewers to things that are culturally unpopular or that make them feel uncomfortable. You draw viewers by presenting things that do not threaten them, things that, as novel as they may seem, do not take them beyond the safe and comfortable. You give people what they want to see, and what they want to see is what they are already culturally acquainted with, by and large.

Since advertisers spend a lot of money on their commercials, they want to know for sure that the programs they sponsor are indeed popular. This has led to their developing ever more accurate polling of viewers' tastes. Today's sophisticated computerized monitoring of television watching ensures that we are more certain than ever before of finding out precisely what kind of programming people most approve of. This kind of sophisticated knowledge of viewer preference has helped make television our most powerful promoter of cultural orthodoxy.

cultural
orthodoxy
and beyond

ERTAIN WAYS OF THINKING maintain and deepen the trance of culture. Many of these thought patterns lie quietly below the surface, largely undisturbed and unquestioned by people. These are the foundational "truths" of our culture, the result of hundreds or thousands of years of cultural evolution.

Overlying this deep cultural bedrock are ideas, attitudes, and values that one might call our cultural orthodoxy. These are the broadly accepted ideas that are consciously thought about and defended against contrary positions. "Correct thinking" can be precisely formulated; in this way the orthodox member of society can be clearly identified, as can the unorthodox.

Orthodoxy refers to beliefs that one must hold to be a true believer within a group. A church or a political party may expend a great deal of energy to promulgate what constitutes the core of its orthodox thinking and to make sure that its members maintain the proper beliefs. There are orthodoxy tests, blatant and subtle, administered to members in the course of their ordinary association with the group. The Catholic Church, for instance, insists that the Creed be recited at every celebration of the Eucharist. Evangelical services are liberally laced with affirmations of orthodox faith. Communist Party meetings include pledges of adherence to the party line. Political parties hold their conventions and, among other things, reformulate and reaffirm their parties' political beliefs. Daily interaction among group members contains subtle messages that indicate whether orthodox thinking is being upheld. In all groups, those who fail the tests of orthodoxy are identified to the membership and pressure is applied to get these people to change their ways. Failure to comply leads to punishment that varies from ridicule to expulsion.

What happens in belief-based groups such as churches and political parties also happens on the broader level of culture. In present-day North American culture, there is an acceptable way to think and to be—our orthodoxy. If you fit within that orthodoxy, you feel you belong. If your thinking conflicts with that orthodoxy, you feel like an outsider, a person on the fringe.

What happens, then, when a current orthodoxy seems to actually undermine the health of the culture? I would like to talk about three orthodoxies that are constantly being displayed and reinforced in everyday life in our North American culture—scientism, moneyism, and bodyism. By examining these three, I do not mean to say that they are the only orthodoxies, or even the principal ones; one could just as well cite the dogmas found in prejudices based on sex or race, or other pervasive orthodoxies. The three I wish to examine here seem to me particularly relevant in the context of this book. Each of these attitudes plays on a hidden promise and a hidden fear buried in our culture. I will say more about them in a moment.

The Culture-Bound Mind

None of us is free of the frameworks and constraints that our culture imposes on our thinking. It would be naive to imagine there exists some cultureless mental space where we can ponder things unhindered. However, we do have the ability to reflect on ourselves and our thinking so we can actually understand something of the influences that affect us. This capacity to be critical of and even to challenge the very cultural context in which we live is the most precious of gifts.

There is a kind of mind, however, which seems to lack this ability to question. It is so hobbled by cultural influences that it simply cannot reflect on the stand it has taken on the basic issues of life. This culture-bound mind knows what it knows, and that is all there is to it. It can adhere to any philosophical position, from liberal to conservative, materialist to spiritualist. You can be sure, however, that the culture-bound mind did not arrive at its position through deep reflection. Rather it absorbed its philosophy from immersion in a particular cultural milieu. So whether it is the mind of a rabid racist or of a devout cult member, the culture-bound mind suffers from the same malady—the inability to imagine something other than what is.

Cultural Orthodoxy and the Media

The teacher and enforcer of cultural orthodoxy in North America is principally the communications media. Every day we receive our dose of indoctrination from TV, radio, magazines, and newspapers. Every item that reaches us is gilded with an opinion, the opinion of the author who formulates the story. Sometimes the opinion is obvious, as in editorials, journalistic columns, and opinion programs of various kinds. Sometimes it is not so obvious, as when the opinion is buried within a seemingly factual news story or documentary report.

The opinions of media people embody values and moral judgments. By stepping back a little from the rhetorical impact of their presentation, we can usually see what they are fairly easily. These values and judgments powerfully affect our country's culture and our thinking. They embody the thinking of the national group mind and therefore have to be taken very seriously.

Although media people express and enforce these values and judgments, they do not originate them. They are spokespeople for ideas in the cultural group as a whole. I believe that, by and large, media personalities do not have the faintest idea what is taking place on the level of group-mind dynamics. Media people seem to be among the more unreflective of group-mind members. Perhaps they have to be that way; otherwise they would constantly be disturbed about their role in mirroring and enforcing the group-mind thinking of the culture. Media people tend to be caught up in the moment. They are able to make their presentation interesting precisely because they have the capacity to milk the moment for all it is worth. That is why the majority of successful media people simply cannot afford to be reflective.

One thoughtful media person once pointed out to me the rather cynical attitude that pervades the media. She said that, in the trade, there is nothing more desirable than a story that can be dramatically presented as fact one day and dramatically denied the next, because then you have *two* stories. My media friend cited the current furor about childhood sexual abuse. For some time the leading dramatic story was about people (usually women) who, through psychotherapy or some other recovery process, began to remember as adults that they were sexually abused as children. All the media fed on these accounts and fired emotions of sympathy and indignation among us, the viewers, listeners, and readers. The prevalence of sexual abuse of children in our society was bemoaned, and calls for greater vigilance went out. Then along came the False-Memory Syndrome Foundation, and the drama of the story completely shifted. The same reporters who had been expressing empathy and anger on behalf of the victims of childhood sexual abuse now presented with equal sympathy and indignation accounts of wrongfully accused parents and other caregivers. These people's lives, they claimed, had been ruined by supposedly false memories obtained in psychotherapy by the same victims the press previously flaunted. Now the story was about the injustices perpetrated by those who claimed that they had suffered the abuse in childhood and made their claims public, bringing charges against the alleged perpetrators, or even by bringing the matter to the attention of other family members. The media's indignation had shifted to how reputations were being sullied and families torn asunder. So now the media had developed two great stories. The fact that they contradicted one another seemed to raise little consternation among media folk. The media-promulgated orthodoxy was converted smoothly from one story into the other with barely a backward glance.

I find it quite easy to spot the current orthodoxy by watching those weekly television documentary/exposé programs, such as *Current Affairs, 20/20,* or *Prime Time.* I say "current orthodoxy" because, as my friend's remarks about childhood sexual abuse indicate, what is orthodox is constantly changing. You can always spot the current orthodox doctrine through the tone of reporters as they interview the various players in the story, and particularly by listening to the closing comments of the show's moderator. In the old stories of childhood sexual abuse, for instance, the victim was interviewed with respect and sympathy, and often the reporter appeared emotionally affected by the pain of the person he or she was interviewing. On those occasions in which the alleged perpetrator was being interviewed, the reporter showed no patience, no sympathy. He or she made it very clear to the audience who were the bad guys and who were the good guys. But when the story shifted to the false-memory issue, the reporters reversed attitudes. Even when the alleged victim was saying the very same things as in the earlier story, the reporter was now clearly reserved and skeptical. Now the burden of proof was on the victim. The accused perpetrator, on the other hand, was treated with sympathy, and the account of the accused was accorded the same unreserved acceptance that had earlier been shown to the "victim's" account. Then at the end of the show, the program host would echo the reporter's sympathies and often comment about what had been "scientifically established" about the matter, pointing out how science clearly sided with the latest version of orthodoxy.

As propagandists for the culture's current orthodoxy, the media exercise a great deal of power. They convey the orthodoxy to the media consumer with a combination of subtlety and drama that is hard to resist. True, there have been ongoing attempts to stand back and look at what the media are doing—how they may be slanting a story, how they may be censoring what is presented to the public—

with the critical reviewers, usually panels of experts on television and radio, doing their best to keep the media honest. But I am afraid that even the experts are not sufficiently aware of the way we all live and work within our web of group minds. Until we give the group mind the respect due it, we will remain unwitting promulgators of its ideas more than we are wise critics of its influence.

Science As Idol

Many of the tenets of our cultural orthodoxy change with the wind. Among those that remain constant is the cult of science as the final arbiter of truth. Within our culture, anything that is scientifically proven is taken as true and adherence to it is respectable. Anything that is not scientifically proven is suspect. Anything that a scientist rejects is nonsense, naive, superstitious, or dangerous.

It is interesting to see how this works. If a scientist says something about any subject, the listener is expected to give his or her opinion respectful consideration. Whether the scientist is a marine biologist venturing an opinion on democracy in the Ukraine or a metallurgist telling us about the nature of the human mind, because she is a scientist, she must be right—or very nearly so. To a member of Western civilization, the scientist is an authority. Scientists' opinions have weight because they practise some kind of science, somewhere, in some area. That their particular scientific investigations cast no light on the subject they speak about makes little difference.

If you watch television, listen to radio, and read the papers, our culture's faith in the scientist soon becomes clear. Our culture holds that because he has "scientific training," the scientist is nobody's fool and we can trust his opinions. It matters not that his "scientific training" is a master's degree in chemistry. By the mere fact that his training is in science, his ideas—*all* of them—automatically command greater respect than those of, say, a person who has spent twenty years studying Buddhist philosophy. Scientific training is believed to grant a person some infallible method of thinking, rock-solid common sense, some deep and universal wisdom that will inevitably lead to the truth. The person who has been indoctrinated into scientific training is thought to have acquired a hard-nosed sense of the real nature of things and will not be seduced into the byways of fantasy, suggestibility, and other foolishnesses to which those without such training are vulnerable. The scientist's knowledge is reliable because he will not accept anything that has not been scientifically "proven." If he says something has been proven to his satisfaction, then we must accept his word; after all, we are not in a position to check his data or examine his scientific work critically. Any questioning on our part would be presumptuous.

Scientism is a problem of culture, not of individuals—not even of scientists. As a matter of fact, scientists number among their ranks a significant number of critics of naive scientism. Reviewing Carl Sagan's *The Demon-Haunted World* in the *New York Review of Books,* Harvard biologist Richard Lewontin makes some telling points about our unquestioning acceptance of scientists' statements.[26] He tells us that scientists are quick to criticize other sources of knowledge, such as descriptions of experiences of ESP or mysticism, as sometimes contrary to common sense and often based on the pronouncements of authorities. But, says Lewontin, some of the most basic claims of science are against common sense and at first glance seem absurd, such as the claim that the pungent cheese I just ate is really made up of tiny, tasteless, colourless, odourless packets of energy separated by empty space. Also scientists depend heavily on the statements of authorities, for they are very hesitant to make pronouncements on matters involving branches of science other than their own, and even areas within their own specialities in which they do not have expertise. When venturing outside their own domains, scientists quote other scientists as authorities and take their word for things, since they too have no way to verify their findings personally.

Many scientists, especially those who popularize science, face an insoluble problem. For they use rhetoric to convince their audience that they should be convinced only by scientifically established facts. Lewontin sums up their problem:

Carl Sagan, like his Canadian counterpart David Suzuki, has devoted extraordinary energy to bringing science to a mass public. In doing so, he is faced with a contradiction for which there is no clear resolution. On the one hand, science is urged on us as a model of rational deduction from publicly verifiable facts, freed from the tyranny of unreasoning authority. On the other hand, given the immense extent, inherent complexity, and counterintuitive nature of scientific knowledge, it is impossible for anyone, including non-specialist scientists, to retrace the intellectual paths that lead to scientific conclusions about nature. In the end we must trust the experts and they, in turn, exploit their authority as experts and their rhetorical skills to secure our attention and our belief in things that we do not really understand. . . . Conscientious and wholly admirable popularizers of science like Carl Sagan use both rhetoric and expertise to form the mind of masses because they believe, like the Evangelist John, that the truth shall make you free. But they are wrong. It is not the truth that makes you free. It is your possession of the power to discover the truth. Our dilemma is that we do not know how to provide that power.[27]

Although most scientists might be reluctant to make statements about matters outside their scientific expertise, it would not be difficult to compile a veritable encyclopedia of inane pronouncements scientists have made on matters relating to other disciplines. A work of even greater bulk could be put together of once broadly accepted opinions of scientists of the not-so-distant past that have been quietly buried, without public funeral. The scientific journals of today are jammed with differences of opinion and out-and-out wars of denunciation between scientists studying the very same data. We have recently seen the publication of a number of significant books about the crucial role played by social, political, and theological opinions of some scientists in collecting their data and formulating their theories. Scientists of the "highest reputation," as they are often introduced on our current-event shows, have even been known to falsify their data and commit other kinds of fraud to back up pet theories.

Despite the distortions of scientism, science itself has served us well. It has developed a technology that provides comforts of a kind unimaginable mere decades ago, and the men and women who have made this possible deserve our thanks and respect. However, it is of the utmost importance to note that science has contributed nothing to philosophy, little to psychology (there are, of course, some who would debate this), and little to our understanding of human beings as living, creative creatures. And when we, as a culture, defer to science or scientists in these matters, we are on precarious ground.

I would like to question the almost worshipful acceptance of the findings of science and the opinions of scientists that is firmly established as a principal tenet of our cultural orthodoxy. This attitude of the rank and file of our culture is tremendously undermining, for several reasons. First of all, it grants one mode of knowledge a monopoly on the truth. In any conflict between an opinion held by a scientist and one held by another learned person, the scientist's opinion is automatically accepted. In our cultural orthodoxy, anything that is "unscientific" is at best suspect and, at worst, worthless. To call an idea unscientific is to exclude it from further consideration and condemn it to oblivion.

Ironically, most of our knowledge is not scientific at all. Very little of what we know comes through scientific experiment and research. We acquire most of it through quite other means, quite unscientific (or to use a more appropriate term) non-scientific means. But in our culture non-scientific modes of knowing—the intuitive, the poetic, the aesthetic, the mystical, the spiritual, the subjective, the directly experiential—are denigrated. They have no official status. The official doctrine is scientism. Other modes of knowledge are a kind of unsubstantial food that some people ingest. They can be allowed and even appreciated at times, as one might indulge a culinary taste for creatures that slink along the bottom of the ocean, but if there comes a moment when one of these modes of knowledge contradicts some scientific opinion, our culture indicates in no uncertain terms where our loyalties must lie.

It is a shame that as a culture we are so philosophically unsophisticated. The philosophy of science long ago delineated the severe limitations of scientific knowledge. The areas of reality to which it could be properly applied and those about which it could say nothing were clearly laid out, and there has never been any serious philosophical challenge to this analysis. Also, the notion that science could provide an accurate view of reality has been rejected. One writer has stated that "great scientists invent descriptions of the world which are useful for purposes of predicting and controlling what happens, just as poets and political thinkers invent other descriptions of it for other purposes. But there is no sense in which *any* of these descriptions are an accurate representation of the way the world is in itself."[28] Nevertheless, while many great scientists are equally great philosophers (witness Albert Einstein) and know very well what science can and cannot do, a great many other scientists have so fallen in love with their methods that they have been loath to subject science itself, as a mode of knowledge, to philosophical analysis.

Science and Materialism

In his *New York Review of Books* piece on Carl Sagan's *The Demon-Haunted World*, Richard Lewontin writes: "Sagan's argument is straightforward. We exist as material beings in a material world, all of whose phenomena are the consequences of physical relations among material entities. . . . Our willingness to accept scientific claims that are against common sense is the key to an understanding of the real struggle between science and the supernatural. We take the side of science *in spite* of the patent absurdity of some of its constructs, *in spite* of its failure to fulfill many of its extravagant promises of health and life, *in spite* of the tolerance of the scientific community for unsubstantiated just-so stories, because we have a prior commitment, a commitment to materialism. It is not that the methods and institutions of science somehow compel us to accept a material explanation of the phenomenal world, but, on the contrary, that we are forced by our *a priori* adherence to material causes to create an apparatus of investigation and a set of concepts that produce material explanations, no matter how counter-intuitive, no matter how mystifying to the uninitiated."[29]

But the problem is not so much with the scientists themselves as it is with our culture as a whole. If some scientists have arrogated to their discipline a status which philosophical examination cannot support, that is their problem. Our problem is that our culture has enshrined this same naive understanding of scientific knowledge and is making no move to question that position. The pity is that this worship of science and scientists makes children of our culture's rank and file. It means that we cannot trust our own intuitive views about people, the world, and life. On the contrary, we must look to scientific authorities to tell us what to think and how to see things.

When I mentioned our culture's three problematic orthodoxies, I said that each has a hidden promise and a hidden fear. The hidden promise behind scientism is that science will provide certain and complete knowledge of the world and life and make us feel secure in this frightening universe. The desire for certain and complete knowledge is an age-old hope. It is the reason that people have needed oracles in every age. Every past culture that we know about and every present culture outside the West has developed and revered its own oracles. So have we, but we do not tend to acknowledge them as such openly. Our oracles are our scientists. Our scientific oracles are given precisely the same kind of naive acceptance accorded to the seers of old.

The elevation of the scientist to the role of oracle is based on a hidden fear. It is our fear that there is no meaning, no sense to our universe—the fear that we exist in a chaotic, random, feelingless, purposeless void. If science can find order and sense in the overall operation of the material cosmos, then we are tremendously grateful to it and its practitioners. It is the ray of hope we are looking for. And if they can find order and sense in certain physical manifestations, then we deduce that maybe they can find meaning in all aspects of human existence. Perhaps they can also tell us what we as human beings are about, how we function, how we should function, where we are going, and how we can get there. This is how our hidden fears put science and scientists in a role that they cannot possibly fill.

To elevate the scientist to the role of oracle and universal adviser has seriously adverse effects on our culture, for it makes the non-scientist a little person who must look to these big people for their truth. In this way, the worship of the scientist provides us with a striking example of what I want to deal with in the next chapter, the Little-People/Big-People Delusion.

New Age Orthodoxy

Today we encounter a way of thinking that is unique in the way it affects our culture. It is the view of the world offered by what has come to be known as the "New Age" movement. New Age thinking owes a great deal to the general shift in consciousness in the 1960s, the moving away from blind adherence to authority in general and to scientism in particular. In many ways it embodied a liberation of thought that was long overdue. The New Age world view espouses definite beliefs: that the world in which we live is not limited to the material; that the human organism embodies vital forces as yet unknown; and that we are spiritual beings whose lives have meaning that transcends the immediate and the everyday. It is characterized by a pervasive optimism based on a belief in the presence of the divine in every aspect of life. One unique feature of the rise of this thinking is the way that it has been disseminated in our society. It is not associated with particular identifiable religious groups or cults, but may be found, in some form or other, in a broad spectrum of people who belong to various religious groups or non-religious organizations, or who have no affiliation or religious creed at all. For that reason New Age thinking can show up anywhere and be communicated in a variety of ways in all media. It has become a significant kind of fringe thinking, not accepted by the majority in our North American society, perhaps, but constantly growing in influence nevertheless over the past three decades.

New Age thinking arose to counter the stale orthodoxies of the 1940s and 1950s, but, like so many creative movements, it shows signs of becoming a new orthodoxy itself with all the problematic features of the other orthodoxies I have mentioned. Its particular form of orthodoxy turns what was originally fresh thinking about life and meaning into a kind of spiritual pablum characterized by magical thinking. New Age orthodoxy provides a simplistic notion of security that is not subjected to sufficient scrutiny. It is characterized by a lack of skepticism and even good sense. Whereas scientism is blind to the limitations of materially oriented methods for investigating the nature of reality, New Age orthodoxy is simplistic in its approach to interpreting human experience and gullible in accepting the ideas of its gurus and authorities. Unfortunately, the boldness of the first wave of New Age thinking is now in danger of being replaced by this orthodoxy and the conservative complacency that so often follows upon success.

Moneyism, Bodyism, and the Vicarious Life

If scientism mis-evaluates science, then moneyism makes the same mistake in regard to money. And, like scientism, moneyism is a manoeuvre to gain security in a world that feels too precarious. While scientism seeks the security of believing that some group of wise people has the ultimate knowledge of the way things are, or could gain that knowledge if they applied their methods long enough, moneyism seeks the security of gaining and maintaining the material means for keeping oneself in existence—forever, one hopes.

The issue in moneyism is survival. In calling on this most basic of instincts, moneyism exerts a great deal of power in our culture. The prime activity of moneyism is the accumulation of money, goods, land—whatever will establish a person immovably on the earth. It is true that moneyism often leads to seeking to acquire the greatest number of comforts possible, but preoccupation with comfort is secondary, a byproduct of one's involvement with procuring what is needed for survival.

If you want to hear the voices of moneyism, listen to phone-in shows, both on radio and television. Participants speak of their fears for their monetary future and the survival of their children in a world in which material security seems so elusive. They express sympathy with those who protect their sources of income at any cost. The elevation of money above all human values has reached a pitch unimaginable short decades ago. Businesses have always placed money first, but there used to be a certain shame in doing so. Lack of concern for employees was always in evidence, but it was covered up, a dirty secret denied to the public. Now, the public is coming to accept this overturning of human values. Business leaders speak of their catastrophic "downsizing" without any chagrin about the suffering involved. The bottom line reigns supreme and money is king.

Fear can do strange things to you. It can make you hate the imagined source of the fear and identify with the real source. Talk shows demonstrate that both of these are at work in regard to moneyism. Those whose financial security is truly threatened hate those they believe are taking their jobs away from them. That is why there is such strong talk about stopping immigration, for instance, for the immigrant is perceived as taking a piece of a rapidly shrinking pie. On the other hand, business practices that embody moneyism and play down human values are often approved, even by those who are the victims of such practices. Incredibly, on these phone-in shows one hears the unemployed declare themselves in agreement with businessmen who call in and tell about situations in which they put their financial gain ahead of the well-being of their employees. After all, it is a dog-eat-dog world, and who can blame them for protecting their interests?—even to the extreme of committing acts against their employees that used to be considered despicable. In this way, many of the downtrodden feel so caught in the fear behind moneyism that they themselves identify with their oppressors and become spokespeople for what is surely an indefensible philosophy of life.

There is also evidence on phone-in shows that people can easily come to envy and even hate those whose jobs are more secure than their own. Government workers especially come in for a great deal of negative comment, because, at least in the eyes of the general public, they are ensconced within the last secure employment base. Envy and hatred are also directed at workers who are still doing all right but want to do better—get better wages or working conditions. The feeling so often is: How dare you want more when I am on the verge of losing all.

Moneyism and the fear of not surviving find expression in the adoption of social policies that downplay the urge to look after one's fellow human beings—which it calls bleeding-heartism. If you fear that concern for the welfare of others will mean you lose your own life's blood, you will be powerfully motivated to look the other way when people are needy and suffering, even when they are literally in danger of losing their existence. Within the frame of moneyism, the plight of the destitute is too uncomfortable to look at head on, for it confronts people with their own worst fear. It must be blocked out or distorted so that those in need are pictured as worthless parasites who simply want to drain others.

Moneyism is a trance based on fear. It cannot embrace higher values. It cannot afford loyalty at the expense of money, so employees who have become dependent on the monied person or corporation cannot count on being considered above the profits of the business. Businesses driven by moneyism dismiss long-time, faithful employees with barely a second thought. Lip service may be given to retraining, psychological counselling, or other services in response to outside pressure and the need to present an image of "doing the right thing." Such services are to substitute for human concern about those who are ousted. After all, the vital issue for the money-driven business is survival, and in that framework, each must think only about his or her own business. Anything else is a dangerous distraction.

And who will find fault with that? In our culture, "taking care of business" is more and more accepted as a primary criterion for decision making. It has come to mean that if money or the good of the business is at stake, all other human values must take second place. This makes it possible to fire without regard for human considerations, to refuse to hire those who will not sacrifice themselves for the good of the business, or to feel justified in creating work pressures that destroy the confidence and creativity of employees. Moneyism recognizes human needs only insofar as they do not conflict with business survival.

Moneyism is destructive because it is based on a fear that is not being acknowledged and dealt with, the fear of not surviving because of a lack of material goods. When fears are not acknowledged, they get out of hand and lead to extreme action. That is the case with moneyism in our society today. Government and individuals take extreme measures to preserve the illusion that one can accumulate enough goods to be truly and permanently secure.

In fact, we can never be truly and permanently secure in this life, no matter how much we possess. Material security is always imperfect. Those who recognize this pursue whatever material security they can find, but they do so in a balanced fashion. That means that other principles and considerations maintain their place in these people's hierarchy of values.

True security can only be the sure knowledge of the nature and meaning of things and not about empty fantasies about science or money. Nor can it be founded on the pursuit of bodily perfection, another of our culture's orthodoxies.

Bodyism is the mis-evaluation of physical power and beauty. Bodyism contains a hidden promise—that we can grasp eternal life and vitality through the body. Its hidden fear is that eternal life is an illusion. Bodyism entails the adoration of a certain image of beauty, the granting of exaggerated importance to physical prowess or athleticism, the worship of youth, and the fear of old age.

Bodyism is promoted through not merely the glamour and sports shows of television; it is also what powers the infomercials advertising everything from beauty creams and hair transplants to dating and sex phone lines. Bodyism is a large part of what sells magazines on entertainment, fantasy romance, sports, and body shaping. Bodyism has a lot to do with who is hired for high-profile television host positions, and it plays an enormous role in determining programming policies.

To be young, beautiful, athletic: that is the ideal of bodyism. It hides a terror of defect, for defect means we are physically mortal, that our bodies will degenerate and die. This terror isolates the elderly from the mainstream of our society. Bodyism fears to look at the old and the process of ageing that we all must go through. As a result, bodyism keeps our society from appreciating the maturation process of old age. Because of bodyism, our culture cannot avail itself of the wisdom about human nature, the meaning of life, moral values, interpersonal interactions, and social mores that can only be acquired through long experience.

The worship of youth that characterizes our culture cripples us in another way: it blocks the creativity of those who are going through the inevitable ageing process. Preoccupation with staying young often combines with the desire to meet the impossible standards of beauty propounded by bodyism in our society. The amount of energy spent in this endless and largely fruitless task is enormous. The other, more creative strivings of the person are pushed aside in favour of this pursuit. The waste of human resources is staggering.

Secretly we all know that the dreams of moneyism and bodyism cannot be achieved. We can never achieve perfect monetary security, nor can we achieve perfect beauty or stay eternally young. That is why another strategy must come into play to compensate for the despair created by these pursuits. In our culture that strategy is vicarious living—living through the experience of another.

Vicarious living is a natural part of human social interaction. The stories of childhood and the fiction of adult life always involve something of the vicarious. In groups, boys and girls, men and women, regale one another with their (sometimes exaggerated) exploits to give each other thrills, or establish status. Vicarious living can create entertainment and it can spur one to achieve similar experiences. However, it can also become a substitute for personal living and the basis for passivity and eventual hopelessness, for it can make you feel inferior to those whom you live through and depressed that you can never achieve what they exemplify. This is especially true when vicarious living is based on images derived from moneyism and bodyism.

The criteria for physical beauty for both men and women in our culture can be deduced easily from the pages of beauty magazines, celebrity magazines, and clips from fashion and entertainment programs on television. They stand as an ideal for all to emulate. Some also experience such images as a reproach when they, under the spell of bodyism, feel desperate to conform to them but know they never can. The shape of the body must be perfect, the skin flawless, the hairstyle au courant, the apparel of the latest style. Every success at meeting the ideal is a source of deep satisfaction; every failure to do so is a blow to self-esteem. Unfortunately, those in the grip of bodyism tend to be much more aware of their defects than their good points. Even those who embody the ideals of beauty in the eyes of most—movies stars and models—are keenly aware of their weak points and consider themselves anything but icons of perfection. It is sad to see a top model or movie star, bodyism's idol, speaking with embarrassment and chagrin of his or her small chin, thin hair, or flabby thighs. In their own eyes, these people do not meet the ideal, and they too suffer the despair that is the inevitable outcome of bodyism. Sadder still are those who, under the shadow of our culture's bodyism, live their lives bowed under the misery and confusion of eating disorders—sometimes even bringing their lives to a premature end. This slavery to bodyism that so many of our children experience and carry as an insufferable burden into adult life must be the most telling indictment of this distorted orthodoxy.

Delusions

Scientism, moneyism, and bodyism, as elements of the cultural trance, all seek security, in the wrong places. Science does not hold the secrets of life. Money cannot establish a truly secure place in the world. Beauty, youth, and vitality do not lead to immortality, as bodyism seems to promise. The "securities" promised by these orthodoxies are delusions.

Is real security possible? Is there *some* basis on which we can be truly confident in ourselves and in life's possibilities? I believe there is. The rest of this book is concerned with exploring the foundations for this kind of security. As a first step, let us look at the possibility of cultural change.

Trancebreaking

Cultural trance, with its bedrock beliefs and less stable orthodoxies, forms the framework within which we carry out the transactions of life. At first glance it may appear that the tenets of cultural trance are unshakeable. Our institutions preserve them, and our daily communications entrench them. Yet change is possible. To some extent our orthodoxies are vulnerable to change, for they embody explicitly formulated beliefs, and can therefore be subjected to question and criticism. Even the more deeply embedded and less explicit attitudes of culture can evolve, given the right circumstances. Deeper cultural change is especially likely when either the culture is frequently exposed to the influences of another culture or the culture has developed the ability to identify and examine its own fundamental attitudes. Both conditions apply to our modern North American culture.

Trancekeepers

In any culture there exists a tension between those elements oriented to preserving the trance and those seeking to break it. Trancekeepers and trancebreakers are both necessary for the well-being of our society, and trancekeepers, as the conservators of cultural sleep, should not be dismissed as detrimental to cultural health.

We need our conservative element, those who for the sake of continuity and stability work to maintain the cultural trance. These people are acutely aware of the value of tradition. They revere the legacy of the past and do what they can to preserve the treasures of previous generations. In this way our society enjoys the security of proven ways of thinking and acting. These are the practices that have worked, that embody our culture's previously hard-won lessons. In promoting the given, trancekeepers renew and deepen the cultural trance. They are the pillars of the cultural community, the transmitters of wisdom, and are respected and honoured for their role. For them, right is on the side of conserving the accumulated wisdom of the past. We may fittingly feel thankful for our trancekeepers, for every day we reap the benefits of living within a culture that, for all its shortcomings, embodies traditional attitudes and ways of life that are nurturing and humane.

One group of trancekeepers whom we recognize as valuable leaders in our culture are our teachers. Working within our educational systems, they transmit the wisdom of the past and help their students become knowledgeable about how to fit in with the principal institutions of society. They work to make people feel at home in their cultural world and comfortable with the ways of thinking in place there. Theirs is a valuable service. We cannot thrive, or even exist, in our society without being taught how to do so. And the more knowledge and skill we acquire, the better we can adapt to the circumstances in which we find ourselves. Many of our teachers recognize this and dedicate themselves to this essential work.

Politicians, too, may be considered among our trancekeepers. They think of themselves as devoted to discovering ways for us to live together in society to our mutual benefit, and to establish and preserve institutions that make this possible. Because politicians are engaged in governing, they are inclined to conservative, trance-keeping thinking. Nonetheless, there are exceptions to that rule, and history presents some striking examples of politicians who in some way or other have broken the mould and become true leaders of their people.

Those involved in the helping professions—doctors, psychiatrists, psychologists, psychotherapists, social workers, nurses—see themselves as there to assist those in need. They also see themselves as representatives of order and stability in society. This is in no small part due to the fact that they are often so closely allied with institutions set up to look after the welfare of society's members. Being attached to these institutions, they tend to speak with the voice of the conservators of the old order, advocates of the cultural status quo. This attachment to institutions and approved procedures places the helping professions solidly in the ranks of the trancekeepers. In large institutions people have to be managed in such a way that they do not impede the operation of the establishment. It must function in the manner that will do the most good for the most people in the shortest period of time. Money must be spent well, and this is most easily gauged according to how speedily the service is administered. Also, methods of treatment have been devised over the years that have proven effective, and there is the tendency to maintain the familiar. In the absence of compelling evidence that another approach would be better, the established technique will be the approved one. All of these factors call for preservation of the ways of the past, so the helping professions by their very nature are trancekeepers.

Trancekeeping is not limited to a few professions. It plays a part in every human institution and is found in every aspect of daily existence. Trancekeeping forces exist in the family, the school, at work, in religious groups, and in recreational life. Maintaining the trance of culture is crucial for our existence. Without it there would be no way to preserve the wisdom of the past, and our lives would be disjointed and in danger of disintegrating. So our trancekeepers have their place and always will.

Trancebreakers

But we also need our trancebreakers. For while trancekeepers provide the supportive backbone of our society, trancebreakers expose and oppose its pathology. Like the disease-fighting mechanisms of the body, they attack the forces of morbidity and dispose of cultural tissue that has ceased to function.

Trancebreakers seek to break the mould, to challenge the ways of the past. Life is movement, and trancebreakers know we cannot afford to keep it frozen in one particular cultural posture. In contrast to our trancekeepers, our trancebreakers are not oriented primarily to recognizing the wisdom of yesteryear. Rather, they think about what might be and how our unexamined and uncriticized institutions keep us from realizing our dreams. They chafe under the yoke of unthinking habit. They are sensitive to the suppression of new thought and creative imagination. Trancebreakers recognize culture as a sleep, and look on that sleep as a state of inertia analogous to death. They call for an awakening; they ask that we let the scales fall from our eyes, that we see things from a new point of view, that we doubt, question, challenge, resist.

Trancebreakers want change. Constructive trancebreakers are aware of the positive contributions of their culture, but they do not want to be limited by the old ways. If they anticipate negative effects from change, they judge the gain worth the risk. They tend to view stability as stagnation and fear that society will decay in the grip of conservative forces. Trancebreakers operate from a vision, conscious or unconscious, of a better future. They are impatient, and feel righteous in their impatience. For them, right is on the side of creative change, though constructive trancebreakers do not want to impose that change on others. Instead of using violence to force change, constructive trancebreakers invite others to freely choose to share their view of the future.

When trancebreaker meets transkeeper there is tension. Each senses in the other a fundamentally different orientation to life and feels threatened by that difference. They know that they will come down on opposite sides of most of the major debates of their society. Each finds it nearly impossible to identify with the other. Conversions are rare. The more enlightened on both sides appreciate the need for the other view, but fight it tooth and nail, nevertheless.

It is very difficult for trancebreakers to be moderate in their approach, because to cast off stifling influences they sometimes feel they have to throw caution to the winds. Yet caution is in order, because trancebreakers often find themselves fighting cultural elements that have served a good purpose in the past. Trancebreakers must realize that in their slashing and burning they could leave in their wake a scorched cultural landscape incapable of renewing itself. In that case their overall efforts would be negative, whatever good intentions might have motivated them. So trancebreakers must take care to insure that their ultimate effects are constructive rather than destructive.

There have been many truly constructive trancebreakers in our own North American culture. Here are a few who illustrate trancebreaking of the most creative kind:

Martin Luther King, Jr. might be called the trancebreaking leader of a trancebreaking movement. King came on the scene in the 1950s, at a time when black people were denied many of their fundamental rights. In many parts of the United States a black person could not take public transportation, go to schools, vote, eat in restaurants, use public rest rooms, and do other things with the same freedom as white people. All over the United States black people were denied equal opportunity in employment and equal consideration for positions of influence. However many people might have disapproved privately, society in general accepted this segregation of races in the United States and believed little could be done about it.

King and his co-workers were trancebreakers both in what they confronted and in how they confronted it. They brought the problem of discrimination to public awareness, and they did it through culturally untypical means: non-violent protest. In a country whose very existence was based on violent revolt, which expanded by using arms to push out its native inhabitants, which had fought a devastating civil war to settle the question of slavery, which promoted the age-old notions of manly aggression as a basis for success in life—in such a country non-violent protest was not the means for radical change that would first come to mind.

King was largely responsible for the civil rights movement adopting peaceful resistance as its method for bringing about change. Peaceful "sit-ins" and non-violent marches were employed as means of saying that full and equal participation by blacks in American life could not be put off any longer. Peaceful demonstrators often met with physical assaults and arrests, but violent opposition did not discourage the non-violent movement. King's peaceful confrontation reached its culmination in the "March on Washington" in the summer of 1963, when 250,000 demonstrators of every race and religion converged on the capital city to show their support for legislation to ensure the rights of black people.

Looking back more than 30 years later, it may be difficult to appreciate what a trancebreaker Martin Luther King was. Although the matter of equality for black people is by no means a dead issue today, we live in a culture that has been significantly altered by the movement King spearheaded. We take for granted many progressive standards for racial equality that exist only because of the work he did.

Jean Vanier, although not well known in North America, is another excellent example of a trancebreaker. In 1964 this son of a Governor General of Canada, former naval officer, and doctor in philosophy embarked on a unique personal journey. He purchased a small house in a town north of Paris and invited two mentally handicapped men to live there with him. He did not know precisely where this adventure was going to lead, but he soon discovered that just through the experience of living with these disadvantaged men he himself began to change radically. He also found out how, as he tells it, the handicapped can be a source of peace and unity in our terribly divided world. This small experiment marked the beginning of a movement which came to be called "L'Arche" (the Ark). In this form of community life, the mentally handicapped, often rejected and despised by the world, can fully develop their capacities and make their unique contributions to the lives of others.

Over the years since that first house was established, L'Arche has grown into a network of communities that span the globe from Canada and the United States to the Ivory Coast and Australia. Vanier's vision was to give back to these people, society's outcasts, their experience of connection. This was to happen in a very simple way—by their living in small communities where everyone is accepted and treated with respect, and where the handicapped and those who are not profit equally from living together.

Vanier became convinced that the handicapped have the ability, through their sufferings, to reveal the inadequacies and impoverishment of the lives of many of the so-called normal. He realized that people are afraid to see the defects and weaknesses in themselves, and that they show that fear by rejecting those with obvious handicaps. He believed that by accepting and appreciating people who are wounded in this way, we can find the courage to accept our own "brokenness" and transcend it by coming together in love. So, in Vanier's vision, his communities are not there simply to help those whom our culture has scapegoated; they are there to benefit all. With this explicitly stated agenda, the L'Arche communities nestle uneasily in our culture's landscape, for they threaten some of the secret, not very admirable beliefs about the value of human beings embodied in our cultural trance.

Sometimes trancebreaking works through deftly applied humour. Successful humour takes the familiar and adds an element of the unexpected, a twist that produces an "Omigod! How preposterous!" surprise that stimulates our mysterious organ of laughter to respond. There is a performance humour that so relentlessly introduces the unexpected, so mercilessly sets us on our ears, that afterwards we find it difficult to regain our balance. In fact, we may never be quite the same again.

Such is the humour developed by the Australian-born Barry Humphries and embodied in a superlative way in his flamboyant stage and television character, Dame Edna Everage. Humphries's humour so effectively destroys our normal, trance-laden way of seeing things that it places him in the first rank of trancebreakers.

Watching Dame Edna is an experience. Virtually everything she does is a "spoof," poking fun at some idea or ideal of our popular culture. She has drawn particular attention to the fantasy of celebrity, playing off the concept of the "megastar," one of the true absurdities of our popular culture. On the one hand she has dubbed herself a megastar and constantly bemoans the "onerous" responsibilities of that role in our society: being unable to go out in public without being swamped by fans, having to rub elbows with boring world leaders, being hounded by producers who want her to star in their movies. On the other hand she frequently has people that many consider megastars (for instance, Jane Fonda, Charlton Heston, Lauren Bacall) on her programs, and typically either casts them in ridiculous subservient roles during their appearances or reduces them to helpless paralysing laughter about their own hyped images and personal foibles.

Dame Edna characteristically marches into areas that are forbidden subjects in our society. She talks about sex, race, the handicapped, death—anything that arouses uneasiness is fair game—without the least concern for conventional sensitivities. She forces her audience to laugh about things that we usually do not consider laughing matters, and in the process she makes people take a second look at things that they do not even want to take a first look at. She forces the secret, the nasty, the embarrassing, the stupid into the light of consciousness, unwilling to leave unexamined any prejudice or pettiness. Dame Edna is thus the epitome of the trancebreaker. The sleeping dogs that our culture goes to great pains to let lie, she rouses with irreverent, satirical jabs. With Dame Edna, Barry Humphries prods us with humour and outrage so effectively that we barely notice that we ourselves are waking up.

Looking at the work of King, Vanier, and Humphries, it is clear that trancebreakers have their own unique visions. Those visions may at times put them in conflict with the powerful guardians of culture's orthodoxies. Think of trancebreakers such as Betty Friedan (*The Feminine Mystique,* 1963), Rachel Carson (*Silent Spring,* 1962), the Beatles, or one of history's greatest trancebreakers, Jesus Christ, and you will see how impossible it is to avoid rubbing people the wrong way. Trancebreakers have to be capable of an extraordinary single-minded determination. And once they have achieved their goals, they must guard against the temptation to bask in their accomplishments—a very dangerous attitude for a trancebreaker.

Keeping the Faith

Some years ago I attended the graduation of my sister and her husband from chiropractic college. They had been attracted to chiropractic largely because of its unconventionality and its scope for personal creativity. Medical doctors tended to look at chiropractic as the next thing to quackery, and chiropractors over the years have in many ways functioned as trancebreakers to the health-care professions. The speaker at the ceremony was the vice president of the American Chiropractic Association, about to become its president. At one point in his talk he admonished the new graduates that even though their training was complete, it was important for them to keep learning. He said, "It is especially important to keep reading in your field. But remember, read only those things approved by the American Chiropractic Association." Knowing how hard chiropractors had to work to have their unconventional ways accepted, I was shocked by this blatant advocacy of dogmatism. After the talk my embarrassed sister enlightened me. The struggle of the chiropractic profession for acceptance as a legitimate health service had only recently been successful, with chiropractic receiving official approval for payment by health insurance companies and government health-care plans. With that victory, chiropractic had moved from the ranks of unconventional fringe groups to those of the establishment. It had not taken long after that before its spokespeople had shifted their role from trancebreakers to trancekeepers. Now they had become advocates of a chiropractic status quo against innovation, and were seeing unorthodox thinking within their ranks as a danger to their newly acquired power.

There is a lesson here. Trancebreakers are not always defeated by a repressive force. Sometimes they are swallowed whole and transformed into trancekeepers, as the chiropractors of America seemed to me to be in danger of doing. Being handed power in society is a seductive enticement for the trancebreaker. Few can keep the faith in the face of that temptation and avoid becoming, in their turn, promoters of cultural sleep.

To sleep, to enjoy the tranquil peace of cultural stability, to be handed the sure knowledge of what is right, true, and proven workable: who would not want that? Considering what cultural sleep has to offer, it is amazing that there are as many determined trancebreakers as there are. Some trancebreakers are driven by an inborn need to question, to take nothing for granted, to expose each idea, each situation, each person to its roots. Taken to the extreme, this attitude would leave nothing standing. There would be no culture, no accumulated riches in society. This attitude is what Robert Lindner calls "negative rebellion," the creative spark of rebellion gone wild and destroying everything in its path, including, eventually, the rebel. Lindner also speaks of "positive rebellion," a rebellion that questions and challenges, but does so with an eye to building. Positive rebellion destroys only what must be destroyed and maintains valuable elements wherever they are found.

Positive rebellion is perhaps harder to find than one might hope. It is found in those who have attained a maturity that is rare among us. It is manifested by people who have overcome the most elusive and undermining deceptions that we face in cultural life: the Little-People/Big-People Delusion.

3

waking up

---

little-people/
big-people
delusion

IS THERE A GROUP-MIND TRANCE that transcends all cultures and affects everyone born into the human race? Is there a way of thinking that entrances all of us without exception? I believe there is a universal trance of this kind. It is what I call the "Little-People/Big-People Delusion."

The Little-People/Big-People Delusion is not limited to particular cultures; it embraces them all. Because we are all subject to this trance, it is very difficult to identify it. Many of us spend our whole lives caught in its spell. Some of us become aware of the delusion and learn to free ourselves from its grip. But those who throw it off do so only with great effort. In fact, the process of overcoming the Little-People/Big-People Delusion is identical to attaining full realization as a human being.

The Delusion

When I was five years old, our family would occasionally have guests over in the evening for a visit and a game of cards. I would usually fall asleep half-way through the proceedings. I can remember periodically partly waking up and hearing the voices of the adults as they talked and laughed. Hearing those voices was a tremendously comforting thing for me. It gave me a sense of security, a feeling that all was right with the world. I could lie there and doze and do nothing, without a care. Everything was being looked after by those all-knowing, all-powerful big people.

Perhaps the deepest and most cherished hope of the human heart is that there is, after all, meaning in life. That somewhere it all makes sense and that things happen for a purpose. We ourselves don't have to know what that purpose is. As long as there is meaning, and as long as *somebody* knows that meaning and can make it all happen, we can feel safe. We can be confident about the future, free of worry. We can live as little people, dozing through our lives, secure in the knowledge that big people are looking after things. The fond hope for this kind of life is at the heart of the Little-People/Big-People delusion.

For the delusion to work we need to believe that there *are* big people. We must be able to identify them for ourselves and tell ourselves that they are there, all around us, keeping watch. It is this need to see big people everywhere that makes us invest big people qualities in very ordinary individuals. The boss, the teacher, the pastor, the doctor, the therapist, the mayor, the president, the royal family, the movie star, the scientist: all profit from this craving.

We even invest the dead with big people qualities. The sages and saints, the knights and heroes, the conquerors and emperors of yesteryear make comforting big people. We even go beyond the realm of humans to augment our list of big people. Alien creatures from other star systems occasionally drop in to check on us. Angels and spirit guides speak to us in our dreams and visions or deliver their messages through mediums and channellers. Devils, demons, and Satan himself are passionately involved in human affairs. Yes, even this is comforting, for if bad spirits and bad angels are so interested in our affairs, good ones must be, too. This whole scheme shows that we, in our frail human existence, are cared for, after all, and included in a greater plan worked out by the biggest people possible.

This brings us to the final, most powerful and all-knowing of the big people—God himself. I say God *himself* because I am speaking here not about the ultimate, indefinable divinity, but about the culturally constructed ultimate big person who, in our culture, at least, has been typically pictured as a kindly (or not so kindly) elderly male. He watches over us from on high, scrutinizing our every move, going through a gamut of emotional reactions to us as we muddle our way through our lives.

Living in Oz

In the movie *The Wizard of Oz,* a disturbing thing happens. When Dorothy and her friends first encounter the Wizard, he is a terrifying figure. All the children in the theatre cringe and grab their mothers' hands as they watch the fierce apparition. But then something *really* scary happens: the Wizard is revealed as nothing but a harmless old man manipulating some crude machines to make people afraid of him. This unveiling is intrinsically more disconcerting than the Wizard himself; it represents a revelation most of us spend our lives trying to avoid, that there are no big, powerful people ruling the world.

We want to believe in our Wizards, even if they scare the life out of us. For, scary or friendly, they show us that people, older, smarter, wiser, more powerful people, are running the show that we call life. These big people make us feel safe, make us feel looked after, understand everything, and, if they deigned to do so, could explain what our lives are about.

Our big people must have three qualities: they must have transcendent knowledge, they must have the power to control the world, and they must be watching over us and judging our actions, for good or ill. That way our big people make us feel safe, show us that our lives have purpose, demonstrate that the world has meaning, and guide us in knowing right from wrong.

The Little Person Stage

When I was nine years old, my father's mother passed away. I went to the funeral. Sitting in the church and listening to the service, I suddenly became acutely aware of what death was. It had never really come home to me before, and then, as I saw death in its starkness, I became afraid. I felt alone and very small in the face of its overwhelming reality. As the choir sang "The Lord Is My Shepherd" in doleful tones, I looked around the church and saw my maternal grandfather sitting there, quietly respectful. I immediately felt better. I had a tremendous admiration for this grandfather. He was a powerfully built, good-looking man highly respected in our small rural community. His physical strength and his unswerving honesty impressed me greatly. When I saw him at that moment in the church, I felt relieved. I clearly remember thinking to myself, "As long as Grandpa is around, everything is all right."

It was a very simple equation for me. While my grandfather lived, I did not really have to think about death. Its devastating inevitability was completely neutralized by the fact that this remarkable man existed in the world. It seemed to me that his mere presence defeated death. I was thankful that he, my "big person," was there to save my little self.

I suppose that no one would find fault with my escape from the contemplation of death. When we are growing up, there are many things that we cannot fully come to terms with, many things that we cannot fathom or control. We need to be able to trust that there are others who do have a handle on them, who do know the right answers, and who can make the proper decisions. In the early years, it is largely our parents to whom we ascribe this godlike quality. They are the big people who, by their very presence, make us feel that all is right with the world. As we grow up, others are vested with that aura of bigness. The teacher, the clergyman, the policeman: these are added to the list of know-it-alls.

Then, in adolescence, we start to delete names from that list. Usually our parents are the first to go. But what may seem like a teenage rampage of iconoclasm really turns out to be nothing of the sort. For while diligently removing names from one end of the list, the adolescent is busily adding them to the other. Among the newcomers may be rock stars, movie idols, radical political leaders, or outcast poets. In any case, there is no lack of big people to whom the adolescent can play the little-person role.

The Pseudo Big-Person Stage

There comes a point where we graduate from being just a little person to being a big person—or at least so we think. This happens when we discover that we know better than others what is good for them and feel ourselves in a position to tell them so. This can happen at any point as we mature. As we gradually assume positions of responsibility and power, we accept these new developments as a confirmation of our growing sense of bigness.

Our first encounters with imagining that we have superior wisdom and power start very early. The little girl knows what is best for her dolly, just as her mother knows what is best for her. The little boy orders his playmates around and defines the rules of their game, something he has learned from his parents, who have defined the rules of his life. Children are constantly playing at being "big" people, practising how to exercise their own domination over others later in life. And why wouldn't they? The role of the little person, as comforting as it is in so many ways, is downright uncomfortable in others. The sense of helplessness, subjugation, even humiliation that goes with being a little person is not a lot of fun. So playing the big person takes away some of the discomfort and provides a respite from the downside of being a little person.

As we enter adulthood as defined by our society, we begin to exercise, by the right given us by family and culture, the power of the big person. We play our "big person" to the "little person" of those we feel we can dominate. We truly begin to see ourselves as big people in those situations, and justify our power plays with the rationalizations society sets up—"Somebody has to be in charge;" "Position has its privileges;" "It's for their own good;" "A parent knows what is best;" "Without order the world would be in chaos;" "My expertise gives me the right." At the same time, the little people who are subject to us have their own rationalizations: "Who am I to question my parents? . . . the pastor? . . . the president? . . . the professional? . . . the expert?"

We play our big-person role as adults for the very same reason that we played it as children, to take away the sting of being a little person in relation to others. It is a painful thing to realize that each day you are subjugating yourself to your big people, that at work, in your family, in your social contacts, and in your engagement with the world at large you willingly place yourself in a one-down position, that in things great and small you choose to stifle your spirit in favour of the security of believing that bigger and better spirits than yours are taking care of things. If you can find someone to treat you the way you treat your big people, if you can entice an equally insecure little person to hold you in awe in some fashion or other, then you experience a momentary relief. And if your insecurity is great, if your belief in yourself is crushed, if your pain of subjugation is unbearable, then you will find as many little people as you possibly can to numb your awareness and anaesthetize your heart.

There is another way we sometimes use to try to save ourselves from the pain and humiliation that comes from seeing ourselves as little people, and it is not a pretty thing. It is by attempting to disable and destroy those we see in the big-person position. This is a continuation of the adolescent desire to throw off the little-person yoke, now pursued in more serious contexts. Here we find those who make an art of being "passive–aggressive," blocking productive action of imagined big people by *not* doing something that the big person depends upon them to do (the person who "forgets" to make a crucial call to one of the boss's clients). Here we find those who try to destroy the people they envy with gossip and calumny. Here we find the terrorists who set out to destroy the power of certain big people (although they do their work in the name of another set of big people). Here, too, we find those who literally take the lives of those people whom they see as big so they can steal for themselves something of their perceived greatness (those who murder rock stars, religious leaders, and politicians).

Entitlement

"I'm amazed to discover the ideas behind my attitudes," a client once said to me. "I get angry because my wife isn't perfect, because my children aren't perfect, because my body isn't that of a 17-year-old athlete, because my life isn't extraordinarily fascinating. I believe I am *entitled* to these things, and more. If I am not getting these things, to which I am entitled, then I am going to write a stiff letter of protest. To whom? To God. No—I think I have to go higher than that to get real satisfaction. I'll write to the person God reports to."

The feeling of entitlement can be crassly obvious or subtly disguised. A person whose job injury has inconvenienced him for a couple of weeks may feel entitled to 10 years of disability payments. The corporate thief may feel entitled to a small bit of the money of a fabulously wealthy conglomerate. The woman who has been an adequate wife and mother may feel entitled to the unending, worshipful devotion of her children. The man who has been reliable in his job may feel entitled to having all of his faults and abusive actions at home overlooked. People may truly believe they deserve these things, that by right or by nature they are entitled to them, and no argument can persuade them otherwise.

Feelings of entitlement grow out of a forgotten memory of a time when the person was indeed entitled to full appreciation, protection, and care—the period of infancy. It may be hard to admit that we secretly wish—even expect and demand—that the entitlement of infancy will last for the whole of our lifetimes. So we find all kinds of reasons to justify our entitlements. While those reasons may seem believable to us, they appear pretty silly to an objective onlooker.

Nicely ensconced within the feeling of entitlement is the Little-People/Big-People Delusion. If this feeling of entitlement continues beyond infancy and childhood, it is because there continue to be big parent-people who are supposed to look after our needs. The bigger those parent-people are, the easier we find it to maintain the feeling of entitlement. If the big parent-person is a wealthy corporation, then who could find fault with a claim to a small piece of its wealth? After all, they are so big that they would never miss it. If the big parent-person is the nation, this is even more undeniable. If the big parent-person is God, then we are surely justified in expecting him to come across with the goods and grant our most cherished wishes. After all, did Jesus not say that God knows when even the smallest sparrow falls?

People with deeply ingrained feelings of entitlement find it very hard to give up their ideas. Argument will not convince them, because they have thought up counter-arguments to the cleverest reasoning. Therapy will not convince them, because they usually do not persevere through that arduous journey. Even adversity will not convince them, because, for entitled people, adversity further entrenches their Little-People/Big-People Delusion and provides them with an endless supply of what they consider justifiable complaints. To the entitled person, remaining in the role of the little person is a very precious thing.

The Authoritarian Family

In families based on authority and structure, children are seen as extensions of their parents. The children may be praised and supported in their undertakings, but only insofar as they fulfil the aspirations of the parents and the "good" of the family. It is very difficult for parents in the authoritarian family to appreciate the creative accomplishments of the children, for their evaluations are based on how well their children have done what was expected of them. The *unexpected*, the creative, is difficult for the authoritarian parent to perceive, much less appreciate. The truly original is considered a threat; it goes beyond the given structure, and the authoritarian family owes its very existence to the preservation and enforcement of that structure. This state of affairs reinforces the Little-People/Big-People roles promoted in society at large. In the authoritarian family, the message is that children are little people, subject to the big parent. When children grow into adulthood, they become big people to their own little people children. But they remain little people forever in relation to their original parents. Every person is assumed to live out his or her life in the Little-People/Big-People framework.

The Nurturing Family

In the authoritarian family, permission is an essential part of life. It is taken for granted that children need permission for everything they do. Not to need permission for something is the exception. Permission is granted by the parent, and this validates any action of the child.

In the nurturing family, permission is the exception. The only ways that the parents hold authority over their children is in matters in which the children's actions may harm themselves or others, or in matters that affect the necessary order of daily living. In everything else, the child's actions are his or her own to determine. In the nurturing family, the child's originality and creativity are recognized and appreciated. The nurturing parent marvels at the individuality of thought and perspective of the child and promotes the child's originality in every way. This originality, this going beyond the given structure, is considered a great accomplishment. This contrasts with the authoritarian family, where it is seen as a great threat. In the nurturing family, the Little-People/Big-People Delusion is given little support. Adults who come from nurturing families find it easier to question that delusion in society at large and are less likely to be seduced by its enticements.

Our Big People

If I were to draw up a roster of our big people, the list would be endless. Being a little person to someone else's big person is a relative thing and can be found in every aspect of life. Nevertheless, there are some kinds of big people that we all seem to need:

We need our preachers, priests, and religious leaders to tell us
how to get close to God.
We need our parents, alive and well, to make us feel that we will
never die.
We need our counsellors to tell us what to do with our lives.
We need our psychics to tell us what decisions to make.
We need our movie stars to keep our dreams alive.
We need our royalty to make us feel we belong.
We need our doctors to tell us how to be well.
We need our bosses to tell us how to be productive workers.
We need our governments to tell us how to be good citizens.
We need our politicians to tell us how we can all live together.
We need our geniuses to tell us what creativity is.
We need our scientists to tell us what the truth is.

Yes, we need our big people. But we do not need them just to be the
promised fulfillment of our hopes and dreams, the omniscient gov-
ernors of our lives, the invincible protectors of our safety. We also
need our big people so that we have someone to blame. It is of the
essence of the Little-People/Big-People Delusion that, in the final
reckoning of things, we are not responsible for ourselves and our
lives. Instead, we have made the big people responsible. If they are
responsible for all the imagined good, they are also responsible for
all the imagined bad. When things go wrong, we are more than
ready to blame our big people and express indignation at their
falling down on the job. Our outcries range from cursing the dentist to cursing God. Yes, for a brief moment we allow ourselves the
luxury of cursing our big people and giving vent to our pent-up
frustration with life. Afterwards we are ashamed of our feelings and
take back our sinful doubts and reinstate the big people in their
original positions. Or else we replace the offending big person with
another, better-equipped big person, who will surely do a much
better job. We switch our dentist or we change our religion, and
then everything is better. Inside us, though, nothing at all has
changed. The Little-People/Big-People Delusion remains fully intact. We do not realize it, but all the qualities we ascribe to our big

people, all the hopes we project onto them, all the wisdom we seek in them, we could seek in ourselves. But to do that we would have to cross an enchanted boundary.

The Enchanted Boundary

The desire, the longing, the urgency to believe that there are big people in the world is very understandable. We want the reassurance that somebody understands this chaotic and unpredictable world, even if we do not. We want to know that things make sense, that life has meaning. The projection of this encompassing wisdom onto "big" people, however, turns out to be a miserable failure. Now and again we rip back the curtain and see that our Wizard is a human being like the rest of us and does not have the knowledge we have ascribed to him after all. We get angry and accuse him of fraud and manipulation. But, really, we have willingly set him up with his trappings; if we were honest we would blame ourselves.

But to deny that there are big and little people is not to deny any differences between people in terms of knowledge or skill; there are such distinctions and always will be. Differences of knowledge and skill in the world mean that we need each other and so depend on each other. It does not mean that one person stands in a position of intrinsic superiority over another, nor that one person has essential power over another, nor that one person can take responsibility for the life of another. We can all learn from each other, while we cannot give away to anyone else our duty to live our own lives and make our own decisions.

One of the most significant moments in one's personal evolution is discovering that the Little-People/Big-People view is a delusion. This is a truly liberating moment for us. From that point on we know that our lives are in our own hands. That moment represents stepping across an invisible boundary from a country in which we exist as children living in blind trust or fear into a country in which we are fully mature people. As we prepare to take that step, we sense that what we are about to do is momentous and that crossing the boundary will profoundly change us. The borderline we are about to cross seems like an enchanted boundary that will almost magically transform our lives. When at last we take that fateful step we are met with the undeniable certainty that there are no big people—there are only people. As soon as that realization hits us, we know that we can never go back, never cross that boundary again.

It may take some time to get our bearings on the other side of the line. Loss of the little person/big person mentality that has been so deeply entrenched in our lives leaves us feeling disoriented, perhaps fearful, for the new landscape is unfamiliar. Learning how to be in a world where we are all just people will take us some time.

Now that we do not look to others for answers, we feel a new kind of freedom. We no longer have to keep up a charade that, deep down, we always knew was false. We no longer have to pretend there is infallibility in the palpably fallible. On the other hand, we no longer need to sacrifice our intuition to the god of false authority, either.

Another immediate benefit of crossing the enchanted boundary is our ability to understand things more deeply. Now we can allow ourselves to ask questions that we could not before. Up to now, to question anything would be to doubt the big people. On the other side of the boundary, doubting was condemned as a sin against the holy spirit, the only unforgivable sin. Now we realize that that holy spirit is within us. We find that to doubt and question are natural and fun. A new excitement about learning bursts forth, because now we can learn for the sheer joy of it, not to prove some doctrine of the old faith. Now that we have crossed the enchanted boundary we cease to look outside ourselves for solace and began to look within. We have a new landscape to explore—that of our inner world—and we discover here the only true source of security. The font of true wisdom, we find, is not some wise big person, but our own inner selves.

Consolidation

Even though once we have crossed the enchanted boundary from the realm of the Little-People/Big-People Delusion we can no longer go back to that region, yet we must face a great deal of consolidation of our new position. As a matter of fact, the whole of the rest of our lives will consist in finding out how to incorporate our new state into life and relationships.

Something of the little-person mentality still remains in everyone who has given up the delusion. Even the person who is aware of the delusion must confront him- or herself constantly, probing for thinking that reflects the old delusion. This process of discovering and integrating the consequences of this great change is ongoing, a process that we never truly finish in this existence.

We will still have hankerings to be taken care of and want someone to give us the answers. Yet always in the background we will remain clearly aware that there is no foundation for such yearnings. Those who are fortunate find companions in their work of consolidation, other people who have themselves given up the Little-People/Big-People Delusion. They may find these fellow travellers among family members or friends, or in totally unforeseen places. In fact, those who cross the enchanted boundary discover some unexpected good news: When you discard the Little-People/Big-People Delusion, you come to realize that we are all interconnected in a way we cannot conceive within the delusion's framework. We all derive from one source and can rejoice in finding a ready-made kinship everywhere we look. I will say more about this in the final chapter.

So it is important to know that giving up little-people/big-people dependency does not mean giving up relationships. Relationships are very important, maybe more important than ever, to one who has crossed the boundary. Support, understanding, and love are what enabled us to cross the boundary in the first place, and they continue to be crucial in the process of consolidation that follows. To establish or maintain relationships that provide this must be a priority for the changed person; the alternative is a kind of loneliness of the most disorienting kind. While many relationships of this kind would be desirable, I believe that a person may count him- or herself lucky to have one or two companions on his or her new path.

The Grand Inquisitor

Not everyone is ready to cross the enchanted boundary. Not everyone is prepared to accept the freedom that is theirs by right. This is graphically portrayed in Ivan's story of the Grand Inquisitor in Fyodor Dostoyevsky's *The Brothers Karamazov.*[30] He posits that Jesus has returned to earth in Spain in the time of the Inquisition. Jesus is immediately recognized by the masses as he walks through the streets, healing people and raising the dead. However, when the wizened old Grand Inquisitor sees him and what he is doing, he immediately has him arrested and thrown into prison. Then the Grand Inquisitor comes to talk with him in his cell. The interview is really a confrontation between the encrusted and rigid group mind of the Church, represented by the Grand Inquisitor, and the Church's loving, charismatic leader and founder. As it turns out, the fossilized group mind wins, at least on the surface. For the Grand Inquisitor informs Jesus that he will have him burned the next day and that the very people who were bowing down to him and praising him as he walked through the streets will be the ones who heap embers on the fire.

The Grand Inquisitor points out to Jesus that when he lived on earth, he gave people freedom. The problem was that people did not want it. They wanted someone to tell them what to do. So although it took centuries, the Church was finally able to completely vanquish freedom. That was the only way to make people truly happy. For, says the Grand Inquisitor, human beings are born rebels, and it is simply impossible for a rebel to be content. By taking away their freedom, people once more enjoy the chance to be happy.

The Grand Inquisitor tells Jesus that he himself and the other present leaders of the Church are willing to suffer the pain of being free themselves for the sake of the people. The people don't want to be free; they want to be told what to do. The Church's leaders will give them the rules and prescriptions they seek: "They will marvel at us and worship us like gods, because, by becoming their masters, we have accepted the burden of freedom that they were too frightened to face, just because we have agreed to rule over them—that is how terrifying freedom will have become to them finally!"[31]

Jesus has badly misjudged human beings, says the Grand Inquisitor. He actually thought them capable of making their own decisions. This was far too much to expect of people. When the Church expropriated freedom from the individual, it made each person's life much easier, like that of a child. The Church's group mind reinforced that way of seeing things. The people came to accept that they were weak children, and as children they could enjoy the child's happiness. By huddling close to the powerful church, like chicks to a hen, they would feel safe. Their leaders would force them to work, and then magnanimously grant them time to rest, for which they would feel grateful. The Church would allow them to sin, as long as they sought permission for their sin so that it would not be held against them. The Church would tell them what to do in every circumstance, and provide them with the security of knowing for certain whether they were doing right or wrong. When Jesus brought men freedom, he brought them a curse, says the Grand Inquisitor. Fortunately, the Church has succeeded in correcting Jesus's work, and people no longer operate under that burden.

In this vignette, Dostoyevsky brilliantly describes the dilemma that people face in contemplating whether to cross the enchanted boundary. They know that if they take that fateful step they will have to give up their craving to be told what to do and how to think. For many, that is simply too great a sacrifice to make. They remain in their trap, bowing to those pseudo-big people who are only too ready to take on the burden of their freedom.

Dostoyevsky fittingly places the dilemma of the enchanted boundary in religious context, in the confrontation between inner spiritual freedom and outer religious constraints. I believe that the struggle with the Little-People/Big-People Delusion will eventually lead to our encounter with the transcendent; in the end the search for oneself becomes the search for God.

Seeking God

To see yourself as other than a little person, you must believe in yourself. If you do not believe in yourself, you will of necessity be driven to find someone else to believe in; you will want to put your life into the hands of those imagined big people. You will beg them to tell you what to do. You may disguise your begging. It may take the form of delegating the responsibility for your physical well-being to a doctor who is, after all, supposed to know more about your health than you do. Or it may take the form of becoming physically or emotionally ill and unable to take care of yourself so that you have to be looked after by some group or institution, which, after all, is set up to see to these things. Or you may join the army or a cult or a religious organization or some other regimented group, which, after all, carries out an important function in our society. Or you may study and work hard to make yourself a part of a corporation or academic staff or medical team or some respected project, which, after all, elevates the quality of life in our society. Or you may become part of some socio-political movement or cause that allows you to lose yourself in something "larger than yourself," which, after all, is a noble thing to do. Or you may seek advice from a spiritual counsellor or guru, who, after all, is closer to God than you are.

There are a million ways to carry on being a little person and feel quite all right about it. There are a million ways to avoid the challenge of learning to believe in yourself. The desire to be told what to do, feel, and think can be met in many fashions and many contexts. And they all involve giving your power to someone else and not having faith in yourself.

What is this self of mine that I am supposed to have faith in? When I look at myself as revealed in what I think and feel and do, I may not be all that impressed. I do not have the solution for a lot of problems. I do not know how to do many things. My stamina flags. My feelings are erratic. My ideas and ideals change from day to day, even from moment to moment. Is this the self I am supposed to have faith in?

We want to put our faith in something certain, something reliable, something that will come through when we need it, something that deserves our trust. Traditionally that something or someone is God. So is that the answer? Is it a matter of not putting our faith in anything human, either an outside person or our own selves?

If that is the answer, I am afraid it is not a very satisfying one. It doesn't tell us very much or guide us very far. After all, what or who is God? The myriad churches, cults, religious movements, prophets, gurus, guides, and spiritual books give us a bewildering array of conflicting answers. Not only are there many different conceptions of God; there are at least as many notions of where to look for him, where to hear his word, where to find his representatives.

The books and writings that represent God say many different things about where he is to be found. The prophets and leaders that claim to speak for God present us with a confusing babble of ideas. The groups that claim to practise the true worship of God confuse and confound us. And because these writings, people, and groups contain so many incompatibilities, they vilify each other, go to war with each other, and even kill each other.

Because of our human limitations, we never find God. We find only manifestations of God. Each manifestation is fraught with contradictions and incompleteness. If we take these manifestations for God himself, we fall into what has traditionally been called idolatry. Idolatry is inevitable when we seek God in the outer world.

Whenever you seek God *outside yourself,* you are caught in the final, most subtle, and most crippling form of the Little-People/Big-People Delusion. You create your big person after your own image and then worship him. You do not realize that the outer world can provide only a shadowy experience of God, and that the truest experience of God takes place within. I do not mean to say in some simplistic way that you, with all your limitations, are God. That would indeed be a poverty-stricken view of the divine, a pitiful idolatry. What I mean is that the clearest manifestation of God can be found in your own experience of your own existence. Your own being is your gateway to the cosmic and the divine.

Beyond the Delusion

Living within the Little-People/Big-People Delusion, we believe that all our worthwhile knowledge comes from outside ourselves, from the big people. We beg them to give us the answers about the meaning of life. Frozen in this outward gaze, we are incapable of looking within to the only true and reliable wisdom. Although preachers, prophets, and religious institutions have their place in the human search for meaning, they cannot replace personal experience. After all the sermons have been preached, after all the prophecies have been uttered, after all the religious institutions have spoken, after all the holy books of the world have been read, each person remains alone on his or her quest. And although we learn our ideas through interaction with the human community and although we depend on the encouragement and support of our personal relationships to persevere in the search, the pursuit nonetheless remains in the end a solitary one. No one can be born for you and no one can die for you: there are some things you simply have to do for yourself. One of them is discovering your ultimate self and, in the end, God within you.

trance zero: faith

"Some people hear their own inner voices with great clearness, and they live by what they hear. Such people become crazy, or they become legends."
  — *Legends of the Fall,* the movie, 1995

Trance as Limitation of Human Experience

I OPENED THIS BOOK by saying that human experience is a web, an interweaving of trance states, a complex tapestry wherein trances nest within trances. The definition of trance as a profound state of absorption and abstraction applies perfectly to every experience we have, every minute of the day. All of our experiences involve some kind of absorption, some concentration, some engagement. And to the extent that they do, they also involve some abstraction, some obliviousness, some unawareness. In other words, human life is a trance-bound life.

This is the same as saying that all human experiences by their very nature involve limitation. We are incapable of having an experience that is not in some way or other limited. If I am aware of writing at my computer at this moment, I cannot at the same moment and in the same mental act be aware of all the previous experiences of my life, all my present involvements and relationships, all my hopes and worries, all my future aspirations, to say nothing of the myriad of sensations and stimuli reaching me every second and filtered out by the censoring mechanisms fortunately at work in my nervous system. From this point of view, my writing at the computer at this moment is not simply limited, it is *severely* limited.

My writing trance exemplifies the limitation that applies to all human experience. Trance, by definition, applies to every experience, and trance by definition means limitation.

Keeping Track

So the problem with trances is not what we are aware of, what we are absorbed in. Rather it is what we are *not* aware of, what we are oblivious to. The problem with trances is that they involve limitation.

On that spring day it was all very well for me to be absorbed in my thoughts about what I wanted to put in my new book (Chapter 1), but I was missing the pleasure of my walk as a result. Gail would have been able much better to avoid the abuse from her counsellor (Chapter 2) if, while she was with him, she could have maintained her awareness of what she was learning about that situation in her therapy sessions. It is fine for a Unification Church member to concentrate on the lecture by Moon, so long as other awarenesses allow that person to evaluate critically what Moon says. The workaholic does well for his business through his single-minded devotion, yet cannot simultaneously consider his family's needs and respond to them.

Trance is everywhere in life. At any moment we both know and do not know. We know what we are absorbed in and we do not know what we are abstracted from. We take this for granted. We do not demand of ourselves that we be aware of everything at once. We do not demand that we figure out what groceries we need while taking an exam. We do not insist that we be aware of our financial obligations while making love. We do not even expect ourselves to be keenly aware of a friend's faults while delivering his eulogy. We have a division of thought, much like a division of labour, that allows us to live and act without confusion, without distraction, without complicating things.

The trouble with the situation is that in reality things *are* complex. If we see only one aspect of reality at any moment, we can make significant misjudgments, which could lead to big mistakes. It is much better for me if, while going over a proposed lease, I am aware of my own sense of a deceitfulness and untrustworthiness in my prospective landlord. Concentrating on the details of the agreement may not be enough to warn me off from signing a disastrous agreement. There is value in my being able, when at work, to maintain my own views in the face of gossip being spread about a co-worker, for if I give myself over completely to the workplace group mind, I may do that person a real injustice. A mother must not let her conversation with a friend blot out her awareness of what is happening with her toddler in an adjoining room. In these situations, it is fortunate that we can be aware of two things at the same time.

Multiple Channels

So although the ability to concentrate totally is of supreme importance in some situations, the ability to move with agility from one awareness to another is essential in others. Doris, a friend of mine, once described to me her experience as a mother of young children. When her children were two and four years old, the circumstances of her life were extremely chaotic, and she spent much of her time in a state of confusion and worry. But whenever she walked into the children's room to feed them or otherwise look after them, she found her state of mind changed radically. She felt herself becoming calm, competent, and attentive. For those moments, her children were her only concern, and it was as though everything else had disappeared. Doris felt as though she assumed a new identity when she walked through that doorway, became a different person, the one the children needed. Put another way, one could say that, on coming into the presence of her children, Doris entered a powerful relational trance within which she could call upon resources that only moments earlier were beyond her reach.

Doris described a period later in her life when, as a psychotherapist, she experienced similar transformations in connection with her clients. She might wake up in a depressed mood in the morning or have a particularly distressing experience during the day, yet her state would completely alter when she walked into her office to begin a psychotherapy session with a client. Her previous mood would be wiped out and she would find herself immersed in a completely focused state. She did some of her best work in those conditions. This ability to switch from one mental state to another is very important if we are to maintain the flexibility we need in order to fulfill what is required of us in life. Although we may not know how we do it, most of us can switch trances and call upon whatever capacities we need in new situations.

In addition to being able to bring about successive trance states, we also seem to have the ability to open up and operate from two channels of awareness simultaneously. This kind of dual or multiple consciousness exists as a part of normal life. The driver preoccupied with a personal problem during his drive home does this. He seems to function from two streams of consciousness at the same time. One drives the car, makes the necessary judgments, and initiates the proper actions for a safe trip. At the same time, his other stream of consciousness is deeply immersed in thoughts about the problem. Some people find their best solutions in just such situations. Apparently, this division of consciousness allows each stream to operate competently and creatively.

While we often do well with dual consciousness, we do not seem to be as good at managing simultaneous *multiple* streams. If the driver attempting some internal problem solving also has to be aware of what is going on with her two children in the back seat, the whole system may break down. As she switches from one awareness to the other, her concentration on each activity is weakened. Often enough, she will end up insisting that the children be quieter than usual because she is afraid of losing the focus she needs to drive safely.

Even though in daily life we may tend to be quite limited in our ability to operate effectively from multiple streams of consciousness, the human psyche may have a greater capacity to do this than we might expect. On the level of the inner mind, we can run any number of streams at the same time. This capacity is not much evident in our daily lives, however, because our awareness of the doings of our inner mind is quite limited. We are much better acquainted with our outer mind.

Multiple Levels of Consciousness

Experiments done more than a hundred years ago show that we can maintain multiple levels of consciousness in the inner mind and keep track of several layers of information şimultaneously. These levels can be separated one from another, so that one level does not know of the activities of the other. This ability of the psyche is graphically demonstrated in multiple-personality disorder (dissociative-identity disorder) in which the person maintains several separate identities, each capable of operating simultaneously with the rest. The person experiences each of the identities as separate from the others and consistent within itself as it thinks its thoughts.

The Ultimate Self

What has been written in this book unquestionably testifies to trance as limitation. Moving from focus to focus defines our life in this world, and the dominance of outer mind concerns in daily life demonstrates that we spend most of our time out of direct contact with our considerable inner resources. But is there perhaps more to it than that?

If in its very essence human experience is piecemeal and limited, how do we get along in the world as well as we do? How are we able to carry on adequately if we never at any particular moment get an overall sense of the whole, of who we are, and what our lives are about? If in healthy lives the outer mind dominates, even though a tremendous amount of subconscious, inner-mind activity takes place at the same time, how are we able to navigate life's complex course without constantly blundering? How can we take into account all that subliminal communication and all that inner-mind activity if they are given such short shrift on the ordinary conscious level of our lives? Also, the human mind's mysterious ability to operate on many mental tracks at once does not derive from the operations of the ordinary consciousness. As I mentioned above, the outer mind, geared to handle the affairs of everyday life, tends to bog down when faced with distractions. So how do we ever succeed in managing the multiple tracks of mental activity that seem to be a normal part of human existence?

The answer is that we have an inner unifying principle, a faculty that directs and guides us as we live out our existences. But if we have a faculty that can co-ordinate our lives, we have no objective experience of it. We cannot stand in the place of that co-ordinating principle and know it from there. If such a thing exists, it has to be something outside ordinary awareness, something in the inner world of the psyche. I believe we do possess this unknown capacity, for without it, not only would our lives lose all direction and meaning, but we could not function at all. The way we operate in the world only makes sense if there is a unifying, co-ordinating factor at work.

Let me emphasize this. The notion of a co-ordinating principle beyond our direct perception is postulated not merely as the result of a spiritual understanding of human existence; it is also required to explain the common facts of everyday life.

The concept of an intelligent unifying principle has been posited by a number of disciplines from a variety of perspectives. Philosophers have developed various versions of this factor. For 250 years the greatest thinkers have struggled with the fact that there seem to be mental processes occurring outside our awareness that nonetheless affect our conscious thinking and behaviour. Some have held that those processes arise from a central intelligence, within human beings yet unknown to them, and not subject to the limitations of a person's ordinary consciousness.

Some have identified this faculty with "nature" and have believed that as nature operates through the human mind, it manifests a wisdom that far exceeds conscious thinking. Many have recognized this wisdom also in dreams, poetry, and fairy tales, which were thought to be channels through which nature reveals itself without the censorship imposed on our conscious ideas.

The mesmerists, who practised a healing art called "animal magnetism," believed that within every person lies a deep, reliable knowledge about what is good for him and what will contribute to his healing. Puységur (Chapter 4) was the first magnetizer to write about his conviction that the trance state made it possible to tap this inner font of wisdom. He held that while a person is somnambulistic (in a deep inner-mind trance), his personality alters notably and he demonstrates an understanding of nature and life unavailable to his normal consciousness. Although Puységur never attempted to explain where this extraordinary intelligence comes from, he had no doubt of its existence.

Toward the end of the nineteenth century, psychologists were trying to deal with evidence of the presence of an inner co-ordinating mental faculty. Pierre Janet's study of hysterics led him to posit the existence of subconscious mental activity operating on many levels simultaneously with conscious thinking. He held that on the deepest level of subconscious thought, there is "perfect somnambulism," or complete awareness of everything the person knows. On the level of ordinary consciousness, however, the person comprehends only a fraction of this knowledge. Although Janet believed that his findings applied only to those who were mentally pathological, F. W. H. Myers posited a "subliminal self," common to *all* human beings, which included everything Janet had talked about and more. Myers believed that the subliminal self was the repository not merely of unresolved psychological conflicts, but also of the greatest powers human beings manifest. Specifically, he found there the source of all inspirations of genius. Pointing out that many of the finest artists describe their creative experiences as the sudden awareness of the whole creative product—the story, the painting, the musical composition—without any knowledge of

having participated in its creation, Myers believed that the subliminal self communes with a kind of cosmic wisdom that gives freely of
its creative power.

Sigmund Freud posited a region of mental activity in the psyche
that is basically unconscious. We can become aware of it if we turn
the searchlight of our conscious mind on it. Freud saw the Unconscious as the realm of instinctual urges, repressed memories, and
psychological defences. He saw its co-ordinating function as resulting principally from an attempt to arrive at an equilibrium between
forbidden unconscious impulses and the demands of the ego.

Carl Jung, on the other hand, posited a mysterious Self that
transcends a person's ordinary consciousness and operates from the
accumulated wisdom of the collective unconscious.

The spiritual philosophies of Buddhism, Hinduism, and Sufism
teach that it is the divine itself that manifests in human beings and
guides them on their life paths.

New Age health practitioners talk about an inner healer that has
all the knowledge and wisdom that a person needs to heal him- or
herself both physically and emotionally.

Hypnotherapists, such as Milton Erickson, look upon the unconscious mind as a source of accumulated learning that can guide
a troubled person through confusions and correct both physical
and mental problems.

Why has an inner, co-ordinating, intelligent but evasive centre
been postulated by so many people who arrive at such a conclusion
from so many different starting points? When you read the literature that contains these speculations, it becomes clear that the conclusion has been reached because it was considered necessary to
explain human experience, to account for the unity, co-ordination,
and wisdom that are obviously there. Some of these historical attempts to define that principle have been partial, because they were
often trying to account for only one or the other aspect of human
experience. I would like to talk about a principle that covers all
aspects.

The names chosen to designate an inner unifying principle have
been many. In my book *Multiple Man,* I refer to an overriding

co-ordinating centre and call it the "Ultimate Self." Since writing that book, I have been trying to come up with a better term, without success. So I will continue to call it the Ultimate Self and define it as a transcendent centre, present in all people, which is the intelligent source of unity and life function and which a person can never objectively know. The Ultimate Self is known only subjectively, being the "I" behind, or beyond, all the "I's" that we experience, the indescribable core that is the ultimate thinker of all our thoughts and doer of all our deeds, the ultimate co-ordinator of all psychic events, and the ultimate agent of all healing in us.

How We Know About the Ultimate Self

Some years ago, I got a graduate degree in philosophy, specializing in two areas. One was medieval philosophy, which, in most of its forms, holds that we can solve the riddle of existence through reason supplemented by faith. The other area was the philosophy of science, which, among other things, deals with uncritical claims that we can solve the riddle of existence through science. Now, there is no doubt that I was interested in solving the riddle of existence. But it quickly became clear to me that neither reason nor science could do the job.

The dissatisfaction that I felt owed to the fact that neither reason nor science touches on personal experience. I was not really convinced by anything unless there was some way that I could connect it to my own experience. St. Thomas Aquinas' proofs for the existence of God, for instance, were masterpieces of reason. But they left me unmoved and certainly did not inspire the type of conviction I could build a life on. On the other hand, reductionist explanations of the nature of reality deriving from physics and related sciences I found equally unappealing. Examining the nature of scientific explanation shows that nothing is really explained at all; scientific theories always remain one step removed from concrete reality and can never bridge the gap. Besides, there is a whole universe of reality that science cannot even enter—that of subjective experience. Science is based on objective observation, the kind of thing that involves measurement and that can be replicated by anyone anywhere. Subjective experience is entirely different. It forms a category of knowledge entirely distinct from the objective. There is no way that objective knowledge can measure or describe the intrinsic nature of my elation at the discovery of a new idea or my love for my family. It can use objective observation to make statements about what happens to me when I say I am experiencing those things. It can measure my pulse and respirations as I experience those feelings; it can observe the alteration in cellular activity in my body; it can analyse the neurotransmitters released in my brain and measure my brain waves.

But none of these observations in any way touches on my actual subjective experience as I experience it. That remains a singular and ineffable fact beyond measurement. The closest anyone can come to understanding my subjective life would be if someone were to draw an analogy to subjective experiences of his own that he thinks are probably similar. So the more I got to know about the nature of human experience and the actual limitations of scientific knowledge, the more I knew I could never be satisfied with that kind of knowledge alone.

In this I don't think I am unusual. Most of us are impressed by experience and little affected by theories. The immediacy of experience can create a sense of undeniable truth in us. Theories never do that. No matter how high one piles evidence in support of a theory, one can never attain that sense of undeniable truth. No matter how thick the dossier of the experiences of *others* concerning the truth of some idea, doubt will remain. Personal experience alone convinces us, and it is to personal experience that I now turn.

How do we know that there is more to us than shows up in objective observations? How do we know that there is something in us that transcends the limitations of our conscious knowledge and intentions? We know through experience. That experience may come in the form of a stunning revelation arising from a mystical experience, or it may come in little happenings that we recognize as arising from something beyond us. Since the majority of us probably do not have frequent access to the experience of mystical consciousness, let me say something about that sense of something "beyond." I can come at this from my own experience only, since I have no direct knowledge of any other.

When I was a young man I was plagued by the suspicion that life was, after all, meaningless. As a member of our modern Western culture, and as a physics and math major in university, I was impressed by the findings of science and feared that what the public spokespeople of the scientific world were saying might be true: that science was the full and comprehensive study of all that exists; that meaning is a delusion; that the spiritual is a fantasy; and that human experiences such as knowing and loving are mere rearrangements of particles of matter (which, in the end, are simply wisps of energy).

But then something happened. I decided that instead of poring over the books that explain the elementary structure of matter and the chemistry of my brain, I would pay attention to my own personal experience. What I discovered was both surprising and elating. I discovered that when I experienced myself as a centre of thought and action, my perspective radically altered. There was no way that my experience of knowing, for instance, could be explained as pouring sand in a bottle, to put it crudely, or, less crudely, the electrochemical exchanges in my grey matter.

Rearrangement of my bodily composition told me nothing about the fact that there is an "I" that knows. This "I" is an irreducible given fact that cannot be explained in terms of anything else. As I continued with my examination of my subjective experience, I learned that what I sometimes think defines my "I" clearly does not do so at all. I might say that "I" am a man or a husband or a teacher or a philosopher or a writer or a vacation-taker or a movie-watcher or an angry person or a neurotic or a psychotic, or anything else I might want. These aspects may be thought of as my socially constructed selves, but none of them describes the essence of the "I." All of these qualities are quite irrelevant to the experience of being a centre of thought and will and action. It would make absolutely no difference whatsoever to my being an "I" if I were *not* a man or a husband or a teacher or a psychotic. I would still have the experience of being a centre of thought, will, and action.

My life is made up of episodes. Situations come and go. Experience follows experience. In the process I change and grow. It is my "I" that remains constant as episodes occur. That "I" would be there no matter what the episodes. The experiences could be anything. No matter what I go through, something stands unchanging throughout. That is the irreducible experiencer itself, the "I."

The phases of life come and go. I am a child—unformed, innocent, curious, open to learning. I am an adolescent—eager, probing, questioning, striving for an identity, learning how to behave and connect in adult ways. I am a young man—building a life, creating opportunities to establish myself, learning how to interact with those who are a part of the stable world I want to be a part of. I am an older man—investigating how to live after those building years, seeing things from a more mature perspective, looking for the deeper meaning of life, aware that my life will end. I am an old man—realizing that life is drawing to a close, reckoning up the life I have lived, taking stock of the legacy I will leave, meditating on the insights I have attained and the values I have formed. Throughout these tremendous changes, throughout all the doubts, failures and successes, there is an "I" who has persevered. It makes no difference what my life has been—it has been mine and mine alone. I, who was born into the world, am still here. That "I" is not the product of this life but a centre of subjective existence that makes the notion of "a life" possible.

From all of this it became clear to me that this "I" of mine cannot be assigned qualities, such as strong or weak or fearful or brave or adventurous or anything else. These qualities may belong to me, it is true, but whether they are absent or present the "I" remains the same. Having these qualities does not change the "I." This made clear to me that the "I" that I am is indescribable. It is a pure subject and can never be the object of observation. Even I cannot observe my "I." I can only know it subjectively, as a subject. If I think I know it as an object, I am mistaken: when I examine any quality that I attribute to it as an object, I realize that I am not describing anything of its essence. I am merely describing some aspect of my personality, not my "I." This final subject, this unobservable "I," is what I call the Ultimate Self.

So what about me as a man or a husband or a teacher or a philosopher or a writer or a vacation-taker or a movie-watcher or an angry preson or a neurotic or a psychotic? What about this multiplicity of states, capacities, attitudes, moods, and preoccupations of which we are all capable? Before taking this discussion further, I would like to refer to something I said about this matter in my book *Multiple Man*.

Human beings are sometimes characterized as tool-making animals. We differ from other animals in that the whole of our practical lives seems to centre around the invention and use of tools. I believe that we can extend this predilection for tool-making to the psychological realm and say that the whole of our *mental/emotional* lives centres around the invention and use of those tools that we call "personalities." By "personality" I mean a complex of psychological characteristics that has a completeness and cohesion. My personality-tools are created in social situations and are geared to enhance my social interaction. By this definition I might say that within my social context I create the personality-tools through which I am a father, a teacher, a philosopher, and so on. This garden variety of multiplicity is an aspect of life we tend to take for granted. We all know we can change—sometimes radically—as situations dictate. We also know that none of these personality-tools exhausts my potentials nor totally defines who I am. These personality tools, these socially constructed selves, are all partial manifestations of me. None of them embraces the whole of my essence.

In *Mysteries* Colin Wilson talks about a "ladder of selves" that demonstrates an order among our various personality-tools.[32] The ladder's sides slant, far apart at the bottom and converging at the top. On the wide lower rungs are our lower selves, characterized by feelings of diffusion, lack of focus, and low intensity. As you move up the ladder, the rungs narrow and the selves located there are characterized by greater concentration. These higher selves show a greater intensity and more of a feeling of being alive. Moving up the ladder, through higher and higher selves, the sides of the ladder eventually meet at a point—what Wilson calls the "real me." He says that the "real me" cannot be identified with any of the selves, even the highest. I believe that Wilson's "real me" is what I call the Ultimate Self. While the higher selves or centres may control certain functions and co-ordinate certain important operations—such as those involved with physical/emotional/mental healing, a self we might call the Inner Healer—and may be to a certain extent described and known, the Ultimate Self remains unknowable.

The Ultimate Self is my centre of knowledge, will, and action. It is also the source of all that I am, including my physical/ organic/emotional being. All of these things belong to my Ultimate Self, but are not what it is. They are a part of my personality, and that is the difference between my personality and my Ultimate Self. Perhaps the best way to express this idea would be to say that all of these things are expressions or utterances of my Ultimate Self.

Since I first realized I had an Ultimate Self, I have many times been aware of a kind of dual experience of self. Usually when saying "I," I simply mean myself as I experience myself in an everyday way, with all of my limitations. But every once in a while I suddenly realize that when I say "I," I just as truly speak as my Ultimate Self. This is a rather stunning experience. I haven't quite been able to get used to it. It is one thing to think about the matter abstractly; it is quite another to experience its reality directly and palpably. The sense of actually being, here and now, my Ultimate Self is accompanied by an indescribable feeling of contact with something beyond space and time and beyond limitation, something that is personal, so personal that it is what I mean when I say I am a person.

"Who" is it, then, that lives my life? I can say with confidence that *I* live my life, but what does "I" mean in this context? The "I" that I ordinarily think of as me, the "I" of everyday life with its personal characteristics and limited awarenesses: this ordinary "I" lives my life. But to a large extent this ordinary "I" does not feel very much in charge of that life. The limitations on the knowledge this ordinary "I" has and the limitations on its control of life events, and even of itself, make the statement "I live my life" seem true only in part. That is why one sometimes hears the lament, "I don't seem so much to live my life as to be lived by it."

So who really does live my life? When I say "I live my life," and mean my ordinary "I," I am surely not wrong. But in the truest sense, my Ultimate Self is what lives my life. It alone has complete knowledge and complete control. And the Ultimate Self is, in the end, the one that determines what my life is to be.

What are the intentions of my Ultimate Self? What is its motivation? I believe that because of our limited knowledge, we cannot grasp the ultimate picture of existence. I think we can only guess at such matters, arriving by analogy at motivations that I, the ordinary "I," would have. Whatever my Ultimate Self might plan and accomplish through my life remains a matter of shaky speculation. This is true to some degree because it seems that the Ultimate Self exists apart from space and time as we know it. Space and time are categories that we use in the objective aspect of our existence. There does not seem to be any reason to associate space and time with the subject, with the Ultimate Self. If this is true, the motivation and goals that define our objective existence may not be a very solid indication of the motivation or goals of our subjective existence. While we may find some kind of consolation through imagining how things work for the Ultimate Self, we also have to keep in mind that we may be way off in our speculations.

Higher Selves

Like Colin Wilson, I believe that there is a kind of ladder of selves that controls and co-ordinates higher and higher aspects of our functioning through our lives in this world. There may be, for instance, an Inner Healer that restores us physically and psychologically. These higher selves are centres of intelligence that we can talk with as we might talk with any intelligent being. When Milton Erickson, for instance, asks his client's "unconscious mind" to cure a lifelong menstrual problem by having a dream about it, he is probably appealing to just such a higher centre.[33] When the menstrual problem is cured, we have to say that his appeal was successful.

I find something similar in my own psychotherapy work. For a long time now I have known that it is not I who heals my psychotherapy clients; rather, they heal themselves in the context of our work together. This means that I rely on an intelligent interior faculty which, for want of a better name, might be called my client's Inner Healer. This Inner Healer 1) has a sure and reliable knowledge of what is needed for this particular person's healing at any particular moment, 2) has the ability to bring about that healing, and 3) is accessible for the therapeutic process. My client's Inner Healer guides me much more than I guide my client. One of the most important aspects of psychotherapy, therefore, becomes watching for what the Inner Healer indicates is needed at each step along the way, and being ready to put aside any preconceived ideas of my own about how this person should be cured. Often my client has pointed out to me what was needed next in the therapy when I myself was at a loss to know what to do. Frequently the solution comes from the client without any identifiable reasoning process on his or her part. Many times I have been surprised to discover that my client has taken a big step forward in the healing process when I was neither expecting it, nor able to account for it. Often I have been extremely thankful to know that when clients were in suicidal or self-damaging states, they had an inner drive to live that got them through, when my ability to help them was very limited. To me, these are indications of the presence of a wise, benevolent, and powerful Inner Healer. For me this Inner Healer is what ultimately makes psychotherapy possible.

If it is true that we have higher centres or higher selves at work within us, the question naturally arises: How can we enlist their help for our betterment? This has been the subject of hundreds of self-help books, treatises on mental or spiritual healing, and essays on spiritual philosophy. There is much practical knowledge to be gained from these manuals. The good thing about most of them is precisely that the approach is practical; they aim for results. Their speculations about these higher centres arise from an attempt to engage the inner mind in dialogue in such a way as to bring about change and healing. Whether the description of the healing power that is mobilized is accurate or even adequate is quite secondary. What counts is what works.

That is not to say that it is not important to find out all we can about the more intrinsic nature of these higher centres. Our need to know about these things is archetypal and urgent within us.

Faith

Faith means believing in something you cannot see or prove. Believing in something also means trusting in that something, putting yourself into its hands.

Each of us needs faith in our Ultimate Self. Although I cannot see it or offer a proof of its existence, I know intuitively that it is there, behind the scenes, the final source of all that I am. I can also trust in my Ultimate Self, because it is at bottom my own essence and must desire my own ultimate good. I am, in my varying states and multitude of experiences, the expression of my Ultimate Self. Even though I do not, in my narrowed consciousness, understand where those states and experiences are leading me, I know that they have a purpose and that there is a plan. I don't have to worry that some higher power on which I depend has forgotten me or misunderstood me or is using me for some purpose other than my own good. That is impossible, since I am the living and constantly connected expression of my own deepest essence, my Ultimate Self.

If I experience suffering or confusion in my life, I can be sure that deep inside me it all makes sense; for if I have an Ultimate Self it is impossible to think that I am at odds with it, and it is impossible to think that my life is meaningless. If I don't understand the meaning, it is because my understanding is limited in my present existence. I have faith that in my Ultimate Self I know very well what it is all about.

Faith in my Ultimate Self gives me a new perspective on the "I" that I experience in the course of my everyday life. Faith banishes the fear and anxiety produced by my limited perspective. This limited "I," this self that is called "me," is *the point at which the Ultimate Self manifests in the world.* This is the only true way to regard myself, the only viewpoint that describes the true state of affairs. Looking at it this way, I respect myself as Ultimate Self manifesting at this point in space and time, while I also acknowledge the fact that this manifestation is limited, partial, imperfect. At the same time, I realize that I have an important task to undertake during the limited existence of this manifestation: to be aware of my true and Ultimate Self, and to work to manifest it better in the world.

Faith in my Ultimate Self forms the basis for my feeling of confidence about life. Faith in my Ultimate Self and my higher selves or centres is the basis for my conviction that there are unity and direction in my daily life. If, beyond and outside my conscious awareness, my higher centres co-ordinate my vital physical/mental/emotional functioning, and if, finally, these higher centres are an expression of my Ultimate Self, then I can feel confident that everything is working together to bring my life into being. This rock-bottom sense of unity is the basis for what I call Trance Zero.

Trance Zero

Trance Zero is based on my notion of trance as a state of profound absorption and abstraction. Trance Zero is the state of being absorbed in whatever is appropriate at the moment, but with a readiness and ability to shift to another focus naturally as needed. Trance Zero is only possible if somewhere there exists an awareness of the whole picture, of all the possibilities, both inner and outer. From this emerges an awareness of where to focus next.

This awareness and judgment cannot emanate from the outer mind. There is no evidence that the outer mind is or ever could be capable of transcendent knowledge of this kind. Instead, we must assume that the awareness and judgment are located in our inner mind, specifically in our higher selves—and, when all is said and done, in the Ultimate Self. My higher selves have access to all inner centres of consciousness and all inner states. One might also say that they have access to a broader awareness of all reality and the collective wisdom of the race and the cosmos.

In Trance Zero, the awarenesses that develop and the decisions that are made remain unconscious and unknown to the outer mind or normal consciousness. They must remain that way. The outer mind has its work to do and would be totally distracted if it had access to such material. This means that in this life, we can never gain full access to our higher selves and, of course, to our Ultimate Self. In this life, the outer mind always exercises a certain dominance over the time and energy of a person. This dominance is set up by nature and is necessary for our successful functioning in the everyday world. We have to accept this limitation of our conscious awareness. In Trance Zero we have to be willing to be guided without knowing.

In life we move from trance to trance, from focus to focus. This roving of attention can be random and chaotic, or it can be coordinated and meaningful. At the point that our higher centres completely oversee this process, we have attained the state of Trance Zero. At that point our intuitive awareness operates freely and fully, guiding our every action, even in the smallest details of daily life. Our life is overseen by an inner wisdom that we can never explain, yet in which we can place complete confidence.

Trance Zero involves faith, because we cannot directly perceive our higher centres and we cannot easily communicate with them. The most our conscious minds can establish is a fragile connection with these higher centres. As I mentioned, attempts at communicating with them are the subject of self-help manuals, books on healing, hypnotherapy, visualization, meditation, spirit guides, and the like. Success at connecting with our higher centres by using the suggested techniques varies greatly. The problem is that because we are all so different and because the circumstances of our lives are equally diverse, any general instructions are bound to be defective. This is why so many people eventually become disillusioned with life-improvement manuals. Even when people work with experienced counsellors and guides who treat them as individuals, they still achieve a relatively low level of success. For most of us, establishing links with our higher selves is a long, arduous process, constantly interrupted by the practical necessity of our involvements with the outer world.

Communication with our Ultimate Self is another matter. The Ultimate Self stands beyond any direct exchange. It is constantly present in our lives, but we cannot ask it questions and listen to its answers. Our thoughts and actions are an expression of its creative plan, yet we cannot check how we are doing directly. Those approaches that seek this kind of information from a "Higher Self" are dealing not with the Ultimate Self but with the higher centres.

There is no way to know exactly what these higher centres look like and exactly how they operate. It may be useful to think of the highest of them as three: the Inner Healer, the Guardian of the Psyche, and the Spiritual Guide. The Inner Healer applies its wisdom to healing the body and soul. The Guardian of the Psyche governs complex psychological manifestations (e.g., forming personalities, establishing defences, co-ordinating dissociative activities, manifesting inspirations). The Spiritual Guide taps a kind of cosmic knowledge concerning our spiritual aspirations. Whether these functional centres are really separate or emanate from one higher functional source, we cannot tell.

No Infallible Gurus

Information gained from attempts to communicate with a higher centre or self is subject to the limitations of that higher self, on the one hand, and the distortions introduced by our conscious and subconscious minds on the other. That is why meditation and visualization exercises, for example, although aimed at contacting the higher self that functions as a Spiritual Guide do not always produce correct information.

The same limitations that apply to information gained from a higher centre apply to what we learn from spiritual teachers. All teachers are subject to their own personal distortions. No teacher can give us a complete answer. No guru is infallible. And even if one were, the limitations of language and our own unconscious filters and censorship would not allow us to get a perfectly clear picture. This means that, unfortunately, we can never develop a fully satisfying understanding of our life and its purpose, on the conscious level.

This is a hard lesson to learn, because we so want to know everything. This desire to know, when channelled into serious personal exploration, can bear good fruit. When the desire to know prompts us to set up external sources of knowledge that we uncritically rely upon—our adored popes, preachers, prophets, channellers, mediums, psychics, shamans, or other spiritual gurus—we lay for ourselves a foundation of sand. We must not give in to the enticement of the guru. In this existence, ultimate answers are not available, so we must be willing to endure the pain of not knowing.

Luckily, we can develop a faith in the Ultimate Self that takes away the pain of not-knowing. Faith in our higher selves must be tempered with a certain caution. Not that they do not exist—they do. Not that they are untrustworthy or deceptive—they are not. They do, however, have their limitations, since they are not the Ultimate Self. Also, by the sheer constraints of human existence, our interactions with them are subject to distortions and misunderstandings. Faith in the Ultimate Self is quite a different matter. On the one hand there is no reason to think that the Ultimate Self is limited in itself (I'll be saying more about that), and on the other, we do not have to worry about distorting its messages, because it does not give out messages to distort.

Faith in the Ultimate Self operates not on the level of belief in the information received, but the direct and unshakeable knowledge of its presence and the realization that it is giving shape to its plan in all we do. This is not a disguised new version of the Little-People/Big-People Delusion. We are not placing our faith in some external big person, for what we have faith in and trust is at bottom our own self.

Inner Guidance

Trance Zero means taking inner guidance seriously. To be guided by what is most profound in yourself—to be truly and completely guided—requires tremendous conviction. For it does not mean being guided only when it makes sense, only when it feels comfortable. It means being guided all the time. If you live from Trance Zero you will indeed be considered either crazy or a legend: crazy when it involves actions that make others uneasy; a legend when the outcome impresses.

There are no half-way measures. If you really believe that your normal awareness cannot muster the comprehension you need to always be aware of what is needed at every moment of life, if you really accept that such comprehension can only derive from a transcendent awareness and if you really want to live from such awareness, then listening to your inner guidance is the only way. Only if you believe that it is possible to tap such inner wisdom will you be able to put aside the objections of ordinary consciousness and live by that guidance.

Of course there will be fear—fear of giving over to something that transcends ordinary awareness and common sense. We all know very well that some of the most bizarre, selfish, psychopathic, and destructive actions have been attributed to inner guidance, inner voices, or intuition. We must face the fear head on and take this objection seriously.

This problem will be discussed in the next and final chapter, but let me say for now that the problem of false conviction does not invalidate Trance Zero. It simply brings home how difficult the process is that leads to Trance Zero.

If you believe in the reality of higher centres and the Ultimate Self, the possibility of Trance Zero follows as a natural conclusion. If you can experience guidance from your profound self on the odd occasion, then you can find ways to experience it more often and more clearly. It is just a matter of working out how to recognize and pay attention to the wisdom that radiates from that source.

A Spiritual Quest

Is the quest to attain Trance Zero a spiritual one? For me "spiritual" refers to what transcends the immediateness of our everyday world. It implies being open to what is beyond the limited, culturally conditioned modes of thought we usually employ to understand who we are and make sense of our lives. So, for me a spiritual quest is a search for a sense of meaning derived from what is most central to oneself—the place of the Ultimate Self, the "I" of "I's." In that sense, the quest for Trance Zero is certainly a spiritual quest.

Striving for Trance Zero is a process, a movement towards acquaintance with deeper and deeper personal truth. The quest for Trance Zero is a hope-generating experience, for as we get closer to ultimate personal truth, we discover that our limited existences are part of an astonishing web of being within which everything goes as it should.

immanence

TRANCE ZERO entails faith. It is based on the belief that we possess inner resources far beyond what we know through ordinary awareness, that we have access to a "higher power" that can see us through the baffling complexities of life.

Transcendence

Trance Zero is possible because this "higher power" lies within. This contrasts to the prevailing cultural view that the higher power is outside us, something beyond the bounds of our own being, something transcendent. In this cultural framework, if we are to find resources beyond the ordinary, we must obtain them from some "other," some separate entity of unimaginable knowledge and power who transcends our puny existence—the entity traditionally called "God."

When thinking is formed by this paradigm of transcendence, we encounter certain problems that seem to defy solution. Two of the most difficult are the problem of free will and the problem of evil. The existence of free will and the presence of evil in the world are problems because any explanation involves intrinsic contradictions.

If God is all-powerful and all-knowing, how could we, as his creatures, have the ability to choose freely from among alternatives? Would not God, as creator of all things, be the source of our "free" actions as well, and therefore the author of our choices? But then, how are our choices free, because if God is their author, we are merely mediators of his action? Also, if God is the true source of our choices, would he not have to be the author of the evil ones as well as the good?

And what about the more general problem of evil in the world? What about all the bad things that happen to good people, the seemingly meaningless suffering of the innocent, and the lack of justice in life? Since these evils exist in the world, must not our all-powerful God be their source? And could he not have created a world without evil? Could he not prevent evil from occurring in our lives? Certainly, if he is all-powerful. But he has not done this. Rather, he has constructed a world in which horrible things happen to innocent people. Now, if God is the source of this evil, how can we think of him as a loving God and feel trust in him or optimism about the future?

It seems to me that our culture's notion of a transcendent God is the perfect embodiment of the Little-People/Big-People Delusion. God is the great and ultimate Big Person who looks after us from above (or some other angle, but in any case from the outside), and makes sure the world runs as it should. Of course, immense practical problems arise from this view, for every day we have experiences that seem to indicate that we are not looked after and that the world is not going as it should. It is a tribute to the power of the Little-People/Big-People Delusion that we can continue to maintain this view in the face of overwhelming evidence to the contrary.

As we approach the twenty-first century, people are filled with forebodings of darkness and disaster. They look around at their appointed big people—their politicians, their teachers, their artists, their religious leaders, their opinion-makers—and they do not feel reassured. They do not believe that this crop of big people has the wisdom and strength to see them through the difficult times ahead. If then they turn for comfort to the image of an all-powerful, all-wise, all-loving, transcendent, big-person God, they are likely to feel equally disillusioned. For most are perceptive enough to realize that the evidence for the presence of such a God in the world is lacking. Living at a time when torturers prosper and the helpless are abused, when the resources of the planet lie in the hands of a squandering few while millions barely survive, when compassion is seen as weakness and ruthlessness as strength, it would take a great deal of delusive thinking to believe that we are protected and safe in the hands of our transcendent Big Person.

Our religions counsel prayer to this transcendent God. Then they have to publish hundreds of books to explain what most people know—that prayer, as taught by them, does not work. Once you accept the paradigm of a transcendent Big Person and once you establish a system of beliefs based on that paradigm, you are confronted with a contradicting reality—something called life. That is why the spokespeople of religion must spend most of their counselling time trying to convince people that what they see happening is not true and that our Big Person truly is in control. Their task is impossible. It turns out there is no plausible explanation of our reality in the framework of a transcendent God. No matter how we explain things, we cannot get away from the unsolvable conundrum of free will and the immovable stumbling-block of evil.

Death, too, forces us to look deeper into things. The death of a human being is thought of as a time of reckoning. Usually the dying are depicted as having to face a reckoning, having to look at how they have lived their lives and admitting their sins and failings. But one could picture another kind of reckoning, one involving a transcendent God shaped according to the Little-People/Big-People Delusion, a know-it-all God who would be called on to give an account of why the world, with all its evils, is the way it is.

In this scenario we might imagine Elizabeth, a seven-year-old girl who was subjected to the most atrocious treatment from infancy, suffering unremitting, unspeakable sexual and physical abuse from both parents, the very people placed on the earth to protect her and help her explore the possibilities of life. This girl had no comfort from anyone, for her tortures were skilfully hidden from outsiders, and she was threatened with the most horrible consequences if she ever told anyone. Then, at the age of seven, her hand somehow slips out of that of her mother at a busy intersection, and she falls from the curb into the path of an oncoming truck and is killed. When she comes to, she is standing outside the gates of heaven before a beautiful throne where our transcendent God is preparing, as is his wont, to pass judgment on her life to see if she can enter. He says, "Well, Elizabeth, of course you can go in! No problem! You never did anything wrong and you fully deserve to be happy forever." He then swings open the gates, revealing a realm of dazzling beauty and light. But Elizabeth does not move. She is preoccupied with a nagging question and is not ready to go anywhere until it is answered.

"God," she says, "you are right in saying that I have never done anything wrong, and so I suppose I should not be kept out of heaven. But tell me this: If I never did anything wrong, why did you devastate my short little life, making me suffer these dreadful things and finally die a painful death?"

"Well, that's easy to answer," says God. "You see, it wasn't I that did this to you. It was those awful parents of yours. They used my gift of free will to carry out those abominable and unspeakable acts, acts that I personally abhor! I made them free, so of course I could not stop them, could I? And I can promise you the satisfaction of knowing that they will be thoroughly punished when they reach the end of their lives. So you can see that I am not at all at fault in the matter."

After hearing this, the little girl stands thinking for a long time. Finally, shaking her head in puzzlement, she slowly enters the kingdom of eternal joy. Our know-it-all God had his answer ready for little Elizabeth.

But what about Esther? She is also seven years old. She was born with cerebral palsy and spent every moment of her life in pain and discomfort. She suffered dozens of seizures a day. She was never able to use her arms or legs and so was unable to do anything for herself. She was in constant pain from her progressively contracting muscles, which distorted her body and threatened to dislocate her hips. She could eat only with great difficulty and had no control over her bowels or bladder. She could not recognize her own name, and never learned to speak. Despite the loving care of her family, at age seven Esther's life finally ends when her tired and deformed body simply stops functioning. Now she, too, stands before the gates of heaven. She too has a question for God, but since she never learned to talk, she does not realize she can put it into words. So she just points to her wracked and deformed body and looks at God with a questioning expression.

God responds, "Sorry about that! But you see, if I had it my way there would have been no disease or suffering on the earth. I had this beautiful paradise thing going when your great-great-great-grandparents, Adam and Eve, threw it all away. They did something I clearly forbade them to do. And since one must never disobey God, they were guilty of a terrible sin. As a result, suffering and death entered the world. Everybody since then has had to put up with it. So you see, it certainly was not my fault." Or perhaps God takes a different tack and answers, "Sorry about that! But you see, in my great wisdom I created the world as a marvellous mechanism that would run according to certain physical laws. As it turns out, this means that sometimes people are in the wrong place at the wrong time and get clobbered as the universe moves along its physically determined path. One person might be standing at a vulnerable spot on a mountainside when an avalanche starts; another person might be torn apart by a shark while swimming off the coast of Australia. In your case, you just had the bad luck of being born with faulty genes, which evolved according to the interactions of your ancestors and the vagaries of the environment. That is what led to your nightmarish life. It is not that I wanted your pain and agony. It was merely the outcome of physical factors that had to be. So you see, I am not to blame." Or perhaps God chooses the simpler approach and replies, "Sorry about that! But—don't ask. It's much too complicated to explain. Take my word for it, it was for your own good. Anyway, it's all over now. So come on in and I will make it up to you."

These scenarios may seem absurd, but they are consistent with the notion of a transcendent God, shaped by the Little-People/Big-People Delusion. I believe that the paradigm of transcendence leads to just this kind of absurdity, because it has us looking in the wrong direction. It has us looking outward, as to a longed-for parent, and ignoring our true riches, our inner resources. It leads to our viewing ourselves as at best helpless and at worst useless. In fact, most religions of transcendence view human beings as miserable wretches, who in their deepest hearts are repositories of darkness and evil. This view makes us reluctant to look within and discover who we really are. It devalues the inner life and projects our inner riches onto the sorry and tattered idol of a God-out-there, who is sometimes formed in the image of our most satisfying human relationships and sometimes in the image of our most feared human taskmasters. In any case, he is always a big person magnified as far as our imaginations are capable of. I believe that if we are to attain to a view of the divine that does justice to both God and ourselves, we must go a different route.

Finding God

In *Mysteries,* as Colin Wilson muses over his "ladder of selves" he asks the question: What is at the apex?[34] I believe it is the ultimate "I," but what does that mean? At that place, where this "I" is beyond time and space and beyond any objective knowledge, is there any way to distinguish between my "I" and the "I's" of other people? Is this the place where all being is one, and if so, is there any way to distinguish the Ultimate Self from the one source of being itself, God?

In his remarkable book *Cosmic Consciousness,* first published in 1901, Richard Bucke, a reform-minded superintendent of the asylum for the insane in London, Ontario, described his experience of "cosmic consciousness."[35] One night after midnight he was travelling home in a carriage at the end of an evening of reading poetry with friends. He was enjoying this reflective time when suddenly he felt himself wrapped in a flame-coloured cloud. For a moment he thought that he had somehow driven into a fire. Then he realized that the light was actually inside himself. Immediately he experienced a feeling of exultation, followed by a sense of indescribable intellectual illumination. Within this blissful feeling, he realized in a flash that the cosmos was not dead matter but filled with a living presence, that the soul is immortal, that all things in the universe work together for good, that everyone will eventually achieve happiness, and that love is the foundation of all existence. All of this took place in a few seconds, but the effects remained with Bucke for the rest of his life. Bucke believed that this cosmic consciousness has been experienced by many of the great minds of history, including Jesus Christ, Siddhartha Gautama (the Buddha), St. Paul, Muhammad, Dante, William Blake, and Walt Whitman. He equated it with the "enlightenment" described by many traditions, such as Buddhism. It brings with it an undeniable awareness of the essential unity of all things, and it involves a sense of both knowing God and being one with God.

Joseph Campbell has pointed out that Eastern religious traditions differ in a crucial way from those of the West.[36] In Eastern tradition, there is an emphasis on personal experiences that go progressively deeper until one finally discovers that, at bottom, we are identical with what is known as "divine." In the West, the view is that God made man and the world, and God is in no way identical with his creatures, but is the ineffable "other," the transcendent One. In the East, one goes within to discover that we are all manifestations of the divine. To encounter God, we simply have to encounter ourselves on the deepest possible level. In the West, we must look outside ourselves to find God; there is an intrinsic gap between human beings and God, a gap that can be bridged only by establishing a relationship with this external God.

These two traditions have clashed for millennia. There is no way to prove one and disprove the other. Arguments based on reason, analysis of data, quotations from authorities: none of these things is of any use in such a fundamental issue. In the end what counts for us is individual experience. We are convinced by an intuitive sense of what is true in the light of what we have seen, felt, and done, and what we have been taught by our culture.

For me, there is a conflict between my experience and what my cultural group mind has taught me. Coming from Western tradition, I have been educated to see God as separate, apart, essentially other. For some reason I have never felt comfortable with this teaching. I could never make it work for me, and I could never have a really satisfying and fulfilling sense of relationship with this creator God. Then at some point I began to become aware of my personal inner-world experience and particularly my experience of my own self as an irreducible centre of knowledge and will. This led me to a view of God and the world very much like that described by Bucke and the traditions of the East.

So when it comes to the question "Is the Ultimate Self identical with the divine?" I personally would have to say "Yes." This is my personal answer to a question that I believe can only be answered personally. Does acceptance of the notion of an Ultimate Self depend on this "Eastern" view of the world? I do not believe so. I believe that the awareness of an Ultimate Self derives directly from subjective experience and is not intrinsically dependent on any world view. It is only when one asks about the next step, the God question, that we see the parting of the ways .

The Immanent Divine

Seeing God as immanent rather than transcendent means seeing everything that exists as a manifestation of the divine rather than as God's extrinsic creation. It means seeing oneself as a unique eruption of the divine into individual consciousness at a particular point in space and time.

I view myself as one of those eruptions, as a centre of intelligence and an agent of free choice in this very particular existence. When I first became aware of my Ultimate Self, a strange thing happened. I felt that if I could move to the centre point of my being I would be aware of myself as God: I would know myself as the one and the same "I" that speaks through all people, through all centres of consciousness. But is that possible? Can a human being move to that place and really have self-awareness as God?

Before tackling that question, I would like to look more closely at the notion of an immanent divine. If the world is God actualizing, then everything is intrinsically part of a whole—everything is united at its source and therefore connected in its manifestations. The universe is a web of being with a direction and meaning, and those of us who carry self-consciousness within that web are especially interconnected as intelligent and free co-operators in the process. We are capable of actually knowing what is happening and consciously participating in the coming into being of God. We can look at each other and really recognize the one "I" in us all. Put another way, you and I are the way God exists at this particular point in space, at this particular moment in time, and in this particular consciousness.

It may even be said that recognition of this fact forms the true basis for social consciousness and social conscience. The reality of the divine in all may be behind striking social statements by spiritual leaders such as Jesus, who said, "Love others as you love yourself," and "If you do it to the least of my brethren you do it to me." We are asked to recognize that God says "I" in each of us, and when we respond to the needs of others we respond to God being made manifest.

We experience love as an unexplainable, irreducible embracing of and well-wishing toward another which is not based on an anticipated return. We are born with the capacity to love, and although we learn about exercising that capacity, love itself cannot be learned. It is just there—a kind of metaphysical instinct. And although our love responses can be blocked or distorted, they cannot be entirely destroyed. Love for another is, I believe, the striving to join (or rejoin) God-in-us with God-in-others. It is the movement to unite all divine manifestations in a network of meaning, a coming home to our true being. True social responses, then, are based on love of God.

The paradigm of transcendence offers no intrinsic basis for connection between all people and all things. It provides no way to understand the experience of cosmic consciousness described by Bucke. In the paradigm of transcendence, if there is a connection, it is imposed from the outside, by establishing a relationship "at a distance." The distance is the irreducible separateness of all beings from each other and from God. Relationship, then, is the disposition and interaction that comes about between two separate beings who become aware of each other. The gap is somehow bridged through intention and effort. Relationship is by definition fragile, for it requires "tending" and continually renewed communication. While this may be an adequate description of connection between people on the psychological level, for me it is not strong enough to describe my connection with others and with the divine at the basic level of being. These connections cannot be accidental, whimsical, one being stumbling upon another; rather they must be intrinsic, a part of the very definition of existence. The paradigm of immanence says precisely that: We are all intrinsically and irreducibly one, because we are all the manifestations of the one divine.

Theologies of transcendence seem to rest uneasy with their own position. Christian theology attempts to reintroduce intrinsic connection in seeing all Christians as part of the "body of Christ." It teaches that the church is the body of Christ, and all of its members, in being a part of that body, are part of Christ and are filled with his Holy Spirit. In that way Christians are taught to see Jesus, and therefore God, in all other members of the church. This amounts to imposing from the outside a certain kind of divine immanence, paradoxically attempting to overcome the intrinsic separation central to the paradigm of transcendence. Unfortunately, this manoeuvre does not really succeed, since it cannot get around the fact that connection between God and people is created through the establishment of a relationship (in this case with Jesus), with all the fragility that that entails.

Free Will and Evil

Seeing God as immanent means seeing everything as a manifestation of God—everything, including our free choices. It provides a workable approach to a crucial question: If God is all-powerful, how can my choices be truly free? How can they be my own and not pre-set and determined by God from the outside? The answer is that my choices are free because they are determined solely from the inside—they are mine. But they are also God's, for in my Ultimate Self there is no distinction between my "I" and God. In this way, there is no contradiction between the existence of free will and the reality of an all-powerful, all-knowing God, because our decisions are in the last analysis the decisions of God. He *is* all-knowing and all-powerful, and we *are* free.

But can this immanent God also be all-loving? This is a serious question, because the paradigm of immanence holds that everything is a manifestation of God, even the evil that we see in the world. Now if God is the author of evil, what kind of a God is he anyway? Must he not be cruel, if he inflicts all the horrors on us that we examined in discussing the notion of a transcendent God? Clearly the notion of an immanent God is only tolerable if we see evil in a different light.

We judge things as evil according to our own perspective. That perspective depends on the knowledge available to us. Things that from one standpoint may seem evil are not so when seen from another. Life-saving surgery from the perspective of someone ignorant of its benefits can seem a diabolical torture. Someone subjected to harsh discipline may judge it sadistic until he realizes that some day his life may depend on what he has learned. On the other hand, we can also misjudge what appear to be good acts. Seemingly benevolent concessions from an employer may be secretly intended to set us up to accept shabby treatment later on. The attentions and gifts of a pimp to a prospective prostitute hide a villainous purpose. So new knowledge and a new perspective can reverse our judgments completely about what is good and what is evil.

We can judge things only from the perspective we have. As we have seen in previous chapters, that perspective is necessarily limited. We are incapable of knowing and evaluating all the factors involved in the events of life. Yet we have to work with what we are given. We can only ask of ourselves that we do our best, for we cannot act from a perspective we cannot attain. When we judge actions or situations as evil, we must oppose those actions or situations. We are morally bound to do so. Having a limited perspective does not free us of our obligation to make moral judgments. Sometimes, because we are only too aware of the limitations of our knowledge, we agonize about those judgments. At other times we act with a confidence derived from the feeling that something is absolutely and clearly right or wrong. Later events may show that we should not have been so confident and that our perspective was badly flawed. Yet this is what it is to be human. We must accept that the limitations on our knowledge can deprive us of important awarenesses. We must live with the pain of knowing that in all good faith we can make serious blunders.

It may happen that we judge actions as evil when in fact they are not, when considered in a broader context of which we are simply unaware. It may even be that we, in our limited knowledge, knowingly choose to commit what we think is an evil act, but nevertheless do so in accordance with a greater plan and a greater good. It could be that for us, with a particular experience of life, this is an immoral act, whereas from a deeper and truer perspective that act is what needs to happen. In other words, we can do good things through a bad intention.

One might object and say that this is absurd. Surely the evil of some things cannot be doubted. Surely it is obvious that some things are abominably and atrociously evil. These things must be evil in some final and absolute way. This feeling is understandable. The conviction arises from our present knowledge and experience of life. But when we try to take into account the whole of being and the meaning of the whole of existence, that knowledge and experience will be woefully inadequate. We are simply incapable of figuring out the truth of existence itself. So it might be that what seems to be undeniably evil is not so when seen from a final perspective.

What if, from the deepest and truest perspective, all decisions made, all actions taken, and all events that happen result in things going precisely as they should? What if through all mistakes, blunders, and downright immoral acts, the world moves on its course precisely in the way God intends? If this were the case, two things would result. Immoral actions or evil acts would occur, because, as these things go, some individuals involved will choose to act in ways they judge immoral. These people would be using their free will to do what they consider wrong. From the best of their knowledge, they would commit evil acts. However, these acts would not be evil in an absolute and final sense, but only evil when judged from the limited perspective of their perpetrators (and perhaps many other people as well). When judged "in the light of eternity," they would not be evil. They would be precisely what had to happen so that God could manifest as he has chosen.

This ultimate perspective is something we simply cannot attain. If we could attain it, we would be seeing things as God does. Even though, in our limited existences, we can never grasp the totality of being in a complete way, we can know that God does just that and that, in our Ultimate Self, so does each of us. This would mean that, over all, there is no ultimate and unconditional evil. On the contrary, all is working together for the manifestation of the divine in a way that no living being can fathom.

From this perspective, the abusers of seven-year-old Elizabeth referred to earlier were indeed immoral and totally inexcusable in their actions. Judging from our knowledge and perspective (and that is what we must do), their actions were atrocious. We must oppose them with all our might, and support whatever penalties our culture has provided to punish those perpetrators. But were we able to gain the perspective beyond, the ultimate overview of the meaning of this existence, we would have to say that what happened had to happen.

In saying this, I realize that I have spoken the unthinkable and, perhaps for many, the unacceptable. All of our thinking about this crucial problem is necessarily formed from within the limited perspectives afforded by our human existences, and we recoil from such thinking and such an uncompromising position. But no matter how impossible such a conclusion may seem to us within our present awareness, it must stand.

The suffering inflicted on Esther must be viewed in a similar way. Even though no culpable human actions were involved in her predicament, yet we cannot ignore the fact that an innocent child was subjected to the most gruesome pain, and, from our vantage point, we must judge that to be an evil. Even so, Esther's life must also be considered to have gone the way it had to go when seen as part of the whole. Like Elizabeth's, it has meaning, purpose, and fittingness in the manifestation of the divine.

I take this stand not without trepidation. It does not feel comfortable. From my everyday perspective it does not even feel right. That is the difficulty in confronting this age-old problem of evil, free will, and an all-knowing, all-powerful God. No one has ever found a comfortable position to take on the matter. At some point one's reason or one's soul rebels against where it seems to lead. Anyone who is bold enough to follow the argument through to its ultimate conclusion will be forced into some corner from which there is no escape, some contradiction to reason, experience, or good sense. That is where I find myself.

I am faced with the inevitable question: Which of the three elements will have to go? Will it be the omniscience and omnipotence of God? Will it be the free will of human beings? Will it be the existence of absolute evil in the world? I will not avoid answering the question. So I will say that I reject the existence of evil—but with an important qualification. I do not deny the existence of evil in a limited sense. In fact, I insist that, in that sense, there *is* evil in the world and that we must recognize it and oppose it. But since I accept human free will and an omniscient and omnipotent divine without qualification, I must stand, with no cosy defence, and say there is no absolute and final evil.

Is it really possible to stomach such an idea? In Dostoyevsky's *The Brothers Karamazov*, the tortured, skeptical brother Ivan cannot. He tells the story of an eight-year-old boy who one day threw a stone and inadvertently struck a hound belonging to a retired general who lived in the area. The general noticed the hound was limping and asked why. He was told what the boy had done. He had the boy locked up for the night, and in the morning at dawn rode out on horseback in full hunting regalia, accompanied by his obsequious neighbours and huntsmen, with a pack of hounds at the head. The local serfs and the boy's mother were summoned to the place where the huntsmen had gathered. The boy was brought before the throng and the general ordered him stripped naked. The lad was paralysed with fear. One of the general's flunkies then ordered the boy to run and the general set the hounds after him. The dogs then tore the boy to pieces before his mother's eyes.

After telling his tale, Ivan speaks of his need to see retribution for this heinous act. He asks how such a thing can happen in our world and how justice could ever be done in such a case. He refers to the explanation sometimes given in such cases, which says that all these present sufferings in some mysterious way help create a future of harmony. Ivan insists that this explanation is not good enough for him. He wants to see that future harmony with his own eyes:

> I want to be here when everyone understands why the world has been arranged the way it is. It is on that craving for understanding that all human religions are founded, so I am a believer. But then, what about the children? How will we ever account for their sufferings? . . . The day the mother embraces the man who had her son torn to pieces by the hounds, the day those three stand side by side and say, "You were right, O Lord," that day we will at last have attained the supreme knowledge and everything will be explained and accounted for. But that's just the hurdle I can't get over, because I cannot agree that it makes everything right. And while I am on this earth, I must act in my own way. . . . If the suffering of little children is needed to complete the sum total of suffering required to pay for the truth, I don't want that truth, and I declare in advance that all the truth in the world is not worth the price. . . . No, I want no part of any harmony; I don't want it, out of love for mankind. I prefer to remain with my unavenged suffering and my unappeased anger—*even if I happen to be wrong.* I feel, moreover, that such harmony is rather overpriced. We cannot afford to pay so much for a ticket. And so I hasten to return the ticket I've been sent. If I'm honest, it is my duty to return it as long as possible before the show. . . . It isn't that I reject God; I

am simply returning Him most respectfully the ticket that would entitle me to a seat. [37]

Ivan is stuck in an insolvable dilemma: he accepts God but rejects God's show, the world as God has made it. He is a believer but casts himself out of the kingdom of heaven because he cannot see how it all makes sense. Ivan is a rebel and proud of it.

Ivan is able to rebel against God because he approaches the question from within the paradigm of transcendence. His is a God-out-there and so Ivan can take his stand facing God. This extrinsic God has to prove himself to Ivan, and, unfortunately, has failed to do so. The relationship between Ivan and his transcendent God has broken down, as such relationships are prone to do.

Ivan says he cannot understand how the suffering of the innocent can ever make sense. He admits his knowledge is limited and may prove erroneous, but he insists that, *even if he is wrong*, he will not accept such things. He says that at some future time his limited understanding may broaden to the point where everything falls into place. But that is not good enough for Ivan. He must rebel for the sake of his own integrity and "out of love for mankind."

The suffering of the innocent is impossible to understand in our limited, earthly state. But if understanding cannot be attained, does acceptance remain a possibility? Ivan, speaking from the paradigm of transcendence, says that it is not. It is just too big an affront to one's sense of what is right, for it means fitting into someone else's idea of how the world should be (that of the God-out-there) and does not include our collaboration in planning it. It means being involved after the fact, a less than satisfying form of participation. However, within the paradigm of immanence, where understanding fails, acceptance may still be possible; the notion that we are all manifestations of the divine allows us to see that the workings of God in the world are our own workings, even when they seem to be most unfathomable. Our participation here is central. We are in on the ground floor of the whole scheme, whether we consciously realize it or not.

Death

In the paradigm of immanence, death is not encumbered with the absurd scenarios I described in the section on transcendence, above. Although death is a time of reckoning, it is also a time of recognition and a time of return. Whatever our state after death may be, surely it involves a recognition of our true condition and a deeper understanding of ourselves as manifestations of the divine. Also, death means moving away from our preoccupation with existence in this embodiment, in this environment with which the outer mind has been so preoccupied. With death, the outer-mind function loses its place of pre-eminence, for it no longer has anything with which to occupy itself, except perhaps memories. On the other hand, the inner mind, which has always been closer to the true realization of how things are, may remain active in our after-death existence.

The continued existence of inner-mind functions may be what is meant by the "immortality of the soul." If the soul is the spiritual principle which has been engaged in this particular embodiment, there is no reason to think that it could not survive death. This depends on the extent to which, at death, we return to our Ultimate Self and existence as God. On the other hand, if the soul does survive death, it may or may not be "immortal," continuing to exist forever. It is hard to see why this faculty would remain in existence once it has lost its reason for being. Nevertheless, we are dealing with things so far removed from our present ability to comprehend that it is very difficult even to speculate here.

In any case, at death we move closer to that from which we came. Perhaps we simply know ourselves more clearly and simply as manifestations of the divine, yet continue to exist as limited beings. Perhaps we will maintain an individuality of a kind that will be the basis for new existences in some reincarnational series of lives. Or we may maintain some other kind of individuality. On the other hand, we may simply become one with our source. We cannot really know whether the return of death involves simply moving a step closer to divine consciousness or completely merging with it. But we can be confident that death is a change that will be most interesting and something not to be missed!

Trance Zero

Trance Zero only makes sense within a paradigm of immanence. If the movement toward our centre means movement toward the source and determiner of all, then we have reason to feel confident in our intuitions deriving from our own deepest selves.

In describing the experience of cosmic consciousness, Richard Bucke commented in *Cosmic Consciousness* that those who have it "are either exalted, by the average self-conscious individual, to the rank of gods, or, adopting the other extreme, are adjudged insane."[38] This brings me back to the quote at the beginning of Chapter 10: "Some people hear their own inner voices with great clearness, and they live by what they hear. Such people become crazy, or they become legends."[39] Trance Zero means becoming aware of our intuitions and living by them. I do not believe that we must have experienced cosmic consciousness to attain Trance Zero, but I do believe that we have to be open to following our inner voices. By some, this may be viewed as madness, and those who attempt to follow this path may at times feel that they are indeed insane. Why would this be so?

Maybe because some who have been brushed by insanity seem to express ideas similar to those we have been discussing. Charismatic Russian dancer Vaslav Nijinsky, who haunted the fringes of madness, wrote in his diary about something that sounds very much like Trance Zero:

> An order of God tells me how to act. I am not a fakir and a magician. I am God in a body. Everyone has that feeling, but no one uses it. I do make use of it, and know its results. People think that this feeling is a spiritual trance, but I am not in a trance. I am love. I am in a trance, the trance of love. I want to say so much and cannot find the words. I want to write and

cannot. I can write in a trance, and this trance is called wisdom.
(*The Diary of Vaslav Nijinsky,* ed. Romola Nijinsky, London: Victor Gollancz, 1937, p. 49)

Nijinsky is saying that when he danced, people thought he was in a trance. But he knew it was not a trance in the way they meant—not even a "spiritual trance." He was "God in a body," the presence of the divine on the human stage. If it was a trance, it was a trance called love, the very love of God shining through him, what I call Trance Zero. Nijinsky felt something comparable about writing his diary. Although at times words might fail him, when he began to write he became the manifestation of wisdom itself.

As so often happens with the insane, Nijinsky presents us with a stark, unflinching glimpse into a profound truth. But as so often happens with the insane, he gets the details wrong, for, as other entries in his diary show, how he applied this awareness to his life was confused and sometimes downright bizarre. He was correct to deem himself and everyone else capable of this unique state, but he was mistaken to believe that he was living according to its guidance.

If recognizing the reality of Trance Zero isn't the same thing as living it, what further is needed? How can we go beyond magical intuitive moments and make Trance Zero a way of life? The answer is by no means easy, for there are no obvious signposts to show the way.

Following your inner voices means living by awarenesses that in some cases seem eminently reasonable and in others irrational. Living by intuition is not easy; it means believing things and doing things for which you cannot provide any clear evidence or justification. In most situations in life, we are expected to be able to explain ourselves to our family, friends, employers, and others. If we cannot give convincing reasons for what we do, we feel we are out on a limb and risk losing credibility with those whose opinion matters to us.

Our cultural group mind gives very little support to those who pay attention to their intuition. I talked before about how we tend to be a proof-oriented society, hesitant to make a move without the evidence, the data to back us up. This arises in part from the naive science-worship that prevails among us. In this framework, to be adult, rational, and sophisticated is to be skeptical about everything that has not been approved by science or scientists. It makes little difference that almost nothing of what really counts in daily life can even be subjected to scientific scrutiny. We maintain the illusion that if we did sufficient research, we would somewhere find a clear scientific stand on most matters, and we bow to any opinion that claims to be based on such research. For that reason, in our culture to say that you "feel" something is true, that you "sense" danger, that you "instinctively know" that something is a wrong decision, makes you suspect. You have no proof, no evidence. You are supposed to be a "hard-nosed realist" (using "science" as the basis for action), not a "wishy-washy dreamer" (following your hunches and intuitions). To use the language of intuition and to base your decisions on intuitive awareness is "irrational," "uncritical," "naive," "rash," "magical thinking." We want none of that.

Scientism alone has not created this climate inhospitable to intuition. Moneyism, too, has had a significant part to play. Here again you hear the language of "hard-nosed realism" (characterized by actions based on the financially practical), this time opposed to "airy-fairy bleeding-heartism" (characterized by actions based on human values and emotion). The implication is that if you give priority to financial feasibility, then you are an adult. If you put the heart first, you are childish and immature.

The problem of living by intuition is not simply facing the hardships created by cultural narrowness. There are other things that make it difficult to do. For instance, how does one solve the problem of judging what is really an intuition and what is not? This is not a simple matter. We can experience powerful convictions that are based not on intuition but on unconscious distortions. We talk about "common sense," yet Albert Einstein perceptively defined it as the sum total of prejudices we accumulate by age sixteen. What we hold as "self-evident" can just as well be the "reality" created by a family group mind formed over generations of skewed experience. A traumatic event in early life can create a psychological state that dramatically colours much of an adult's response. Societal, ethnic, religious, or cult group minds can so dominate a person's thinking that he may be utterly convinced of something that, outside that influence, he would deem highly questionable. The strength of our conviction about what we believe does not guarantee that we believe according to intuition. Some of the strongest and most unshakeable opinions are held by people gripped by blind bigotry or psychotic delusion.

How, then, can a person ever fully trust intuition? How can one be sure it arises from the deepest, most trustworthy part of oneself? We can only reach that kind of confidence through a long and arduous journey of self-discovery. While this may not be the answer we want to hear, I am afraid it is the only possible answer. Anything else would amount to an underestimation of both the complexity of human life experience and the richness of the human psyche.

A Process of Self-Discovery

At this point in books on popular psychology, there is usually a series of "exercises" that you can practise in the quiet of your home to bring you into touch with the deep inner knowledge you need to change your ways or that help you create mental images that will revolutionize your life. I am afraid that these exercises are for the most part a response to the insistence of today's readers on the means of instant transformation—like working one's way through a book about Prozac and finding at the end, pasted to the back cover, a little packet containing a half-dozen tablets for immediate ingestion. As a psychotherapist, I have worked with hundreds of clients who have read thousands of these manuals and spent thousands of hours carrying out these practices. And in too many cases, they have ended up disappointed, even despairing.

Not that these popular psychology books have nothing good to offer. Quite the contrary. They are often gold mines of valuable psychological and spiritual information. The problem arises from the "quick fix" attitude that desperate readers so frequently bring to them and the prospect of a speedy transformation sometimes promised in the book. Those who use these books as helpful aids in their ongoing personal work, and not as quick-acting medicines for their ills, will find a great deal that is worthwhile there. But no matter *how* you do it, quick this process is *not*.

The only answer to the question "How can I learn to recognize my intuitions and live by them?" is that we must set out on a highly personal, highly individual, difficult expedition of self-discovery that removes, one by one, the hidden sources of distortion that block our acceptance of what we know intuitively.

A Western Contribution

Distorted intuitions often derive from blocks and confusions that exist in the inner mind on the level of the personal unconscious. The distortions may not be recognized, and even if they are, their causes may remain a mystery. Any process that attempts to uncover and remove these blocks to intuition existing in these inner recesses of the mind is bound to take time. Mere intellectual understanding will not resolve such problems; the kind of distortions involved here are those that arise from emotionally charged personal experience. They can only be overcome through methods that can alter emotionally fixed patterns of thought and feeling.

Western psychology has made a unique contribution to our purification process by directly tackling this level of experience. The great psychological pioneers—Pierre Janet, Sigmund Freud, Carl Jung, Milton Erickson, and others—have taken psychological dysfunction as their starting point and made great strides in ferreting out their sources and bringing about change. The practical techniques evolving from their work constitute what has come to be called psychotherapy. The techniques differ remarkably from one school of thought to another, yet all share a concern with healing problems on the level of emotionally ingrained, distorting forces operating in the inner mind.

Other Paths

But psychotherapy and therapeutic counselling are not the only roads to our resolution of conditionally based sources of distortion. Sometimes life itself gives a person the opportunity to resolve and transcend those difficulties. I have had the pleasure of knowing many people who have never had an hour of formal therapeutic work, but who, through their determination to be ruthlessly honest with themselves, have come as far as any analyzed person.

Hidden sources of distortion arise from more than psychological problems in our pasts. Just as often, they arise from ongoing current individual and group-mind trance influences. It is precisely in this area that I believe the knowledge of trance in daily life can be a great help in carrying forward the process of purification.

To understand trance is to appreciate the true nature of human experience, both in its potentials and its limitations. To understand trance is to realize that at the very same moment that we become aware of something, we make ourselves unaware of other things. To understand trance is to appreciate the power of concentration, focus, absorption. It is also to recognize that we have to cut out much of what impinges on the present moment and pushes forward from past experience in order to live successful lives in this world. To understand trance is to realize how the tremendous reservoir of experience concealed in the inner mind can affect the way we think, feel, and act every day. To understand trance is to know the central role that reality creation plays in every moment of our lives. And to understand trance is especially to develop a healthy respect for the influences of the many group minds within whose ambits we exist.

Learning to recognize and follow our intuitions is not just a matter of removing distorting influences and blocks. It is also a matter of attention and the confidence that comes from experience. The intuitions may be there, but if we do not pay attention to them, we cannot follow them; and if we do not feel confident that following our intuitions is the right thing to do we will not carry through. Developing attention can be a matter of simply learning the habit of looking at our consciousness as an ever-active source of intuitive flashes and urges. Confidence in following our intuitions comes from experimenting, from letting them guide us and then evaluating the results. Only experience can overcome the culturally ingrained attitude that every thought must be analyzed and every action must be justified.

Optimism

The paradigm of immanence that I espouse in this book is the very essence of optimism. It holds that everything is as it should be. Furthermore, it implies that Trance Zero is a realistic possibility for human beings, since we are not intrinsically evil or defective beings who need to be saved from our weakness and depravity by a transcendent God. One might well ask whether it is possible to maintain such optimism about people and life when confronted with the facts of what human beings are really like. I believe it is.

My optimism is based on the conviction that you and I are the way God exists at this particular point in space and this particular moment in time. This means that at bottom we can be neither defective nor evil. It also means that we are the repositories of a deep inner wisdom, a divine wisdom, that is ours if we can simply learn to tap it. This wisdom is available to our intuition and becomes a part of our lives in Trance Zero.

My optimism has stood the test. Over the thirty years that I have worked as a psychotherapist, I have been privy to the intimate thoughts and impulses of murderers, abusers, thieves, lawyers, teachers, labourers, politicians, psychotherapists, media personalities, and men and women of the cloth. I have worked with young and old, naive and sophisticated, poor and rich, sane and psychotic. And in all this work I have found no reason to lose faith in people, no reason to despair. Even the most disturbed among us are capable of reaching into their own depths and discovering the divine that shows itself there.

I do have one major concern. It arises not from those I have seen in therapy sessions, but from a particular category of person who will never seek this kind of help: the psychopath. I refer very specifically to that small percentage of the population that is absolutely incapable of feeling empathy for other people. These are the Saddam Husseins, the John Gacys, the Paul Bernardos of the world who torture and kill without the slightest feeling for their victims. These are the career pedophiles who do not experience the least compunction for their crimes and who, given the chance, would repeat their abominations without hesitation. These are the swindlers who steal the life savings of the elderly without a second thought for the suffering they cause. I am speaking about the true psychopaths who, mostly through genetic defect and partly through childhood experience, feel no connection with their fellow human beings.

According to Robert Hare, a pioneer in research on psychopaths, these people are typically glib and superficial, egocentric and grandiose, deceitful and manipulative, impulsive, have poor behavioural controls, crave excitement, lack responsibility, have shallow emotions, and lack empathy.[40] The psychopath is, in fact, the prototypical example of someone totally walled off from the inner depths of being we have been investigating in this book.

I am not referring here to those who have committed atrocities because psychotic distortions have horribly twisted their view of reality. David Berkowitz, the "Son of Sam" killer, with his grotesque sexual fantasies and his fascination with torture was probably psychotic, rather than psychopathic due to distortions in the depth of the psyche rather than a *lack* of psychic depth. This must certainly also be true of the case of Joseph Kallinger, a multiple murderer who believed he had been commanded by the Devil to carry out his monstrous acts.[41] Mental disturbance of some kind is also clearly present in those murder–suicide tragedies that are all too frequently reported in the news. Sadly, the perpetrator's thinking is often so twisted that he actually believes he is doing his family a favour by taking their lives. Mental disorders may also be involved in lesser crimes, and we see evidence of this in those men who brutalize their wives and children, and also experience periods of remorseful lucidity.

I speak about the atrocities committed in distorted mental states not to diminish the evil of the acts committed or to conjure up pity for their perpetrators. I want to contrast the state of the psychopath with that of the psychotic to emphasize the truly disturbing characteristics of the psychopathic mind. We experience a special kind of fear in the presence of a true psychopath (think of the movie *The Silence of the Lambs*) because we sense that we cannot call on anything in him that would be the basis for empathy or compassion. The psychopath is totally incapable of any depth of feeling. Berkowitz or Kallinger may create feelings of horror in us, but they do operate from a depth of feeling, as incredibly twisted as those feelings may be. As perverted as the murder–suicide perpetrator's compassion may be, it is nonetheless a kind of compassion. The psychopath is incapable of even that.

The psychopath is plagued by shallowness, an inability to feel at any depth. This unadulterated superficiality is what makes the psychopath so dangerous. He may very well feel no more emotion when causing the painful death of a fellow human being than he does when swatting a fly. And why? Not because of some psychotic delusion about his action, but because he simply cannot contact anything inside himself that deeply connects with another human being.

When we encounter people in our lives, we take it for granted that a connection can be made between us. Even those in the grips of psychoses make something of their inner selves available to us, something that can become the basis for communication and empathy. This kind of connection can never be made with a psychopath. Unfortunately, psychopaths learn to present responses that mimic depth of emotion. They become very good observers of behaviour and adept at giving people what they want. They can learn to be incredibly charming and often appear emotionally responsive and sensitive to the unwary. For that reason, one of the great challenges of our time is to develop the ability to recognize the psychopath and protect ourselves from him or her. I say protect ourselves, because there is little evidence that anything can be done to treat the psychopath. With our present knowledge, there is no operation, no injection, no therapy that can change a psychopath. Until treatment becomes possible, we must protect ourselves. Whether that means imprisoning indefinitely psychopaths convicted of violent crimes or carefully avoiding non-violent psychopaths who may cross our paths, we must understand the danger realistically.

I have devoted some attention to the problem of psychopaths because I believe they illustrate extreme disconnection from the aspects of the soul we have been discussing. If, in my Ultimate Self, I am a manifestation of the divine, and if I have higher centres of wisdom and guidance that can become the basis for experiencing Trance Zero, then I recognize in the psychopath a person who has, for reasons yet unknown to us, never been given access to these depths. The psychopath is walled off from everything except the most transient and insubstantial. That means that, unfortunately, the psychopath, in this present lifetime, anyway, is not in a position to undertake the inner search that can lead to connection with what in us is most human and most divine.

Before leaving this matter, let me say that I have been concentrating on human beings as manifestations of the divine, but the same thing could be said of all that exists. We can say with equal truth that other living beings and material objects are the way God exists at that particular point in space and that particular moment in time. Intuitively we know this. Why do we feel wonder at other kinds of living things and never blame them for what they are or do? Why do we admire the beauty of "nature" and accept its ways? Because we have an instinctive awareness of the presence of the divine. If we allow ourselves to see deeply, we will accord the same wonder, admiration, and acceptance to human beings.

Approaching Trance Zero

Earlier in this chapter I asked the question: "Can we human beings attain self-awareness as God?" This question has preoccupied many spiritual traditions. Some Eastern traditions in particular have attempted to answer it by describing stages of development through which the person eventually attains full realization as God and escapes the bonds of earthly existence. They use methods of meditation that allow us to perceive the true nature of this reality and move toward an awareness of the ineffable One behind all that exists. They prescribe methods of purification and detachment meant to help us realize in a practical way the illusory nature of our limited existences. What is beyond this reality is roughly described by the term "God," but devoid of the anthropomorphic attributes we tend to attach to that being. The final goal is union with the divine. They say that the process by which it is attained is long and arduous, and few (e.g., Buddha, Jesus) reach it in this life. Those who do may choose to retain their existence as physical beings in this world in order to teach those who want to follow them into their own liberation. In this understanding of things, there seems to be room for the experience of being fully and directly conscious of oneself as divine while still existing as a human being.

Those of us who have not attained this state have to take the word of others on the matter. This means believing and accepting the personal experience of another and using it as the guide for oneself. That would be all right if one simply accepted this second-hand experience as a provisional basis for experimenting for oneself. Unfortunately, that is not the way teachers of this path usually present it. More often than not they require unconditional trust and do not tolerate any doubts about their teachings. Here we are again confronted with the phenomenon of guru-ism, which, in my opinion, is full of pitfalls and has done as much harm as it has good. I have personally been unable to feel comfortable as a guru's disciple. I am unable to go down a path where I cannot question and doubt. I am glad to learn from others, but I cannot learn when I am expected to turn off parts of my own mind.

So, to the question "Can we human beings attain self-awareness as God?" I would give a personal, provisional answer. I have not experienced it. I believe I have not known anyone who has experienced it. I have read no accounts of spiritual attainment that convince me that their authors attained it. Nor have I heard convincing first-hand accounts of anyone who has met anyone who claims to have experienced this state. So while I am reluctant to say that it is intrinsically impossible, I think it very unlikely. I believe that in this life we are always involved with the outer mind and our embodied existence to such an extent that to move into a God-consciousness would be impossible.

But what about Trance Zero?

That is an entirely different matter. I see no reason to say we cannot fully attain Trance Zero. Trance Zero does not in any way require withdrawal from the everyday world. It does not require the maintenance of some other-worldly state. On the contrary, Trance Zero demands our full engagement in the realities of our embodied human existence. Trance Zero is totally oriented to dealing with ordinary daily life—and in the most creative way possible. So there is no reason to doubt that a person could be so in tune with his or her intuition as to achieve a full state of Trance Zero.

Nevertheless, it does seem that, for most of us, Trance Zero is never a complete and finished state. Rather it is a destination toward which we travel. Once we cross the enchanted boundary of the Little-People/Big-People Delusion, our path becomes clearer and more direct. But it is still an arduous journey, one that requires a never-ending questioning of existence as it reveals itself to us.

NOTES

1 See Adam Crabtree, *From Mesmer to Freud: Magnetic Sleep and the Roots of Psychological Healing* (New Haven: Yale University Press, 1993), and *Animal Magnetism, Early Hypnotism and Psychical Research from 1766 to 1925: An Annotated Bibliography* (White Plains, New York: Kraus International Publications, 1988).

2 *Multiple Man: Explorations in Possession and Multiple Personality* (Toronto: Somerville House Books, 1997 (reissue)).

3 In *A History of Hypnotism* (Cambridge: Cambridge University Press, 1992), Alan Gauld thoroughly discusses both the problems involved in attributing specific phenomena to hypnosis and the controversies surrounding the definition of the term. *Theories of Hypnosis* (eds. Steven Jay Lynn and Judith W. Rhue, New York: The Guildford Press, 1991) presents the many different ways of defining and looking at hypnosis today. Robert Baker (*They Call It Hypnosis* (Buffalo: Prometheus Books, 1990)) examines the question of whether it is possible to even say there is such a thing as hypnosis.

4 *The Adventures of Sherlock Holmes* (New York: Ballantine), pp. 133–34.

5 Josephine Hilgard and Samuel Lebaron, *Hypnotherapy of Pain in Children with Cancer* (Los Altos: William Kaufman, 1984).

6 Ernest Rossi, *The Twenty Minute Break* (Los Angeles: Jeremy Tarcher, 1991).

7 Lawrence LeShan, *How to Meditate* (New York: Bantam, 1974).

8 William Styron, "Darkness Visible," *Vanity Fair,* Dec. 1989, pp.212 ff.

9 John Bentley Mays has also written compellingly about this debilitating state. See Mays, *In the Jaws of the Black Dogs* (Toronto: Penguin, 1995).

10 See Henry Ellenberger, *The Discovery of the Unconscious* (New York: Basic Books, 1970), p. 318.

11 Ernest Rossi and David Cheek, *Mind–Body Therapy: Ideodynamic Healing in Hypnosis* (New York: Norton, 1988), p. 191.

12 Dennis K. Chong and Jennifer K. Smith Chong, *The Knife Without Pain* (Oakville, Ont.:C-Jade Publications, 1994).

13 Ernest Rossi and Margaret Ryan, eds., *The Seminars, Workshops, and Lectures of Milton H. Erickson,* Vol. 3 (New York: Irvington, 1986), pp. 9–12.

14 *Journal of the Society for Psychical Research,* 76 (1982), pp. 301–13.

15 Henry Corbin, *Mundus Imaginalis or the Imaginary and the Imaginal* (Ipswich: Golgonooza Press, 1972).

16 Andrew Greely, "Why Do Catholics Stay in the Church?" *New York Times Magazine,* July 10, 1994, pp. 38–41.

17 Jean Jacques Rousseau, *On the Social Contract,* trans. and ed. Donald Cress (Indianapolis: Hackett, 1983), p. 17.

18 Tony Judt, "The New Old Nationalism," *The New York Review of Books,* 41, no. 10 (May 26, 1994), 46–47.

19 Bandler Richard and John Grinder, *The Structure of Magic,* (Palo Alto: Science and Behavior Books, 1975), pp. 10–11.

20 Charles Tart, *Waking Up* (Boston: New Science Library, 1987), pp. 85 ff.

21 Robert Lindner, *Prescription for Rebellion* (New York: Reinhart, 1952).

22 *Ibid.,* p. 16.

23 Wilhelm Reich, *The Murder of Christ* (New York: Noonday Press, 1974).

24 *Ibid.,* p. 16.

25 *Ibid.,* pp. 3–4.

26 Richard Lewontin, "Billions and Billions of Demons," *The New York Review of Books,* Jan. 8, 1997, pp. 28ff.

27 *Ibid.,* p. 32.

28 R. Rorty, "The Contingency of Language," *London Review of Books* 17 (April 1986), 3.

29 Lewontin, pp. 28 and 31.

30 Fyodor Dostoyevsky, *Brothers Karamozov,* trans. Andrew R. MacAndrew (New York: Bantam Books, 1981).

31 *Ibid.,* p. 305.

32 Colin Wilson, *Mysteries* (London: Hodder & Stoughton, 1978).

33 Ernest Rossi and Margaret Ryan, eds. *The Seminars, Workshops, and Lectures of Milton H. Erickson,* Vol. 3 (New York: Irvington, 1986) pp. 17–18.

34 *Mysteries,* p. 36.

35 Richard Bucke, *Cosmic Consciousness: A Study in the Evolution of the Human Mind* (New York: E.P. Dutton, 1923), pp. 9–10.

36 Joseph Campbell, *Myths to Live By* (New York: Penguin, 1972).

37 *The Brothers Karamazov,* pp. 294–95.

38 *Cosmic Consciousness,* p. 3.

39 *Legends of the Fall* (the movie), 1995.

40 Robert Hare, *Without Conscience: The Disturbing World of the Psychopaths among Us* (New York: Pocket Books, 1993), p. 69.

41 For a detailed account of this case, se Flora Rheta Schreiber, *The Shoemaker: The Anatomy of a Psychotic* (New York: Simon and Schuster, 1983).

*This book is set in Garamond, a standard
typeface used by book designers and printers
for four centuries, and one of the finest old styles
ever cut. Some characteristics of Garamond
to note are the small spur on the "G", the open
bowl on the "P", the curving tail on the "R",
and the short lower-case height and very
small counters of the "a" and "e".*